BEYOND INVISIBLE WALLS

The Series in Trauma And Loss

Consulting Editors

Charles R. Figley and Therese A. Rando

BEYOND INVISIBLE WALLS

The Psychological Legacy
of Soviet Trauma,
East European Therapists
and Their Patients

Edited by

Jacob D. Lindy, MD
Robert Jay Lifton, MD

USA	Publishing Office:	BRUNNER-ROUTLEDGE
		A member of the Taylor & Francis Group
		29 West 35th Street
		New York, NY 10001
		Tel: (212) 216-7800
		Fax: (212) 564-7854
	Distribution Center:	BRUNNER-ROUTLEDGE
		A member of the Taylor & Francis Group
		7625 Empire Drive
		Florence, KY 41042
		Tel: 1-800-634-7064
		Fax: 1-800-248-4724
UK		BRUNNER-ROUTLEDGE
		A member of the Taylor & Francis Group
		27 Church Road
		Hove
		E. Sussex, BN3 2FA
		Tel: +44 (0) 1273 207411
		Fax: +44 (0) 1273 205612

BEYOND INVISIBLE WALLS: The Psychological Legacy of Soviet Trauma, East European Therapists and Their Patients

1 2 3 4 5 6 7 8 9 0

Printed by Edwards Brothers, Lillington, NC, 2001.
Cover design by Nancy Abbott.

A CIP catalog record for this book is available from the British Library.
∞ The paper in this publication meets the requirements of the ANSI Standard Z39.48-1984 (Permanence of Paper).

Library of Congress Cataloging-in-Publication Data
Lindy, Jacob D., 1937–
    Beyond invisible walls: the psychological legacy of Soviet trauma / Jacob D. Lindy, Robert J. Lifton.
       p. cm. — (Series in trauma and loss, ISSN 1090-9575)
    Includes bibliographical references and index.
    ISBN 1-58391-318-1 (hbk. : alk. paper)
       1. Psychic trauma—Europe, Eastern. 2. Post-traumatic stress disorder—Europe, Eastern. 3. Psychic trauma—Russia (Federation) 4. Psychic trauma—Russia (Federation) 5. Communisim—Psychological aspects. 6. Psychotherapy—Europe, Eastern. 7. Psychotherapy—Russia (Federation) I. Lifton, Rober Jay, 1926– II. Series.
RC552.P67 L559 2001
616.85¢21¢00947—dc21   2001037439

ISBN 1-58391-318-1 (case)
ISSN 1090-9575

to our cousins

CONTENTS

CONTRIBUTORS

Chapter Authors

Nora Csiszer M.D. was chief psychiatrist at the Crisis Intervention/Suicide Prevention Unit at Karanyi Hospital in Budapest, Hungary. She holds that position at Erzsebet Hospital, Budapest, currently.

Eva Katona Ballagoddard M.D., also a psychiatrist, was research associate on the same unit. She continues to have the title of senior lecturer at the Postgraduate Medical School, Budapest, Hungary. Dr. Katona has emigrated to London, England, where she continues to work as a psychiatrist specializing in work with drug addicted patients.

Heike Bernhardt M.D., a pediatrician and psychiatrist, also worked as a psychotherapist within the former East German State. She helped develop and direct a clinic for East Germans who experienced psychosocial crisis following reunification with West Germany. She continues to live in Berlin. She currently practices psychotherapy with adults and children and writes about the history of psychiatry and psychoanalysis in Germany.

Ion Cucliciu M.D. was a physician and psychiatric resident at the Bucharest University Hospital, and political advocate for change during the late 1980s and early 1990s. He is currently living in Paris, France, where he has completed studies as a psychiatric fellow. He works as psychiatrist at the Robert Ballanger Hospital.

Dr. Fyodor Konkov, a practical psychologist, worked both as a therapist at a suicide hotline in Moscow and as a trauma therapist and consultant with Russian "Afghansi" veterans and with survivors of the Armenian earthquake. He is currently living and working in the United States where he was most recently on the staff of the Santa Clara Community Mental Health Center.

Vasko Muacevic M.D. was professor of social psychiatry at the University of Zagreb, Croatia. He was senior psychiatrist delivering mental health services to the Croatian military and at refugee camps. He continues to live in Zagreb where he is professor emeritus at the University.

Levon Jernazion Ph.D. was a practicing school psychologist in Yerevan, Armenia. He has emigrated to the United States where he lives and conducts a private practic in psychology in Glendale, California.

Anie Kalayjian (RN.C., Ed.D.) is professor of psychology, Fordham University, New York. She works with the United Nations and ives and works in New York City. She organized a mental health intervention following the Armenian earthquake.

Jacob D. Lindy M.D. psychiatrist and training and supervising psychoanalyst, is director of Cincinnati Psychoanalytic Institute, Cincinnati, Ohio.

Robert Jay Lifton M.D. is professor of psychiatry Harvard University, Cambridge, Massachusetts.

Other Contributors

Ivo Banac Ph.D.	Yale University, New Haven, Connecticut
Yitzhak Brudny Ph.D.	Hebrew University, Jerusalem, Israel
Robert Jenkins Ph.D.	Yale University, New Haven, Connecticut
Susan Marrs	Seven Hills School, Cincinnati, Ohio
Arthur Martirosyan	Kennedy School of Government, Harvard University, Boston, Massachusetts
Michael MacPherson M.D.	Liaison with Eastern Europe, Berlin, Germany
Anette Schwartz Ph.D.	Yale University, New Haven, Connecticut
Mark Steinberg Ph.D.	University of Illinois, Urbana, Illinois
Jos Weerts M.D.	Liaison with Western Europe, Gouda, the Netherlands

ACKNOWLEGMENTS

The idea for this book took form as Russian and East European trauma therapists were first interacting with us, their Western counterparts, during *perestroika*. The new political climate enabled our working together to study and help survivors of the Chernobyl disaster, the Armenian earthquake, and Russian veterans of the Afghanistan war, and provided the opportunity for some of them to work by our side in Western disasters. It became clear that, if only the window of opportunity would remain open long enough, the East Europeans would have an even larger story to tell—that of their trauma under Soviet rule. This book is the result. Michael MacPherson (liaison with Eastern Europe), Jos Weerts (liaison with Western Europe), and Jacob Lindy, then president of the International Society for Traumatic Stress Studies, set out to assist East Europeans in telling this story, and served as a facilitating group for the project.

Many people and groups helped us. During the organizational phase, Claire Ryle and the Esselon group, and leaders of the International Society for Traumatic Stress Studies (ISTSS): Yael Danieli, Robert Pynoos, Bessel van der Kolk, and Bonnie Green helped Jacob Lindy together with Boris Tsygenkov and Yuri Alexandrovsky to plan and carry out the (then) Soviet Union's first international conference on posttraumatic states, Moscow, September 1989. They participated in that conference and heard officially sanctioned Soviet colleagues report on their work with survivors of the Chernobyl disaster, the Armenian earthquake, and the Afghanistan war.

Jos Weerts, then of the Dutch Survivors Organization ICODO, together with the European Trauma Society, arranged for younger front-line therapists from Eastern bloc countries (not aligned with the older power structure) to meet with trauma clinicians from the West in Nordvijkerhout, the Netherlands. Michael MacPherson, a Scotish physician living in West Berlin who had maintained contact under difficult conditions with East European clinicians in the years which preceded 1989, arranged for a number of clinicians including Fyodor Konkov from Russia to attend.

The next year he arranged for us to meet Heike Bernhardt from East Germany and Ion Cucliciu from Romania at the ISTSS meeting in Amsterdam.

The form of the book—narratives of case reports of patients traumatized during the Soviet era, along with the commentary of their therapists whose own traumas had not been so different from those of their patients—first took shape in 1991 when, late one night Fyodor Konkov told us informally of his experience during the assault on the Yeltsin White House and the details of some of his clinical work going on at that time.

Over the next two years, the group of clinicians who are authors in this book expanded. Yael Danieli introduced us to Nora Csiszer and Eva Katona (Hungary) whom one of us (Jacob Lindy along with Bessel van der Kolk) visited in Budapest through the Hungarian Psychiatric Association, World Health Organization, and the Koranyi Clinic. Fyodor Konkov, having worked with earthquake survivors, suggested we contact Anie Kalayjian who in turn invited Levon Jernazian (Armenia). Jacob Lindy's colleague, Fedor Hagenauer, recommended Vasko Muacevic (Croatia). A more in-depth meeting with Ion Cucliciu was possible in Bucharest in 1992 through the efforts of Dr. Romila, the Geneva Initiative, and the Free Romanian Psychiatrists. Following months of correspondence and dramatic changes in Eastern Europe, the participants were ready to move into the next phase of the work.

Leadership of the project during the writing phase fell to both Jacob Lindy and Robert Jay Lifton. Here we found the assistance of still more groups and individuals to be indispensable. Four days of presenting first drafts to each other in Cincinnati in October 1993 were pivotal to the cohesion of the group and came about with the support of the Cincinnati Psychoanalytic Institute and its Research Fund, also the Center on Violence, John Jay University, and the University of Cincinnati Traumatic Stress Study Center. Faculty of the Cincinnati Institute hosted the East European therapists and read early versions of the chapters. These included James Titchener, Louis Spitz, John MacLeod, Janet Newman, Richard Honig, and Anna Ornstein. Guest American faculty with Eastern European roots were regular participants during the meetings and included Larry Rotenberg and Fedor Hagenauer. Also crucial at this juncture and thereafter was Susan Marrs who read and edited many drafts insuring that the English prose preserved the voices of the East Europeans. She traveled with us to Berlin and acted as diplomat and peacemaker as well as catalyst for the writing.

During the editing phase, a two-day interdisciplinary scholars' workshop on the project occurred at the School for International and Area Affairs at Yale University through the efforts of Gaddis Smith, and included contributions from Bob Jenkins, Ivo Banac, Yitzcach Brudny, Mark

Steinberg, Anette Schwarz, Dori Laub, and Tom Holquist who read and discussed early drafts of the chapters. Many of these scholars wrote the historical sketches following each chapter. Uwe Kaminsky helped with historical background and Lisa Hock helped with translation within the chapter on the German Democratic Republic.

Michael MacPherson arranged a final meeting of the contributors to the book in the former East Berlin. This reaffirmed the integrity of the chapters, in light of the rapid changes which were occurring in Eastern Europe and the former Soviet Union. Walter and Sonja Suess, the Gauck Commission, Humboldt University, and the Polish embassy were most supportive. Dori Laub, through the Yale University Center on Genocidal studies, arranged for us to meet with Catherine Merridale in New Haven in 2000. Her perspective was most helpful as we brought the book to closure.

We thank Melinda Russell, Donna Kinney, and Rita McLaughlin who helped at different phases with manuscript preparation and logistics. Gladys Topkis edited several chapters. We thank the editorial staff of Brunner/ Routledge, especially Katherine Mortimer and Bernadette Capelle for their many useful suggestions.

We thank our wives, Joanne Lindy and Betty Jean Lifton, who, as professional colleagues as well as partners, offered good advice as well as crucial support.

Jacob D. Lindy and Robert Jay Lifton

PREFACE

This is their story. We are its midwives.

The East European psychotherapists who speak of themselves and their patients in this book treated survivors of political trauma before, during, and after the fall of the Soviet Union. Theirs is a riveting story of psychosocial adaptation in six different cultures to the longest and most pervasive period of politically engendered trauma and loss in the twentieth century. The two of us joined with our colleagues to complete a series of case reports interlaced with parallel memories from the therapists' own lives. Powerful culturally specific traumas reveal themselves, producing in individuals and families both adaptations and symptoms. In the treatments, countertransferences arise as, unexpectedly, therapists realize they, too, are affected by trauma and loss similar to that of their clients. The treatments, which by their very existence represent ethical paradoxes, turn out to be windows into the persistence of irrational and dynamic forces, of multigenerational adaptations, and of character change in Eastern Europe. They shed light on the puzzling history of the years following the dissolution of the Soviet Union, and trace how deep roots of ambivalence towards freedom grow in an arid soil of trauma and loss.

During the project we have come to know the authors of these chapters, to see their self-awareness in action both in their lands and ours. We have come to respect the witness they bring to the traumas of the Communist era as they narrate the inner lives of their patients (survivors, their children, and grandchildren) and their own deep responses to them.

We admire the ingenuity our colleagues used to find and create safe enough places to carry on genuinely therapeutic work in the context of a political philosophy which, in its undiluted form, was anathema to the principles of privacy, privileged communication, trust, and personal growth. Their cases occur in the final years of the Soviet era, the risky opening up of *perestroika*, and the period of change and stress which followed.

The authors came to our attention by virtue of their clinical work in the field of traumatic stress during a time when Western therapists were just learning of the scope of traumas like those of the Afghansi veterans, Chernoblyl, the Armenian earthquake, and the plight of former political prisoners. They were active in the reform movements which overthrew their governments. As one therapist (Dr. Cucliciu of Romania) explained to us, when it is the political system which causes our patients' trauma, how can the psychotherapist NOT be political. Now these therapists face together with their patients a world of change and uncertainty.

For clinicians interested in trauma and loss, *Beyond Invisible Walls* presents the effects of political imprisonment, forced psychiatric hospitalization, and secret police harassment on survivors and their families. Symptoms such as depression, suicidality, posttraumatic stress disorder, and eating disorders are traced to political as well as intrapsychic factors. Institutionalized across generations, these politically generated stressors produce behavioral adaptations in individuals and families which were useful in the Soviet era: for example, caution, even paranoia (Dr. Csiszer) (Dr. Katona); guilt and the inability to be free (Dr. Bernhardt); dissimulation, splitting (Dr. Cucliciu); self-discontinuity (Dr. Muacevic); intergenerational emptiness (Dr. Konkov); and despair (Dr. Jernazion, Dr. Kalayjian). But today the same personality traits contribute to difficulty in adapting to the changes after Communism.

Psychotherapists will learn in this book of special strains on the therapeutic frame created by intrusive third parties and other challenges to privacy, strains which exist, of course to a lesser degree, in our own practices (see Chapter 9). They will also learn how, officially, the Communist State tried to obliterate the very idea of an internal world, banning Freud and his insistence on the value of the individual, as arch enemy of the collective.

For clinicians aware that their own personal traumas and losses serve both as a source of passion for their work and as a source of potential countertransference, there is the opportunity to examine treatments in which therapists, subject to the same political oppression as their patients, have undergone trauma and loss similar to that of their clients. A central value of the book is its ability to show in vivid form how the therapist's self-awareness is indispensable for the recovery of the patient (see, for example, cases of Dr. Bernhardt, Dr. Cucliciu, Dr. Csiszer, and Dr. Konkov).

For students of ethics, law, and social policy, even the existence of the treatments is interesting in states opposed to individual freedom. As the therapists look both at their patients and at their own experience, they open a window into the violation of human rights under Communism. Heike Bernhardt was spied on by professional members of her own medical and psychiatric faculty; Ion Cucliciu was interrogated by secret police;

Levon Jernazian held revolutionary documents while his friends were in prison.

For family therapists there is the intriguing interaction of familial roles, psychopathology, and the "informer ecology" of the Communist State. For example, in the post-Soviet era, guilty parents who were informers for the State projected blame onto others, even their own children (Dr. Bernhardt). Family dynamics point to missing and covered up stories of parents and grandparents who were killed for political expediency or disappeared in the gulag (Dr. Konkov).

For students of personality development and of early childhood education there is discussion of the effects of political education and premature separation of children from mothers in compulsory State nurseries (Dr. Bernhardt). In East Germany, for example, some of the inhibition regarding work and freedom seen in youths today has its origin in the harmful effects of the State's inculcation of one's primary duty to authority rather than authenticity to the self.

For students of public health the book identifies the epidemic proportions of trauma and loss in Eastern Europe as well as innovative ways to address different populations of survivors: for example, a clinic dealing with psychosocial problems of joblessness in East German youth absorbed into the West (Dr. Bernhardt), efforts to identify and work with networks of former political prisoners in Romania (Dr. Cucliciu), and efforts to address the problems of those wrongfully diagnosed with psychiatric illness because of their behaviors as dissidents (Dr. Csiszer).

It is our hope that this book will be read by all therapists seeking to increase their understanding of the multigenerational effects of culture, trauma, and loss, and by interested readers trying better to understand the legacy of the Communist era. Also, we hope the book will be read in Eastern Europe, both by therapists and others interested in increasing the dialogue about trauma and loss between the generations.

Introduction

A young doctor living in East Berlin in the early 1980s was considering escaping to the West. She felt her earlier respect for her country's ideals had been tarnished. Her efforts to reform from within had brought her harassment from the secret police, the Stasi. Understanding the impact this culture, a remnant of an older culture of terror and informing, would have on her future children and her tie to them, she elected not to marry, and not to have children. One night, she had the following dream:

> I was searching for something. I saw a long pole and knew this would help. It was very tall and flexible. I realized that with this pole I could vault over the wall that divided the two Berlins and escape to the West. I ran towards the wall, planted the pole solidly, and flew into the air. The vault was very successful. It was also miraculous. Bullets were flying about me, but all were missing. Soon I was aware that I was directly over the top of the wall and high above it. Without warning, I struck an invisible barrier. It knocked me from the sky. I fell back to the ground on the Eastern side.

The image of this young woman striking an invisible wall as she tried to vault away from her home in the East captures her experience of confinement by invisible psychological forces. Cseslaw Milosz (1953/1990) foresaw how East Europeans caught in the world of Soviet totalitarianism would show signs of a "captive mind." This woman's wish to leap into the world and mind-set of the West even before the wall had fallen, was clear and conscious; yet an equal opposite force kept her on her own side. Perhaps she wished to retain socialist ideals although tarnished, and even feared that the psychological accommodations she had unconsciously learned in order to adapt in the East would effectively repel her from the West. The dream represents to her an internal and therefore invisible wall that divides the self and would persist even when the actual wall that separated the East from the West would disappear.

In the cases of our East European colleagues and their patients, all survivors of trauma in the Communist era, we find the image of invisible walls recurring in two forms: walls which unconsciously preserve outmoded ways of adaptation (for example, guilt, sacrifice, dependency, and paranoia), and walls which maintain silence between generations (where traumas and deaths of parents and grandparents at the hands of the State go unmourned while succeeding generations feel a void in their identity). The first kind of wall represents the enduring personality traits and unconscious emotional defenses reinforced during the Communist era, which persist today as internal blocks to adaptation in a freer society. The second kind of wall divides an older generation from their children. Parents deceived children in order to protect them. Children grew up with an empty space where true knowledge of their relatives ought to have been.

This book is told through the voices of our colleagues, therapists from six countries inside the former Soviet bloc. It concerns their witness to trauma from the Soviet era and its continuing effects in the lives of their patients, their patients' families, and in themselves. The therapies occurred in the years of *perestroika* and after in Russia and Central/Eastern Europe. As the narrative thread in a given treatment unfolds, we note how, around moments of discord or empathic strain, traumas of the patient resonate with traumas of the therapist. We see shame at the pressure to yield to oppressive authority, guilt taken on when crimes belong to an older generation, disdain at the sacrifice of one's autonomy; we see yearnings for connection between children and their parents and wishes to avoid grief and mourning. Through this double exposure we gain a remarkable experiential look into the culturally specific trauma of the Soviet era and the unconscious defensive adaptations to it which have been part of its aftermath. Where unconscious aspects of patient and therapist overlap we see trauma affecting culture and culture affecting trauma, phenomena which continue to spill over into the post-Soviet period.

During the treatments the patients came to understand themselves better as they struggled to reconnect the broken threads of their lives, and similarly therapists came to understand themselves and their society better as they struggled to integrate parallel experiences. In overcoming the inner walls which split off one part of the mind from another, and in breaking down the walls that separate communications between parents and children, the book offers viable models for individuals and groups within society to confront the past. These treatments provide a road map for communication (applicable to families and groups as well as individuals) which addresses a legacy of silence, miscommunication, and suffering in these years of transition following the Soviet era.

The Patients: Search for Connection

The patients described in this book presented with a wide variety of clinical problems which turned out to be trauma-related: some were typical of posttraumatic stress disorder (PTSD) which we see in other settings: recurrent intrusive images, difficulty sleeping, alienation, psychic numbing, depression. Others are less common: phobia, obsession, eating disorder, work inhibition, suicidal behavior, and the attempt to erase an earlier diagnosis of paranoia. The patients and their relative endured a variety of political traumas: harassment, random searches by secret police, arrest, confinement, stigmatization, abuse by psychiatry, torture, thought reform, imprisonment, and labor camps. As part of the earlier terror/informer ecology (see Chapter 2), they were exposed to the era of complicity with the post-totalitarian state, and their awareness of the political trauma to key family members and friends strongly colors their own core dilemmas and identity today.

In addition the patients were exposed to an intrusive ideology which was destructive to their autonomy and growth, and which in the views of these authors was traumatogenic even to the ordinary citizen—one not subjected to the more extreme forms mentioned above.

The patients' ages range from children to the elderly. Most lived in large cities although they and their family had a variety of rural experiences. Most are men, but in the course of their treatments, significant women in their lives interacted with the therapists. The psychopathology of all the patients was severe enough to interfere significantly with interpersonal relations and subjective distress, but only two were seen in an inpatient setting. The treatments usually lasted several months.

Either the patients themselves, or their missing relatives whose stories they are trying to reconstruct, were charged with an array of misdeeds and suspicions: having belonged as students to pro-Western political parties, having a relative who emigrated to the West, being overheard engaging in political debate, or refusing to give a dog to a KGB official, or simply belonging to the wrong group at the wrong time, being a priest or a Jew or a bourgeois or an intellectual or a student. In the course of their treatment they tried to reconstitute various broken threads of their lives, a father–daughter relationship, a father–son relationship, mourning for a best friend-turned-enemy, familial acceptance of an ostracized relative. They also tried to integrate traumatically fragmented pieces of themselves. These patients and their families experienced a malignant adaptive paranoia in which survival meant concealing one's feelings, opinions, ideas, and heritage even from one's children. As a result, their children felt cut off from knowledge of their own past, from the emotional life of their parents, and from the causes and values their parents held dear. As permission was gradually granted to ask questions in Central and Eastern Europe, the results were revolutionary, internally as well as externally.

The Therapists

Living with Contradiction

In their youth, these reform-minded therapists had been loyal Communists. They wrote prize-winning essays on the glory of the new age and the demands and sacrifices placed on the new Communist man. They joined Communist youth groups, and in one case even founded a new one, more rigid and idealistic than the others. In time, all became disillusioned with the power structure that implemented those ideals, ultimately rejected the Communist Party, and all entered a field that offered some expression of empathy and altruism although they understood that it was heavily infiltrated by secret police. Nearly all were asked to join the KGB or its equivalent and had somehow dealt with party officials who felt they had a right to confidential information supplied to the therapists by their patients.

Most were in their late thirties at the time of the fall of the Berlin Wall. They served in a variety of clinics, most of which were founded during the period of *perestroika* such as suicide prevention services, and twenty-four-hour hot lines. Their formal education had been heavily phenomenological, pharmacological, and behavioral in orientation; reading in Western family systems theory and social psychology seemed roughly compatible with an official mind-set, but in Russia, from 1929 to 1989, no work by Sigmund Freud had been published. Western psychodynamics had been the target of official ideologues. Nonetheless, a Russian version of the unconscious had evolved and interaction with the West around this topic had begun (Miller, 1998).

Because they were interested in psychotherapy, yet practiced as psychiatrists and psychologists in a formal climate which repudiated the subjective self, it was difficult to find role models within their own field. They tended not to idealize their teachers via the formal educational track with which Westerners are familiar, where our teachers become our models for ways of listening and developing technical skills. Empathy and humanness were not particularly valued capacities. Unfortunately, many of the authority figures within the profession were implicated in collaboration with the secret police. Interestingly, we learned that the intellectual moorings placing them within the tradition valuing humanistic, intuitive, and empathic skills came from banned, or dissident, writers. Through these writers, they came to believe that the road to the subjective self was via a search for authentic memory: "What is past is not dead; it is not even past. We cut ourselves off from it; we pretend to be strangers" (Wolf, 1976/1980).

Mind-set of the Reformer Clinicians

The language of the reformers, like the language of dialectic materialism and applied Marxism–Leninism which they opposed, is filled with irony and contradiction. An illustration of the types of contradiction to which they were accustomed occurred when Russia, the new Communist State, contradicted its philosophy by allying itself in 1941 with fascist Germany, the arch-enemy of the Russian people. In terms of dialectic materialism the new pact was an illustration of the point that the practical is superior to the ideal. The therapists, as children, to demonstrate their mastery of this dialectic, wrote essays on topics such as "why less is more" (comparing the Communist East with the Capitalist West).

Similarly, the dissident writers, reacting to the untruths in that dialectic, also chose a language filled with ironic contradiction to express themselves. Cseslaw Milosz (1953/1990) speaks of a world in which one's success is measured in the capacity to convince others that what you don't believe to be true, is true, a term he called *ketman*. Vaclev Havel's protagonist, Hugo Pludek, in *The Garden Party* (Havel, 1963/1993), an ironic play on dialectic thinking, checkmates his Marxist colleagues by out doublethinking them, but when his father asks, who are you anyhow, he replies in riddles that that is a question with no answer. Milan Kundera (1967/1992) describes his characters' lives in terms of a dictionary of misunderstood words and uses "the joke" ironically to refer both to the offense of his protagonist which takes him to political prison, and the mentality of his political captors. Manea (1990) calls the complex contradictions inherent in maintaining grand ideals about the common man while living in a world in which the common man has nothing, mystification. Lydia Chukovskaya's *Sofia Petrovna* (1967/1988) converts her love for her doomed son into ashes by burning his letter, throwing the flame of his love for the ideals of the revolution on the floor, and stamping on it. In the end, Aleksandr Solzhenitsyn's Ivan Denisovitch (1962/1991) must make the most of his absurd and lethal prison world by keeping his perceptions clear. The prison guards, he says, don't have it so easy here either.

Such clarity of perception, while living in a world full of contradiction, also characterizes the language of these reform-minded therapists. Dr. Csiszer and Katona speaks of organized irresponsibility, of the simultaneous presence and denial of trauma, and of communism without community; Dr. Bernhardt sees her patient Karl seeking prison for safety, while her patient Hans obsessively washes himself so that his informer parents can have clean hands. Dr. Cucliciu understands his patient Mihai who, rather than hating his torturer, finds him fascinating.

Grounded in their sensitive critiques of the Soviet world from the inside, these therapists kept alive a humanistic tradition which had been abandoned as the State took over the mental health field, banned Freud, and diverted the purposes of that field to its ends. Like Havel's character Joseph Gross in *The Memorandum* (Havel, 1966/1993) they had their own diagnosis for the times: "We're living in a strange, complex epoch. As Hamlet says, our 'time is out of joint.' Just think, we're reaching the moon and yet it's increasingly hard for us to reach ourselves; we're able to split the atom, but unable to prevent the splitting of our personality; we build superb communications between the continents, and yet communication between man and man is increasingly difficult."

Ideology of the Cold War: Freud as Antithesis to Bolshevik Thought

The therapists in this project were more aware than we how elements in Freudian thought had come to represent the antithesis of the Marxist view of psychology. Miller (1998) describes how Soviet ideologues as late as the 1960s, fearing the intrusion of Western psychodynamic thinking in literature, the arts, and psychology, called forth a major attack on Freud. From the Marxian perspective, psychology must commandeer the psyche to the lofty struggle of historic class war. So, intellectually, Soviet psychology was at war with Freud. Freud, they said, worked with the base instincts—sex and aggression, with self-indulgence over social commitment, with an internal rather than an action-oriented external self, with a childhood which was deterministic rather than an adulthood which was rationally directed towards the State's ends. As we shall see in the next chapter, this logic ultimately led psychiatry to become an agent of the State, a perpetrator in its own right. For opposition to the State must represent some psychic abnormality of the mind, and thus became the rationale through which psychiatry via the KGB became the State's instrument to contain dissent in psychiatric hospitals. But for now, we wish to highlight the sympathetic chord which Freudian thought resonated within the dissident-clinicians.

Treatment Under Impossible Conditions

Conducting genuine psychotherapy under these circumstances entailed considerable risks, and all the therapists assume or have indeed learned that they had extensive secret police files which charged them with such offenses as disseminating religious literature, teaching patients ideas against the state, and engaging in pro-democracy activities. How they managed to function in systems which (although they were changing) continued to attack their values, and spied on and harassed them, is a central feature of what these therapists have to teach us.

Soviet culture strained each element of the therapeutic frame and the working alliance in these treatments: a safe space, confidentiality, trust, neutrality. The very effort to create a therapeutic setting in a totalitarian society is filled with contradiction. How can the patient feel safe when the secret police could be listening, or at least exerting pressure on the therapist? Perhaps the therapist himself is a member of the KGB. There are philosophical contradictions between an individual's wish to integrate his life experience and the State's wish that he subsume his life to the goals of the State. Symptoms themselves could be seen as affronts to the state. Symptoms carried trauma-specific cultural as well as psychodynamic meaning.

But nonetheless, powerful treatments did occur. As we reflect on these treatments using a psychoanalytic perspective, we see that feelings which the patient irrationally placed on the therapist (transference) and feelings which the therapist, in response, irrationally placed on the patient (countertransference) make dialogue characteristic of the inner world of the totalitarian state come alive in the therapist–patient interaction reflective of dialogue between the informer and the betrayed, the captor and his victim, the purged parent and his orphaned child, the true self and a false self.

Despite enormous obstacles, these therapists chose creative ways to treat people within the old system; they also took on challenging roles within the reform movement. Dr. Bernhardt, for example, opened a clinic for East Germans confused and disoriented by the sudden merger with the West; Dr. Csiszer established a suicide prevention clinic; Dr. Cucliciu ran for political office in Romania; Dr. Konkov joined Afghani veterans inside the Yeltsin White House while tanks rolled towards them; Dr. Jernazian marched with his political friends in Freedom Square in the Armenian capital, Yerevan; and Dr. Muacevic prepared for the inevitable casualties of ethnic warfare.

Reflecting on the years of even inadvertent complicity, the therapists do not excuse themselves from the implications of belonging to a professional group that broke the public trust by joining in the State's oppression. They agree with Havel (1979/1986) that we are all responsible. How could millions be governed in such a system, they ask, if we didn't all cooperate? Dr. Cucliciu explains: "the division between those of us who promote change and those who oppose it is an artificial one; both exist within the self." They see that understanding the historical aggressor with empathy is as much a part of the task that lies ahead as is identifying groups victimized by the totalitarian state.

It is from this broad yet at times painful position of responsible self-awareness that the therapists in this book, witnesses to trauma in their patients and in themselves, take their position. They carry with them wounds analogous to those of their patients and a powerful humanistic tradition whose roots go deep in their culture and history.

The Cultures

The therapists, as they listened to each other, found a remarkable constancy in the nature of the State-imposed trauma of their regimes—a trauma-specific, Soviet-imposed culture. They also underlined the cultural uniqueness in the differing areas. The six countries represented in this book represent six different languages, four distinct alphabets, and five religions prior to Communism.

The histories of their respective countries involved rivalry, tension and war, occupation, and partition of land at each other's hands. Romania currently occupies land populated by Hungarians; Armenia has experienced Russia as its savior and its vicious master; Germany had occupied four of the other countries in World War II.

Traumatic conditions towards the end of the Communist era differed. The Romanian experience was the most brutal. The German Democratic Republic was the most regimented. In Hungary, a unique set of forces gave Communism a softer face. For Croatia, Tito's Communism had repressed ethnic rivalries. Armenians saw their plight in sweeping terms, as slaves and martyrs to the forces of history. Russian trauma, brutal by any standards, is complicated in today's survivors by the problem of its own enormous losses and its aggressor role with the others in Eastern Europe.

How We Worked Together

Between 1990 and 1993 we had been introduced to our core group of therapists (see Acknowledgments). They had corresponded with us about difficult patients and their own reactions to working with them. Some of these letters were clearly censored. They invited us to visit them in their countries and at their clinics. We saw them with their patients and colleagues, and even joined them at the sites of disaster to work with survivors and caregivers. For more than two years, the idea of this book simmered in our minds, and by 1993 we were ready to set out on the task of writing it. We asked each therapist to select one or two cases that illustrated some aspect of trauma from the old regime which was part of the clinical illness with which the patient presented. We did not restrict the use of the term "Soviet-era trauma," as we wanted to learn from the East-European therapists themselves the range of its usefulness for them, given their difficult experiences under Soviet rule. Then we asked each to develop a chapter with five sections: 1) a subjective narrative of the professional life of the author; 2) the clinical settings and the various roles in which he or she worked; 3) the treatment process; 4) the therapist's experience of the treatment and subsequent reflections about it; and finally 5) some commentary on the personal journey of the therapist during the years of change in Europe.

Therapists used clinical notes as their data base, although in some instances they could only use memory, as written confidential notes were dangerous at the time. Dr. Cucliciu used audio tapes of the sessions. Each therapist completed a written case summary following the traditional medical format of presenting problems and symptoms, psychiatric history, evaluation of mental status, initial diagnostic impressions, course of psychotherapy, and discussion. With a first draft of this write-up in hand each therapist presented informally to the book's working group in Cincinnati in October 1993. These oral presentations lasted three hours each. They were conducted in English, and when nuances of meaning were unclear to one's colleagues, another mental health professional conversant in the language of the author served as translator. The oral presentations and the discussion among our group were recorded and transcribed (authors were free to stop the recording at any point they wished, and did so for a variety of reasons including concerns of potential harm that might still come to persons if identified). We then collated the written summaries and joined them with the earlier correspondence and essays in process, together with transcriptions of those oral presentations. We organized these written and spoken fragments into the above pre-set outline, entirely composed of the author's words.

In the months following the presentations, we asked many questions about the treatments, mostly focusing and expanding the therapists' reactions to dilemmas in the cases. Studying especially the oral presentations in Cincinnati, we tried to discover the voice of each therapist. Next we worked closely with each author to rewrite the chapters in the first person singular, trying to convey those voices to an American readership.

Therapists formulated their cases based on differing schools of treatment: social psychiatry, family systems, behavior modification, Gestalt, psychopharmacology, and psychodynamic psychotherapy.

Their formulations, nonetheless, were empathically arrived at from an intersubjective point of view and were therefore compatible with psychoanalytic understandings, even though this perspective had been largely absent from their official training (see Dr. Muacevic's chapter for an exception). Dr. Csiszer uses an evenly hovering attention; Dr. Bernhardt reflects on her having become a repository for her patient's family's projections; Dr. Cucliciu struggles with the countertransference and uncompromising authenticity: Dr. Konkov explores the layers of meaning in symptom formation; Dr. Jernazian searches with his patients for an inner self, and Dr. Muacevic interprets in an epigenetic context. All participated in a self-scrutiny about the meaning of these cases to the therapist and the role of self-awareness in the process of the work together. Such activities were not alien to these therapists; they were part of the fabric of their identities as altruistic healers within the reformer/dissident mindset. As mental health professionals, then, it is not surprising that they felt comfortable with us using the vocabulary of transference and countertransference, and were, more broadly, willing to explore a psychoanalytic frame of reference with regard to their patients and their treatments.

It is not surprising that, as the reformer-clinicians took stands against the Communist *weltanschauung*, that they also turned (at least temporarily) to Freud for a language to help them explain those internal phenomena which had arisen as their patients and they themselves had fallen prey to Communist oppression. Thus Freudian thought, officially reviled for so long as the antithesis of Marxist dialectic materialism, became one of the philosophic languages of the successful revolt from Communism.

Working with these clinicians, collecting data, communicating those data to each other, and reflecting upon their meanings, has been a lively process in which newer layers of meaning emerge and inevitably the story winds up being told in a way that is different from its first version. Finally we met as a group once again in Berlin in 1995 to insure that the evolving manuscripts were true to the authors' memory and intent, and remained in touch as the project took its course.

Empathic Strain and the Search for Meaning

As in work with other traumatized populations (Lindy, MacLeod, Spitz, Green, & Grace, 1988; Wilson & Lindy, 1994), therapists are prone to countertransference reactions. Here, therapists found that, in the search for empathy with their patients, they unexpectedly ran into blocks or powerful affects in themselves which forced them to confront their own lost stories of family members who were purged or ostracized. In their interactions with their patients, therefore, these therapists often unexpectedly experienced intense emotions such as especially warm feelings of identification or the opposite—feelings of rejection, isolation, fear, or anger. In each case, this intense reaction was a clue to ways in which the patient's wound—a legacy of the Communist era—connected with the therapist's wound of the same traumatic history. What we as readers observe is that, as the therapist acknowledges and works through more of his or her own story, the patients too are better able to acknowledge their past. It is also important to note that as these transference–countertransference crises get resolved, each therapist remains successfully within the frame of the treatment mode he or she has chosen, whether it is a social psychiatric intervention, a family systems intervention, behavioral/existential therapy, or dynamic therapy.

The next chapter, Legacy of Trauma, introduces the reader to the traumatic history of Eastern and Central Europe under Communism. Then, in the following six chapters, therapists in individual countries describe their background, the roles they played as mental health professionals, and specific case studies which contribute to our understanding Soviet trauma. Each chapter contributes something additional to our understanding the complexity of the psychological legacy of the trauma today. Editors' Notes set each author and set of cases into context, and Chapter Highlights summarize the clinical significance of the cases.

Finally, thumbnail sketches of the sociopolitical history of each specific country by scholars in Eastern and Central European history, sociology, and literature follow each chapter. This gives further background to histories with which many Americans are unacquainted, and expands the unique cultural perspective on the forces producing the traumas and the environment in which recovery is to take place.

In each chapter authors explore a different element of the sociocultural milieu of Communism in depth. Drs. Csiszer and Katona select the manipulation and control of social structures. Dr. Bernhardt highlights pedagogy; Dr. Cucliciu, the origins of brutality; Dr. Konkov, the presence of intergenerational schism; Dr. Muacevic deals with ethnic diversity; and Drs. Jernazian and Kalayjian, the godless state. For each of these areas, the authors suggest that their compatriots both adapted to the stressors around them, and also found expression for resistance to them. In Hungary people were complicit with the State's control of social structure, but held on to deep Western cultural traditions as a resistance. East Germans reacted with obedience to the State-controlled pedagogy, but retained their own view of ideal socialism. In Romania, people split off part of themselves to survive, but retained an authentic part in order to hope. In

Croatia, people accommodated to ethnic suppression, but longed for a day of national reckoning. And in Armenia, people succumbed to pagan power by unconsciously activating an inner slave, while drawing ultimately on an even deeper Christian tradition which gave them sustenance.

Each individual chapter offers insights into the practice of mental health in the former Soviet Union and the Eastern bloc countries, the roles our profession played in complicity with the post-totalitarian state, and the roles our colleagues played in the revolutions which overthrew them. Most important, as each chapter elucidates, survivors internalized adaptations to trauma and loss which cannot now be easily discarded. They became cautious, and withdrew from confrontation; they unconsciously yielded to the power of the state; they sacrificed while others exploited them; they projected guilt and responsibility onto the outside; they denied trauma; and they fabricated the truths of their own and their parents' lives; they became complicit with corruption. To the degree that these adaptations persist, they affect the ability of East Europeans to adapt to the changing circumstances of the present.

In Chapter 9, Dr. Lindy refines the lens of observation to those critical moments of empathic strain between patient and therapist during the treatments, pointing out that in the parallel psychological dilemmas they are experiencing, in the room is a larger psychohistorical window into the lasting sequelae of the years of Soviet oppression. And in Chapter 10, Dr. Lifton widens the lens to encompass six psycho-social-historical dimensions involving the complex interaction of forces on all these levels.

We hope that these case stories and accompanying accounts of therapists' internal reactions to them will become a guide for many others to face trauma and loss from totalitarian oppression within families and across the generations.

Legacy of Trauma and Loss

Jacob D. Lindy

Divided Cities, Divided Minds

Trieste, Jerusalem, Sarajevo, and Berlin are cities which, because of their key locations and political divisiveness, have been partitioned in response to the trauma of politics and war. People and armies stake out green and red zones; people and armies build barbed wire fences and masonry walls. Once the partition has endured, the inhabitants on one side of the wall come to have a different view of themselves and of events in the world outside from those on the other side. The events, once shared by all before the partition was erected, now turn into different histories. Leaders on one side draw their past, present, and future in sharp contrast from those on the other side. The barriers are said to protect the inhabitants on one side from warring behavior on the other, but they make the practical management of the city a nightmare, interrupting metro lines, telephone service, distribution of goods and services, and disrupting life-long connections with friends and relatives. Maintaining the barrier comes at a high cost in terms of soldiers, guards, and loss of life for those who attempt to break through the partition. The Iron Curtain, dividing East from West, was one such wall; Berlin, just one segment.

So too with the mind. In the posttraumatic condition, a state in which the "stimulus barrier of the ego" is overwhelmed, barriers form to protect the psyche from repetition of the overwhelming state of trauma. Later these isolated segments of thoughts and feelings become alienated, split off from the rest of the mind. They no longer perceive or communicate

13

effectively with either the outside world or the mind as a whole. Indeed, posttraumatically, each split-off section of the mind composes its own history. Each compartment, such as the victimized self, or the warrior self, selects or represses memories which add up to radically differing views of the past, present, and future. Maintaining these dissociations comes at a high personal cost, as energy is absorbed protecting the splits in the ego or partitions in the mind as though by an internal military, always fearing attack.

Those citizens living within divided cities while under siege experience a sense of despair and numbing when they consider the past and the future. They therefore concentrate on a disembodied present as though it were an eternity. Walls of silence and misinformation between the generations serve to keep these disconnections in place.

And what happens when the walls come down? Physically, architects and city planners might design a reminder of the old barrier. Vienna's ringstrasse stands where the outer walls of a medieval city stood; and tourists gather at China's Great Wall; new high-rises dot the site of the fallen wall in Berlin, and soon, perhaps, a memorial of the Holocaust. Commerce returns, and in time, the old city re-equilibrates. Telephones and subway lines once more connect people, and relatives visit without encumbrance.

But what of the psychological walls—speechless partitions which formed to protect individuals from the pain of trauma and loss incurred during the conflict which divided the city ? These walls of course are invisible. And often these remaining barriers lack words. Yet they still divide families, and they still divide minds. When the physical barrier is removed we are tempted to conclude it must be gone. We see only an architect's reminder. But how are we to judge the silent walls of trauma. When are they gone? When is there free commerce between all parts of the mind and true resumption of connectedness between the generations? In truth these invisible partitions change very slowly. They continue to invoke caution and fear, alienation and distrust, even as the external signs of geopolitical division (as in the case of the Iron Curtain) seem to have disappeared. We shall return throughout this book to the metaphor of psychological walls or partitions which have formed in the presence of trauma and loss, especially in Chapter 9, but for now we must look at some of the history in Russia and Eastern Europe which produced them.

The therapists who write of their experiences in this book grew up in Yerevan (Armenian SSR, now Armenia), Bucharest (Romania), Budapest (Hungary), Zagreb (Croatia), East Berlin (German Democratic Republic, now Germany) and Lvov (Ukrainian SSR, now Ukraine). Geographically, these cities lie along the cusp of an arc sweeping north and west from the Caspian Sea to the Baltic Sea, with Moscow, the center and vortex, twelve hundred miles away. They lived on the outer edge of the Soviet partition. From the West we saw this arc in Churchill's terms, an impenetrable Iron Curtain; from the East it was Solzhenitsyn's (1962/1991) barbed wire fence, built by the hands inside to mark the outer boundary of a vast but failed experiment, behind which all were prisoners. The home cities of our patients and therapists felt the brunt of suspicion and political repression as they lined the divide separating two warring world views.

Waves of Trauma and Loss

In this chapter we present a historical overview of trauma in the Soviet era, a past which the therapists and patients in this book share, and to which they bear witness. The three generations who constitute their families suffered successive waves of violence and death throughout the twentieth century. For those caught in these waves, there were traumatic losses and radical discontinuities in their experience of themselves, their families, and their world. Soviet political repression is the central focus of this book and primary source of trauma and loss for the patients and their therapists. But political repression became so folded in with war, genocide, famine, natural and man-made disasters, and disease that precise distinctions are difficult. Survivors find that they cannot isolate an atmosphere of political repression from these additional catastrophic traumas which complicate them.*

Grasping the height and forms of these waves of trauma and loss is not easy, especially for readers in the United States and Canada. One problem is that the shear size of each wave is enormous. As Merridale (1996) points out, "scarcely a single family can have escaped some direct experience of premature death in this period (1914–1921), a pattern that would be repeated several times in the next few decades." (p. 4) Second, the sources of trauma and loss within each wave are complex, not simply limited to a single form of trauma such as political repression. And third, those who tell its history may speak from within only one psychological compart-

---

*For example, the famine of 1931–32 began as Stalin was enforcing collectivization, deporting prosperous farmers, and forcibly seizing all produce from the farmers of the Ukraine for redistribution (threatening them with arrest for "hoarding" if they did not comply). When, shortly after, crops failed and widespread starvation and famine occurred in the Ukraine, the causes seemed to be both political and natural. Another illustration of overlapping categories is during the Nazi advance into Russia in the early 1940s. The State assigned political prisoners (or zeks) as shock troops promising "rehabilitation" for bravery. But in fact, the zeks found themselves pinned between two foes intent on killing them, the advancing enemy and a *zagradotriad*, a Soviet unit instructed to kill them if they tried to pull back. (Beevor, 1998, p. 85)

ment within the still-divided city of the mind. For example, there is the perspective of the young adult reformers and their dissident elders. Another is that of an older generation still loyal to now-shattered Soviet ideals. A third is the view of children who in the past unquestioningly accepted what they have been taught. Also, we in the West find it difficult to relinquish our own biases, formed on the other side of the divide.

In this chapter, we shall identify four separate waves of trauma and loss chronologically. Then we shall describe some unique psychological dimensions of each form of trauma: political repression, war, ethnic killing, natural disasters, disease and famine. From time to time as it seems necessary for the narrative, we will include differing perspectives on the same history. Mostly our vantage point towards this history is that of the East European therapists, but we include as well views from other portions of the divided city above, for some of their patients and their families continue to see the world within the walls of a partitioned past.

Historians of Russia divide the waves of trauma and death into three time periods: 1914–1922 (World War I, revolution, civil war, disease and famine, 23–26 million deaths); 1926–1939 (political repression, collectivization, industrialization, famine, and the purges of 1937–38, 10 million deaths); 1939–1945, (second world war, 26 million deaths) (Davies, Harrison, & Wheatcroft, 1994). To these we wish to add the post-war years, 1947–1953, in which Soviet political structure was exported to Eastern Europe. Later, we will describe the post-Stalinist totalitarian State in which the therapists themselves grew up, a State which, while less brutal, continued the same traumatizing institutions.

The First Wave: 1914–1922

The first wave of trauma and loss for peoples of Russia and Eastern Europe in the twentieth century came in the form of the First World War and an estimated one million war dead. With its end came the collapse of over-arching political structures, not only of the Russian but the Austro-Hungarian and Ottoman empires as well. Civil war, epidemics of disease, and famine followed. And the Russian Communist Revolution began. With it, political oppression played an important role in the loss of life of those who were perceived to stand in the way of the Revolution's progress. Both therapists and patients in this book lost grandparents in this way. Losses on all sides were enormous. Between 1914–1921 Russia lost twenty-three million lives. Extensive epidemics of disease were associated with war damage and disruptions of sanitary conditions in cities such as Petrograd (Merridale, 2000). Famine contributed substantially to the death toll as well. Elsewhere, in another part of the region, Turks carried out a genocide against Armenians, causing another million deaths (Kuper, 1988).

The Second Wave: 1926–1939

The impact of the wave of violence, trauma, and death between 1926–1939 is of special concern for this book, as it occurred in conjunction with Stalin's purges and his revolution from above, where he instigated vast social and economic programs, while drawing an ever-shifting boundary around who was within and who was outside the new State. Political repression, and the police state institutions to carry them out, became a primary cause of trauma and death. These purges charged people with crimes against the State; interrogated, harassed, and ostracized them; punished their families; tortured them to inform on others; confined them in labor camps, often under arctic conditions; subjected them to long political imprisonment and, often, killed them (deJonge & Morrow, 1986). This wave of violence also set the precedent for a reign of terror in Eastern European countries which would fall under Communist rule later.

Political executions directly accounted for 1.5 million deaths. Revolutionary collectivization of agriculture, combined with famine created unspeakable conditions including cannibalism. Adding deaths from relocations of individuals, forced industrialization, particularly the deportation of the so-called middle-class farmers or kulaks, there were ten million deaths (Merridale, 1996).

The Third Wave: 1939–1945

War struck again between 1939 and 1945. And for much of that war, Russian land was the field of battle. This time Russia's toll alone was "in excess of twenty-six million premature deaths, some in combat, some related directly to the war, but many also products of a continuing campaign of state repression" (Merridale, 1996, p. 3). The countries of Central, Southern, and Eastern Europe were annexed by fascist Germany between 1939 and 1944. Indeed, the national armies of Croatia, Hungary, and Romania entered the command structure of the Fuhrer. Hungary, for example, sent 245,000 troops to fight with the *Wermacht* in Russia. Some 50,000 were killed or froze to death, 70,000 were taken prisoner or disappeared. Hungary's five-month reign of terror by the Arrow Cross in 1944, a final destructive fascist effort, led to " little but ruined cities and ruined lives" (Hanak & Held, 1992, p. 202). In the former Yugoslavia, between 1941 and 1945, besides invasion and occupation, there was a fierce civil war causing suffering in excess of World War I. Deaths in the southern Balkans as a result of occupation, civil war, and genocide were about 1.1 million people (Djordjevic, 1992). Among the therapists and their patients, stories of parents and grandparents who fell in this era are common.

The Post-War Years: 1947–1953

Stalin's policy of political repression, while most cataclysmic during the purges of 1937–38, was actually a continuous process before, during, and after the Great Patriotic War. It reached a second height following it. This new wave of political repression occurred when strong men applied Stalin's methods to the new "socialist" republics of Eastern Europe. The wave of political repression between 1948–1953 followed Russia's victory in the Great Patriotic War against the Axis countries. The USSR now occupied the countries on her western flank who had invaded her. To protect against future German aggression, and to expand her own sphere of influence, the USSR exported the Communist revolution to the occupied countries of Eastern Europe. Militant Communists like Matyas Rakosi in Hungary, Gherghe Gheorghiu-Dej in Romania, and Walter Ulbricht of East Germany took power. Most had been educated in Moscow during the war. Their regimes repeated in every detail the world order of Moscow and the paranoid political style of Joseph Stalin. In Hungary, for example, between 1949 and 1953, over 750,000 came under investigation for suspicion of political deviance. Of these, 150,000 ended up in prison or in concentration camps. About 2,000 were executed in trumped-up charges and thousands were maimed in brutal investigations (Hanak & Held, 1992).

In the former Yugoslavia between 1946–48, Tito consolidated his partisans into the Communist Party. He eliminated former Nazi collaborators, harassed non-Communists, conducted farcical trials of political opponents, and executed his rival antifascist leader, Mihailovic. Returning anticommunist refugees from Austria were executed en masse. By 1947, there was radical agrarian reform, distribution of church property, and large estates. Kulaks were sent to prison by the thousands. In addition, when Tito broke from Stalin, "more than 50,000 were mercilessly tortured and massacred in the same manner as medieval heretics" (Djordjevic, 1992, p. 331). In East Germany, Ulbricht unleashed a reign of terror in 1952 with liquidation of private holdings, agricultural collectivization, and a strong secret police. That secret police organization ultimately imprisoned 200,000 of its citizens (Priebe & Denis, 1998) Another measure of the severity of conditions was that 200,000 per year were leaving via West Berlin (Croan, 1992). For our East European patients and therapists, these were the hard days of which their parents had spoken, days that, although not part of their own memories, colored their perceptions. The case of Mihai (Chapter 5) captures the brutality of these times.

After Stalin, and the leadership of the first round of strongmen in Eastern Europe, periods of political repression seemed to ebb and flow. The amplitude of continuing waves of violence and death tended to be smaller in size and less in brutality. But the institutions of political repression remained in place, especially the Party and the secret police, effectively controlling society and to a significant measure molding the psychology of individual lives. We shall return to the subject of trauma and loss during the post-Stalinist totalitarian state and during the post-Communist period later in this chapter, as they provide the historical context for the lives of the therapists' current generation. But first, let us turn in more detail to major specific forms of trauma and loss which relate to the legacy of trauma in the Soviet era: political repression, war, ethnic killing, and "natural" disaster.

Forms of Trauma and Loss

From the point of view of trauma studies, each trauma survivor population has a certain morphology, characterized by demographics, types of trauma experiences, social supports both at the time of trauma and afterward, and attitudes of the recovery environment to their trauma and loss (Green, Wilson, & Lindy, 1985).

On the one hand, individual survivors are likely to have experienced a series of traumas since each wave contained different forms of trauma, and since a given survivor is likely to have endured more than one wave. For example, Drs. Csiszer and Katona calculate that their patient, Mr. E., experienced thirteen separate traumas (Chapter 3). On the other hand, each specific form of trauma carries with it its own special psychological tones, and presents special problems for recovery, grief, and mourning. We will describe each form separately as each entails a different recovery or mourning process. We begin with the primary form of trauma, for purposes of this book, political repression.

Political Repression: Zeks, Kulaks, and their Families— Citizens and their Revolutionary Duty

At first, it appeared that there was some pattern to those who became the victims of political repression, as they represented positions in society generally thought to constitute a threat to the new revolutionary Communist regime: mainstays of the old order, clergy, ultra-nationalists, fascist supporters, and middle class. Soon, however, the list kept enlarging to include any whose criticism was seen as dangerous to the state: intelligentsia, students, those with contact with the West, artists, and the professionals; those who opposed collectivization, and so-called prosperous farmers (kulaks). Even loyal members of the Communist Party became targets. The latter were dangerous because they commanded loyalty and therefore might inspire separate leadership initiatives. They were arrested and charged with political crimes. Here, however, the charges were more intricate. In the specious show-trials they were accused of deviations to the left or right, were tortured, producing copious confessions of wrong-doing, all so that the great social experiment could go on under the single leadership of the leader. The lesson was clear: No one was immune from the eyes of the State, and any could be caught in the web of political repression (deJonge & Morrow, 1986).

Once arrested, victims were separated from their families, interrogated, tortured, forced to inform on others, sometimes brainwashed, sent to slave labor camps, often under arctic conditions for what turned out to be in-determinate terms. Later, some were sent as shock troops against the advancing Germans. While loyalty often developed in the camps among the *zeks*, there were at times powerful forces turning one political prisoner against another. Upon discharge from prison, they were still ostracized, often lost their families, were harassed and alone.

Those political prisoners who were killed or who died in the camps were buried anonymously. They, as enemies of the state, were denied funerals and ritual. When their families learned of their deaths (often years later), traditional means of mourning were both officially and prac-tically prohibited. Out of fear of further reprisals, widows destroyed pho-tographs and letters. The result was that no vehicle existed for children to learn from their parents and families who these deceased relatives were (Merridale, 2000a). In time they could only be alluded to by a lie, as if their life story were submerged in a vague blanket of sacrifice for the Great Patriotic War.

Now, in the post-Soviet era, the therapists join a generation who are keenly interested in learning about their murdered relatives. How did they live? What did they think? How did they die? But there are other questions as well. Who were the revolutionaries who carried out their "citizen's duty"? How many people did they kill? How many people did they report on, before or after someone reported on them? Some now wish to re-engage an arrested multigenerational grief process; they want to connect with their legacy. Others face intergenerational questions about relatives who perpetrated crimes.

War: Veterans, the War Dead, and their Families

War constitutes another form of violence and death. Circumstances of death or survival in the battle for Russia were often horrendous, accom-panied with freezing conditions, starvation, and disease. Populations were both military and civilian, men, women, and children. Children who sur-vived Stalingrad lived in the ground for four months, and "were swollen with hunger . . . afraid to speak, to even look people in the face" (Beevor, 1998). The specific trauma experiences included a full range of injuries, captivity, exposure to grotesque bodies and body parts, and the impact of killing as well as seeing others killed. In Russia, death in war, unlike being victimized by political repression, was a patriotic act to be revered by mourners and celebrated by the State. Families held on to photos of the deceased, and told stories to children and grandchildren. While traditional religious rites were denied, there was a stoic social solidarity which provided support for the bereaved. Bodies were buried when possible, and where the bodies could not be retrieved great monuments were created making communal grieving possible and comforting. Veterans who survived became heroes of the Revolution, receiving medals, pensions, and becoming revered educators of the young. While the tragedies of war were horrendous, the quality of the recovery environment as an aid to the healing of its aftereffects was generally positive.

The trauma and loss from World War II is a large subject unto itself. It is not the primary focus of these cases, but trauma during that period produced a layer of stress and adaptation indispensable for understanding the patients and their families in this book, such as Viktor and Mr. E.

Ethnic Cleansing and Genocide: Jews, Armenians, Bosnians

For the therapists, patients, and their families, we cannot appreciate the background of trauma and loss without considering the Holocaust, the genocidal killing of six million Jews in Europe, men, women, and children, mostly from East/Central Europe and Germany. All of the countries in which our therapists and their patients live participated in this slaughter. Hungary, for example, gave up 500,000 of its Jews to extermination in the genocide at the end of the war. Even on Belorussian and Ukrainian land, 1.3 million were killed. And such history is part of the life stories of patients and family members in this book. Mr. E. was harassed and threatened for helping Jews. One therapist's father was interrogated and threatened with deportation for helping Jews; another therapist lost relatives in the Holocaust, and was denied access to the knowledge that her mother was a hidden Jew. Interestingly, during our project when Western historians openly critiqued East European governments' brutality in the Holocaust, some of our East European colleagues reacted vigorously and defensively, seeing their countries, instead, as more benevolent: perspectives rooted in their own education and anti-Nazi leanings.

Nor was the Holocaust the only form of ethnic killing. Earlier in the century, in Turkey, there was the willful destruction of more than one million Armenians, many of whom were placed on a forced march into the desert with no means of survival. Even today the policies which placed this genocide into action are not acknowledged. Once again, losses affected the traumatic background of patients and therapists. And official denial rubs salt into the wound. Two therapists lost family members in the Armenian genocide and remember their grandparents' accounts of the survivors' horrors.

Finally, some may have initially thought of the losses in the Balkans during the 1990s largely as military action. It is now clear that they have been enflamed by ethnic hatreds and manifest themselves in ethnic cleansing as well. The patient Josip was exposed to both.

Survivors of genocide and their children must integrate perhaps an even more heinous aspect of human nature than political repression or war; namely, that another group would wish to and in fact did try to destroy all members of their group simply because of ethnic origin.

Famine, Disaster, and Disease

The waves of death which swept through Russia and Eastern Europe also contained more than their share of natural and man-made disasters. The famines of 1921 and 1931–32 were unimaginable, with reports of cannibalism of neighbors and children occurring with some frequency especially in the 1931–32 famine. The latter famine was, in the minds of many, including our reformist-therapists, a direct result of political decisions to collectivize farms at any cost, to relocate the more prosperous farmers (kulaks), and to starve farmers and their families while feeding those comrades engaged in the massive new industrialization. Here, the victims were rural and of all ages. Officially, the Soviet Union denied these deaths by famine. In the aftermath, the survivors, feeling unacknowledged and ashamed, denied themselves even the memory of the tragedy. Public policy at the very least exacerbated trauma, and at the worst cut off emotional exploration of its psychological integration as a means of adaptation. An almost equally horrendous loss of life by communicable disease accompanied the ruined cities of the Russian civil war period. The simultaneous presence of catastrophe, neglectful governmental policy, enormous numbers of death, and official denial became a pattern. We are able to see how political reactions to the Armenian earthquake of 1988 added to the trauma of those who suffered. The government failed to protect its citizens through adequate building codes, and failed to mobilize effective rescue operations. Officials minimized loss of life and damage. They accused victims of excessive complaining rather than acknowledging the legitimacy of their suffering and grief. Survivors of natural disasters such as the Armenian earthquake (Chapter 8) are bitter that the State failed to provide safety, to mobilize effective relief, and to acknowledge loss and grief. In these ways they feel the state contributed to their trauma. Reactions of civilians near Chernobyl also consider these disasters in political terms.

Psychological Context

An Ecology of Terror

We turn, next, to the general emotional climate in which Soviet political repression worked. One way of grasping the larger picture of how fear of political trauma and death affected so many people under Communist totalitarianism is to think of the stories of the patients and therapists in this book as having occurred within a single ecological system of terror.

Let us imagine living in a city undergoing purges in Russia or Eastern Europe. A secret police agent (such as Mr. R., Chapter 8) arrives in his black car, terrorizes a household, pulling out a father (such as Mr. E., Chapter 3) in the middle of the night. This sets off a series of traumas that spread far beyond the agent himself and the man he seizes. The victim is interrogated, imprisoned, tortured (like Mihai, Chapter 5). Upon release, in order to maintain his integrity and protect his family he abandons his wife and daughter. But his effort at anonymity fails; he is again harassed by secret police or perhaps placed in a psychiatric hospital against his will (as was Mr. E.).

His wife is officially forbidden to grieve her loss; rather she must do something to erase the shame his arrest has caused. She must also care for her daughter, who is being denied school opportunities because she carries the shamed name of her father (Chapter 3). The wife divorces her husband but feels guilty, depressed, and angry at her decision. To move on with her life, she changes her name. The family fabricates stories to account for the father's disappearance (Dima, Chapter 6). At the same time, surviving adults fear that a young adult in the next generation will also disappear into a vast system of political prisons or *gulag*. A child grows up with an inner emptiness, deprived of a father and unable fully to see through the fabrications. In this atmosphere the child unconsciously blames the father for abandoning him or her.

Years later, in different political times, the survivor yearns to return, but there he will find no home, no wife, and no family. The abandoned child, now an adult, yearns for the parent she lost.

The original victim, under threats to his family or under torture to himself, revealed the names of friends whose comments could be construed as politically dangerous or he may even have been forced to torture other prisoners (Chapter 5) to demonstrate his commitment to the new order. Now, the pain and suffering of new victims complicates his own. Moreover, during much of his imprisonment the victim was probably kept in near lethal arctic weather, where physiologically he functioned on a subsistence level. He probably watched many others die from illness and from beatings. While he made friends in prison camp, he also often felt distrust: Anyone could be an informant for the state (Chapter 4).

Costs of Survival

In the minds of our therapists, those who survived such trauma did so at enormous personal cost. They passed on a legacy in which personal initiative and creative ideas were dangerous; actions, behaviors, and even choice of words needed to be monitored; contradiction, hypocrisy, and lies must be ignored; and feelings themselves were an ever-present source of danger, for they might lead to precipitous action that could be seen as an action against the State. Surviving spouses, denied information or rites of mourning, in turn, denied their children any remembrance of the lives of parents and grandparents caught in the purges. Survivors of political repression were still thought of as shameful and dangerous to their offspring who were adapting to the new system. Alienation seemed inevitable since acknowledging connection to such "rats, pigs, vultures" endangered the educational opportunities and, at times, the survival of their families (Merridale, 1996, p. 5).

Grief and Bereavement in the USSR

Those who grieved such losses were deprived of traditional funerary ritual. Bodies were not washed and carefully clothed nor were objects given to assist in the hereafter, rather they were disposed of in mass graves or cremated. Religious ceremony was denied. Also, the opportunity for remembering was officially and practically violated. Official documents about the deaths were hard to come by. When, later, families were informed that their relative had died, the reports were often lies, such as death secondary to infection. Further, because the charges were that the relative was an enemy of the State, it was necessary for the family to burn photographs, letters, and documents (Merridale, 2000a). There was no recognition of the victim's suffering, or the family's pain. In fact, complaining would only lead to additional victimization. Both grief and mourning were arrested. Politically active parents withdrew their emotional attachments to children, as if that would protect them and their children from danger and loss. Instead it produced an inner emptiness for all.

A Culture of Informing

An even more pervasive stressor than political imprisonment was the constant threat of being reported to the secret police and the pressure its officers could bring to bear on anyone to divulge information that would endanger someone else. Indeed, the entire network of human interaction described in this book was infused with the adaptive value of informing on others (Chapter 4). Children had been taught that reporting free speech was a service to the State. Adults were bombarded with propaganda about omnipresent spies from the capitalist West determined to destroy the great people's crusade. Advancement in one's career went hand in glove with informing on others and then joining a party knit together by a fratricidal commitment to reform. And finally, if one was arrested, torture and threats to family would probably result in some form of informing, regardless of the victim's principles.

Victim/Persecutor Split

Thus, central to the psychological legacy of the Communist years is the fusing in the same person of the roles of being the one terrorized and of the informer, of being victimized and of persecuting others. In the patients presented in this book we see highly principled individuals forced to turn against their fellows by becoming persecutors; and we see KGB members crushed by the system with which they had identified, thus becoming its victims. Such an atmosphere pervaded not only the world of public interchange but most private homes as well. It affected people in every sphere of life, including (as we shall see later) psychiatry itself.

Today the children and grandchildren of that father, his wife, daughter, and friend, even the secret police officer, make up the general population. They, too, are caught up in the legacy of trauma. Their modes of adaptation have been molded by two or three generations of survival in the ecology of terror, and their defensive repertoire is different from those seen in the West. They suspect there is much they do not know about themselves and much their parents sacrificed so that they might live. While most people contain the remnants of trauma and loss in silent ways, perhaps like a rent in the soul, a few, like the patients in this book, become identified as psychiatrically ill; they threaten suicide (like Hans, Chapter 4, and Dima, Chapter 6), they develop psychosomatic disorders (like Karl, Chapter 4), they have recurrent nightmares (like Viktor and Josip, Chapter 7), and they seek counseling and therapy. Others, not quite seeing themselves as patients, nonetheless seek out therapists in more informal but no less significant ways (like Mr. E., Chapter 3, and Mihai, Chapter

5). The therapists who listen learn that their patients' experiences are not so different from their own.

Post-Stalinist Totalitarian State

The legacy of Soviet trauma continued beyond Stalin's years. While there was generally less overt brutality, the swells and wakes of political repression were part of a more stable but paranoid environment. Kruschev revealed Stalin's crimes, and permitted Solzhenitsyn (1962/1991) to publish *A Day in the Life of Ivan Denisovich*. But not long after, excessive revisionism became a crime. Dr. Konkov remembers his family reading Solzhenitsyn's book as serialized in the newspaper, but one day the publications stopped without explanation. He also remembers his father going to Czechoslovakia with the military to put down the revolution there. It was a topic which father and son never mentioned.

Eastern European socialist republics saw movement towards market economies, and some political liberalization only to be suppressed by conservative backlashes. They, too, became accustomed to a paranoid way of life. Romania in particular became harshly repressive under Cseausescu, even as others, such as Hungary, became more open.

During the years of the post-Stalinist totalitarian State, the form and structure of government—the one-party system, State ownership of economic activity, State control of the arts, the omnipresent secret police— were unchanged. Everyone worked for the State, was paid by the State, was housed through the State, and received his or her food from the State. In the post-Stalinist era people became accustomed to complying with the dictates of the State, and developed coping styles that would permit them to function in a world in which they must deny their individuality. They knew how to adopt a false self, a *ketman* (Miloscz, 1990), to dissimulate in deference in the line of the center. They tried to become invisible for the "eyes" of the regime, because, as Dr. Konkov says, "the regime just does not like visible people, and they will fabricate a reason for prosecution." They tended to accept abuse of power, repression of culture, absence of free expression, falsifications, and hypocrisy as a way of life, in short, to " live within a lie" (Havel, 1986, p. 52). For the individual person accepting such a reality, depression and paranoid tendencies were adaptive. The resultant paranoid atmosphere was the order of things. Patients as well as their therapists being seen even in the late 1980s and early 1990s accepted it as part of the psychological atmosphere of the post-Stalinist totalitarian State.

Perceptions as Children

The years of early childhood for therapists in this book were the Brezhnev years. The therapists, as children, were taught and accepted without question the purposes of the Marxist-Leninist revolution. As mentioned earlier, they were young pioneers who won prizes for their essays on intricacies of the difference between the apparent world (capitalist materialism) and the real one (communist idealism). America and NATO were the capitalist enemy. The Communists were the "good guys."

They learned quite early that, regarding political matters, there was one expectation only: that the views presented in the media *on that particular day* were the right views (no matter what view was expressed yesterday or might be expressed tomorrow). Holding any other views risked public attention and danger.

Even if the therapists, as children, had wanted to learn about the history of political repression in their country, they would not have been taught anything on the subject. Teachers did not teach about the repressions, and students did not learn about them. Like an African-American child in a school in the South who tried to learn about the lynching of African Americans by the Ku Klux Klan, fifty years earlier, such information was simply not taught, nor was it in the textbook (Loewen, 1995). One reason for this was that the local school board which determined the text would have been controlled by active members of the Ku Klux Klan. In fact, there would have been a conscious effort to pass over this "dark period" in our otherwise bright American history, rather than to draw attention to the fact that the practice continued. Those who taught would have no intention of encouraging the child to consider intergenerational linkages which might have identified the lynched figure as kin. Similarly the Russian and East European therapists, as children, knew of the existence of political repression in the Stalinist era, but their teachers did not want them to know that similar practices continued, nor that this history contained the personal stories of their own parents and grandparents.

The therapists reached maturity as Gorbachev came to power. They were now suddenly living in a world in which it was acceptable to speak more freely. The corruption and hypocrisy of earlier years were coming to light daily. Faith in Communist ideology had eroded. Still, a discrepancy existed between what people said in public and how they felt. The therapists felt they must be most careful not to reveal private views in settings where informers could cause trouble

In the later Gorbachev years, it became clearer that the system would not last, and a new layer of pain emerged: guilt over complicity with such an inhuman system. This latest layer of the trauma legacy separated children from their parents and grandparents as those in the older generations continued to deny the trauma of the past. Gradually the younger generation, no longer so intimidated by government, grew angry at the continued hypocrisy. They now insisted on living within the truth (Havel, 1986).

A number of the cases in this book have their traumatic origins in the post-Stalinist totalitarian State. Mr. E. (Chapter 3) was held against his will in a psychiatric hospital. Hans (Chapter 4) was deeply affected by his parents' informing activities; Mr. R., a member of the KGB, blamed the Soviet State for the death of his daughter (Chapter 8). Vahan discovered his bureaucratic position was the source of his illness (Chapter 8). Among the therapists, some were interrogated, others informed on by their teachers and colleagues, and others harassed.

Psychiatry as Victim and as Perpetrator

The therapists were practicing in a field which showed the strain of being both a victim of Soviet attack and a perpetrator within its system. Soviet theoreticians took very seriously the ideology of the self in relation to the collective. Soviet man, an action oriented worker, was non-reflective by nature. He was to be well indoctrinated in childhood, responsive to conditioning in accordance with the behavioral science of Pavlov, and amenable to the *weltanschaung* of Soviet Marxism-Leninism. Dependency upon the state was a given, and compliance or reduction in individuality was a useful adaptation. Work, while idealized in theory, was to become an assignment from the state, to which the worker was to respond with adaptation and sacrifice. Genuine dissatisfaction with the state was not a complaint but a crime, or as the ideologues would argue, a mental illness. Their view of the new Soviet man is someone who would sacrifice all for the collective good of the new wave of history.

Freudian thought represented the antithesis of the Marxist view of psychology (Miller, 1998). Freud, they said, worked with the base instincts, sex and aggression, with self-indulgence over social commitment, with an internal rather than an action oriented external self, with a childhood which was deterministic rather than an adulthood which was rationally directed towards the State's ends. Reflection, particularly self-reflection, which could lead to doubt or inhibition of action in the cause of the State, was seen as a reactionary and destructive psychological tendency. While the sixties began with Kruschev permitting the publication of *One Day in the Life of Ivan Denisovich* (Solzhenitsyn, 1962/1991) it was quickly followed by a more reactionary frame of mind. Under Brezhnev, Soviet ideologues called out their forces to attack Freud's system of psychology which centered on the value and meaning of the intrapsychic world (Miller 1998).

Stated differently, opposition to the State must then represent some psychic abnormality of the mind, and psychiatry, in this less brutal state, would become a more discreet instrument to confine political dissidents on the basis of mental illness. The impact of all these ideas violated the mental health field and its practitioners. As psychiatrists succumbed to these forces, they, too, joined the ranks of those who were traumatizing others in the name of the State. In Russia, and to some extent in other Eastern European countries, the psychiatric field came to represent a perversion of its ideals. Psychiatrists condemned political dissidents to psychiatric internment, distorting diagnostic nomenclature in the State's interests. Psychiatrists informed on each other and on their students and teachers. Psychiatrists and psychologists affirmed the political notion of the absence of an inner life, influenced by early childhood experience and unconscious universal forces. Psychiatry, like other aspects of Soviet life, was both victim to Soviet trauma and a perpetrator within its system. World psychiatry, in turn, banished the USSR from international recognition in psychiatry for its practices.

Later, when change came, it is no accident that Freud, the apostle for individual meaning, and the forbidden enemy of the State, would become rehabilitated. After all, he was a theoretician whose ideas about conflict and compromise formation were steeped in Hegelian dialectic philosophy. Indeed, his language of internal psychic life would become one of the means of expressing the awakening in Eastern Europe and Russia.

Revolution and Stress in the Post-Soviet Period

Most of the therapists were active in the reform movements and revolutions of 1988–1991. Guiding their thoughts and actions were concepts articulated by such dissidents as Vaclev Havel who insisted that what he termed "the post-totalitarian state," characteristic of Communist systems in the 1980s and after, was the responsibility of all who participated in it, thereby establishing a climate for ordinary citizens—especially the young—to challenge the status quo. They momentarily abandoned their skeptical inclinations, becoming more hopeful and even temporarily euphoric as citizens' groups led overthrows in each of the Eastern European states. For many, including the therapists in this book, the changes which came with the defeat of Communism were a welcome opportunity for a new life. They felt more than ready to heed Havel's call, and were prepared to meet the new challenges. In the months and years that followed they struggled to understand the forces that were working against as well as for the changes.

For others, however, including some of their patients, the collapse of the Communist states in Eastern Europe brought insurmountable problems of their own: economic hardship, disillusionment, and violence. Older patients like Mr. R., identifying with the Party, became depressed at the sudden loss in prestige (Chapter 8). Others, like Hans' parents, denied overtly the extent of their loss, and hurled themselves into new forms of work, but unconsciously passed on problems to their children. Some youth, like Karl (Chapter 4), were afraid to enter a new world in which they would be accountable to be free, so now, in a state of clinical regression, they faced instead the threat of addiction and violence.

Also the post-Soviet era has been marked, in the former Yugoslavia and to a lesser extent in Armenia, by a resurgence of ultra-nationalism, ethnic hatred, and war. In these places the collapse of Communist states unleashed the powerful and destructive forces that had been repressively contained, exacerbating Viktor's old PTSD and exposing Josip (Chapter 7) to abusive violence, detention camps, and refugee status.

Towards a Taxonomy of Soviet Trauma

A climate which permits and encourages studies of survivors of trauma during the Soviet era, particularly political repression, is beginning in Russia and its near neighbors. There, psychiatrists and survivors themselves are more likely to think in terms of trials of the soul, rather than psychopathology or Posttraumatic Stress Disorder (Merridale, 2000a). Meanwhile, East German, Hungarian, and Croatian mental health professionals have vigorously entered this area as a legitimate field of study. Armenian researchers have joined those from the West in studying survivors of the earthquake (Goenjian et al., 1995) and Ukrainian researchers have joined those from the West in studying survivors of Chernobyl (Havenaar et al., 1997).

There are now group-level studies of political prisoners in the former East Germany. Examples include those arrested, imprisoned, and harassed by the secret police (Ehlers, Maercker, & Boos, 2000); some work on political dissidents held against their will in psychiatric hospitals (Adler & Glutsman, 1993); treat Holocaust survivors and their families in Hungary (Eros, Vajda, & Kovacs, 1998); and work with soldiers and refugees in detention camps in Croatia (Kozaric-Kovacic, Murasic, & Ljubin, 1999; Martic-Biocina, Spoljar-Vrzina, & Rudan, 1998).

While the individual stories in this book—those of patients and their families and those of therapists and their families—hardly constitute a representative sample, they do give a sense of the range of trauma experiences endemic in the post-Soviet world. We offer, below, a beginning typology of Soviet trauma and loss. We include categories of current-day trauma as well. The extensiveness of the list underlines how likely it will be that a given survivor will have experienced multiple traumas.

- Those who were victims or perpetrators in the culture of terror and informing
  1. Being informed on without their knowledge
  2. Secret police interrogation, torture and harassment, and being forced to inform on others
  3. Political imprisonment (long term)
  4. Psychiatric gulag
- Those whose grief for relatives who disappeared or were killed as a result of the above
  5. Arrested grief in their spouses
  6. Arrested grief and identity-processing in their children
  7. Arrested grief and identity-processing in their grandchildren
- Those who suffered from the forced displacements of collectivization and industrialization
  8. Kulaks being forced out of agrarian settings
  9. Others being forcibly removed from their homes to accomplish the state's ends
- Those suffering in the post-Soviet era
  10. Identity crises in youths
  11. Identity crises in adulthood
  12. Depression in pensioneers
- Those who suffer in war
  13. Civilians caught in warfare
  14. Subjects of ethnic cleansing
  15. Refugees
  16. Soldiers with PTSD
- Other disaster populations
  17. Famine survivors
  18. Earthquake survivors
  19. Nuclear accident survivors
- Perpetrating roles
  20. Citizens performing their duty
  21. Camp guards
  22. Secret police operatives
  23. Psychiatrists who confined dissidents

For clinicians interested in the wider public health dimensions of the aftermath of the Soviet era, the categories above help to define populations of special interest.

Throughout the book we shall return to these survivor groupings, noting creative ways of reaching out to them, considering ways to promote a receptive environment for recovery, and providing alternatives to the massive suppression of individual grief and mourning enforced during the years of Communism.

Those of us who work with trauma and its recovery are aware that the nature of the recovery environment is important for its constructive processing. The world of the Soviet Union and the Eastern bloc countries was a world which denied the trauma its citizens had experienced. It doctored documents, withheld news, and condemned those who complained. It minimized statistics. On a more personal level, it blocked ritual, destroyed individual memory, and made the telling of stories about the deceased dangerous. One of the most profound effects of the period of *perestroika* and the revolution which followed was the beginning of a new era in which a more positive recovery environment has been forming in which people are freer to engage arrested grief if they choose. One of the purposes of this book is to model that re-engagement.

The events which constitute the trauma and loss of the Soviet era are fixed and awesome in their scope. Also, the therapists, in the course of their lives, have understood the scope and meaning of the events in radically different ways: as loyal patriotic Communist children, they minimized and generalized the losses in the name of the collective state; as truth-seeking reformer-clinician adults, they dwell on what they know and do not know of their traumatic past, seeking in it clues to their and their country's identity. Like those behind the divided walls of partitioned cities, and like the split fragments of the traumatized mind, differing parties view the same history differently. We encountered these divisions as we wrote this book. We have tried here to portray in this discussion primarily the perspectives of the therapists as we came to know them. Their mind-set is one that is sharply ironic and from within the reform/dissident culture. It is sometimes subtly and sometimes boldly at odds with common assumptions in the West. And it is a view which bristles at those who, from the outside, set about explaining to them what their history has or has not been. It sometimes even bristles at views held by fellow East Europeans who have their own history of enmity with each other.

In striving in this book both for the subjective truth which bears witness and for historical balance, we have maintained throughout the project a lively interaction with a cadre of historians, sociologists, and literary critics as well as the therapists themselves. This group of academics, whom we met through two symposia at Yale University (New Haven, CT), has a formal presence in the book through the historical sketches which follow the case narratives at the end of each chapter.

In this way we shall return to the specific histories of Hungary, East Germany, Romania, Russia, Croatia, and Armenia in more detail, as they intersect with periods of Soviet political repression. In this way we add another anchoring point to the history of these turbulent and traumatic years.

3
CHAPTER

Hungary

Editors' Note

Nora Csiszer and Eva Katona, two psychiatrists working at a Crisis Intervention/Suicide Prevention Unit in Budapest, Hungary, describe the powerful awakening which they experienced both personally and as part of Hungary's experience in the 1980s and early 1990s.

The Soviet-influenced culture they describe is less harsh than in other countries in this book, allowing for some of the less traumatic aspects of the Communist era to emerge, such as absence of dissent and absence of responsibility. Dr. Csiszer presents a patient who illustrates Communist society as one which is unable to tolerate dissent and to take responsibility. Mr. E. is a man attempting to set right the abuses which he suffered at the hands of Hungarian psychiatrists who, because of his dissident views, labeled him paranoid, hospitalized him against his will, and substantially altered his life by marginalizing him from society. These psychiatrists were functioning as they did throughout Russia and Eastern Europe, especially after 1970, as agents in a reporting culture, an indispensable link in the whole repressive apparatus which punished dissident behavior by involuntary psychiatric internment (Adler & Glutsman, 1993). Dr. Csiszer's patient also highlights the theme of adults who, because of their political activities, became cut off from their children. Mr. E., now a seventy-year-old "warrior" of political trauma during both the Nazi and Communist regimes, left his daughter as Dr. Csiszer's father did her. Indeed, Mr. E.'s

33

relationship with his daughter has many similarities to Dr. Csiszer's own relationship with her father. Painfully, she acknowledges having carried within her a cold, empty space left by her own father who absented himself from her life when she was six years old for political reasons. In this chapter Dr. Csiszer describes how the patient, through the treatment, and the doctor, through self-reflection, fill in the missing stones of an intergenerational gap. They do so eventually with warmth rather than guilt and anger.

In the early 1970s, under Brezhnev's rule, many psychiatrists in Russia and other Eastern European countries joined the ranks of those who were perpetrators in the name of the State (Miller, 1985). Psychiatrists condemned political dissidents to psychiatric internment, distorting diagnostic nomenclature in the State's interests. Dr. Csiszer puts her own psychiatric colleagues on trial as it were, as she examines anew the culpability of those who condemned her patient because his views were a nuisance to Communist society. It is ironic that Hungarian psychiatry, which may have moved beyond the other countries in this book, is the country able to examine in writing in this case the question of abuses by psychiatry during the totalitarian and post-totalitarian years. Such openness has been lacking elsewhere.

Dr. Csiszer identifies as a traumatized population those whom psychiatry has harmed through misdiagnosis. While most of those marginalized by such experiences will likely stay away from psychiatrists in a freer world, others, like Mr. E, will request rehabilitation, a clearing of his name. Responding to those requests on a larger scale can become a portal for empathic mental health outreach as illustrated in Dr. Csiszer's case.

The story of Mr. E. raises important questions about resilience in survivors of traumas (McFarlane & Yehuda, 1996). Throughout his narrative we see in Mr. E. a person with great hardiness, one who refuses the position of victim or patient (Schwarzer & Jerusalem, 1995). He does not dwell on intrusions or traumatic dreams, and while there is some numbing initially he is involved with his neighbor, the treatment, and his doctor.

Finally, Dr. Csiszer's case points out that in the sweep of historical trauma, individuals exposed to political traumas of Eastern Europe were rarely exposed to a single trauma, but more typically to a series of traumas. Indeed, this serial nature of trauma is well illustrated and is a component in the longitudinal history of trauma survivors which we need to study more (Laufer, 1988).

Dr. Katona's narrative raises a different issue—the generation of hidden Jewish children who had not been told of their Jewish lineage until the period of change in the 1980s. Their experience is both similar to and different from other Hungarian Jewish children of Holocaust survivors (Eros, Vajda, & Kovacs, 1989). The reassessment of who they are contains both a de-idealization of those who kept them from truth, and a renewed search for identity which could not have occurred without that knowledge during adolescence. For many, like Dr. Katona, this is a special and ongoing journey.

In summary, the chapter offers the chance to ask questions about the psychology of those labeled dissident in Eastern Europe, the risk of pathologizing their personalities, and the troublesome matter of doctors and ethics in totalitarian states. Certainly Mr. E. offers a good illustration of the protean self in the twentieth century (Lifton, 1993).

As with the case of Dr. Katona there remains the intergenerational yearning to learn what father did, why he did it, and what were the values he meant to transmit in the process.

Hungary: Replacing A Missing Stone

Nora Csiszer
Eva Katona

An Introductory Reflection

I held the small stone in my hand, rotated it, and palpated its broken edges. The stone, a gift from a former patient, served as a paper weight on my desk, guarding my unanswered official correspondence: questions about differential diagnoses that needed to be answered and notes from medical meetings that needed to be recorded.

The stone was still in my hand when the telephone rang. It was Dr. Eva Katona, my friend and colleague for more than fifteen years. She explained, perhaps more enthusiastically than I listened, that she had a letter from our colleagues in America, inviting us to write about our experiences as psychotherapists in Hungary, and asking that we travel to America for a working meeting to discuss the project.

I was cautious. The invitation was to write about our experiences, our subjective experiences. Such reflection would be neither easy nor painless. A focus on countertransference seemed to call for self-exposure, but I thought some things are better left unsaid. Some pains need to remain private ones.

Yet, I thought, if we psychotherapists cannot be open, who can. So many of our people, Hungarians, East Europeans, suffer from the legacy of the post-totalitarian world. And so much remains hidden. I placed the letter from America on the pile, setting the stone on top. So they wanted us to tell our story. But, I wondered, can they hear it?

During the period of increasing political openness that characterized the 1980s and early 1990s, we two women, Dr. Katona and I, worked as psychiatrists at the Crisis Unit of the Karanyi Hospital, Budapest, Hungary. We learned many things about our country and ourselves during those years, our present and our past. We came to view ourselves and our work differently. This is our story.

Hungary: The Soft Dictatorship

We shall begin in the mid-1980s. At the time, we felt fortunate to be living in Hungary, the "jolliest barrack of the Eastern bloc." In comparison to other countries in the region, ours was a soft dictatorship, a phenomenon which had started over two decades earlier. Gradually during that period, the country saw open challenges to cherished assumptions regarding the central economic planning of a Communist State. The government was experimenting with a limited private economy, a phenomenon completely unknown in other socialistic countries, and at the same time, implicitly tolerating a previously forbidden ideology, namely, the consumer's society. There were already government efforts to provide a better quality of life for its citizenry—a bigger flat, a car, freedom to travel, and freedom to get goods or products. The iron curtain dividing us from the West no longer separated us so absolutely. There were special efforts to improve the public climate, with some easing of communication and an opening of borders between Austria and Hungary. Now, for the first time in decades, if you had money and a visa, international travel was possible.

Consistent with these general policies, freedom in scientific life was also increasing. Dr. Katona and I were able to communicate with the international scientific community, and it became easier for us to travel to different conferences. For nearly fifteen years now we have been able to publish what we write. In general, those who do scientific research in our country have had easier access to the West than have those in other socialist countries and, with it, easier access to Western products and amenities that have made life and people feel a little better. In the past several years the Hungarian government also began to tolerate publications by the opposition. Previously these publications were secret, but now they began to be more freely circulated and more widely known in the country. These positive changes were of course in stark contrast to the severely repressive climate of the 1950s which we shared with other Eastern European countries under Soviet domination.

Complicity and Dissent

But even under this soft dictatorship, our people, all of us, suffered in profound ways. We numbed our individual hopes and responsibilities;

we cut off the continuity with our past; we sacrificed our own authenticity on the altar of collective irresponsibility. Faced with the "reality" of socialist life, we continued to adapt best by compromising both outwardly and inwardly.

For even a soft dictatorship is not a pluralistic system. In fact, during Hungary's eleven hundred-year history we have had only two short periods of democracy. One was in 1919 following World War I; the other was from 1945 to 1948 after World War II. We do not have the cultural microstructure of a well-developed democratic country which values autonomy, independence, dissent, and conflict resolution. Moreover, even a soft dictatorship tolerates no real dissent. It has one leader and one very powerful party—Socialist Party. This system carefully defines and restricts the area of acceptable socialization, including the ideas that can be expressed and the interpersonal networks that can be maintained. There is only one correct way of socialization and no alternative. For example, if one enjoyed hiking and also had concerns about the environment, in America one could join the Sierra Club, find friends with similar interests, and become politically involved as an environmental activist. In Hungary such a club would not be allowed because it would deviate from the central policy. So this is how we lived; our teachers showed us and told us, and there was no other way to do things; everyone lived the same way. And those who objected were labeled "deviants."

As psychiatrists, of course, we are called upon every day to see people who exhibit deviant behavior. We examine them, we listen carefully to their stories, we diagnose them, and we recommend disposition. People with suicidal, delinquent, drug addictive, and alcoholic behavior fall into this category. But historically in the socialist totalitarian state, psychiatrists were also called on to establish diagnoses in individuals whose deviant ideas and behavior were thought to threaten the collective State. Sometimes our actions as psychiatrists contributed to this collective irresponsibility. Sometimes the careers of those with deviant ideas came to an abrupt halt in the examining rooms of our very own psychiatric hospitals. (We shall look more carefully at a case which raises these issues later in this chapter.)

Organized Irresponsibility

A society which tends to punish independent dissent and conflict tends to produce two types of psychological adaptation: One is submission to autocratic power (abdication of responsibility), while the second is a kind of numbing or laissez-faire attitude towards political and social phenomena beyond one's control (disavowal of responsibility). When responsibility is both abdicated and disavowed, the result is "organized irresponsibility." As Havel tells us (1986), words come to mean their opposite in a post-totalitarian society. In this way, "organized irresponsibility" is an ironic play on the traditional Communist phrase "collective responsibility." But when collective responsibility simply doesn't exist, and when individual responsibility is forbidden, then the result can be only an organized irresponsibility.

In Hungary, everything was hidden behind the false concept of collective responsibility. As a collective society all we did, we did together, so one could never find the person who was truly responsible for this or that. But adapting to a false concept comes at a high price, because it corrupts one's inner voice. It produces a spoiled moral environment where we learn not to care about each other, and to worry only about ourselves. Words and terms, even life itself, becomes permeated with hypocrisy and lies. In this vernacular, responsibility means irresponsibility, order means disorder, and government means anarchy. The conditions in which this is the true state of affairs we call "mystification"(Manea, 1990, p. 308).

Hungarian "mystification" had its roots in the period from 1948 to 1953, when we were led by the father figure, Matyas Rakosi, known as the "best pupil" of Comrade Stalin. Rakosi of course posed as though he alone was responsible. But he didn't take responsibility; he spread it on the party, and on the nation, so that the way we lived was their decision. And things didn't improve when, upon Stalin's death, Rakosi was removed from power. The Communist Party leadership, under Russian influence, simply continued the same without him from 1953–1956. In 1956 the revolution against the totalitarian regime led to very hard times. People were tortured and other traumas occurred as a result of the regime but our parents wouldn't discuss these things with us. Then, from the end of 1960s life in Hungary became lighter and a little easier.

Trauma, Denial, and Sacrifice

In the history of the past forty years, including the Nazi occupation, World War II, the Russian occupation, and the formation of the socialist state, trauma often filled the lives of ordinary citizens. In general such individual traumas received little or no attention by a society which acknowledged only its falsely idealized collective socialist image. Moreover, because traumas were not worked through, they were passed on to the second and third generations. Parents tried to keep secret the effects of the Holocaust, of purges, imprisonments, and torture. The losses, devastation, sufferings, and defeats could not be expressed openly either at the public level or on a very personal level. We were not allowed to talk about such trauma. Parents and grandparents tried to keep us safe by not telling us who we were.

Individually and as a society we were unable to face the past; we were unable to grieve. During the time of openness during the 1980s and 1990s, many of us therefore came to the conclusion that we had been living in a lie, and that subtly, by our silence, we were part of the lie. This knowledge at first crept slowly into our consciousness, and then the change occurred very rapidly, almost like awakening in the morning with a radically new view of our world.

We may ask, who is it that permitted the totalitarian and post-totalitarian regimes and their traumas to occur? And who is it that contributes to the silence which prevents our healing? We believe almost all Hungarian people became involved in a certain way in permitting these traumas to occur and in enabling the silence to follow. For how can it be that all ten million Hungarians opposed the Communist regime? Of course this is not possible, so we were all part of the old regime and we have to deal with that truth and go on from there. These questions bring up the real question of collective responsibility, and they raise another question: "Who may accuse whom?"

Social Movement Directed from Above

During the past forty-five years there was a sudden transposition in social class in our country which had a great impact on people's behavior and ways of thinking. The new Communist regime, especially in the 1950s, offered people—who for generations had thought of themselves as simple peasants—the opportunity to get higher education, to become the first generation of an intellectual family. While this represented unprecedented opportunity, it also entailed a loss of traditional milieu, interpersonal support network, and a sense of a traditional world order. Individuals pulled out of their traditional settings sometimes found themselves in the midst of severe anxiety and stress. These people, now in their sixties, comprise one group of individuals with neuroses whom we see in our practice today. Disillusionment with ideals, the large gap between the promise of Communist society and the reality of everyday life, the wide distinction between what one ought to be and what one can really become, all these contributed to a traumatizing atmosphere. Further, much of the original social mobility did not occur spontaneously. It occurred after World War II with the Russian occupation and the move to industrialize Hungary, altering its traditional position as the "bread basket of Europe." Changes in people's social/political/economic position often occurred abruptly and almost always as a result of centrally based decisions. All movement was directed from above. While it has been in some cases over thirty years since these decisions were made, we still see the psychological aftermath today.

Communism and the Absence of Community

Since the Socialist State was to be the one controlling force in people's attitudes and behaviors, new potentially disruptive interpersonal networks or micro-communities were not permitted to exist. In the new order there would be only family and state. Church groups and gatherings of those who shared common interests, hobbies, or special characteristics were forbidden. Such groups were prohibited in order to stamp out individuality. First and foremost, one had to be part of the collective societal whole. Instead of a pluralistic society, we experienced Orwell's symbiosis of family and television. No other communities or groups were available to help people share thoughts. All groups that did form in order to object to these directions were seen as a threat against the leadership, so they were marginalized, forbidden, and labeled as deviant. In order to survive, one succumbed to a passive life strategy. People did not act on their feelings. They did not join the opposition. As a basic feeling, permanent sacrifice became the life strategy of survival. This sacrifice has significant consequences that we see in our patients and ourselves.

The roots of individual and collective traumatization originate in a specific Hungarian political, economic, and social history. Today's experiences of deteriorating economic life conditions and the rise of unemployment make it difficult for the young democracy. All of this contributes new stress and serves to elaborate the old trauma. It is these larger historical forces and the social and individual consequences which have produced trauma. By remaining complicit with a worldview which denies our trauma and inculcates sacrifice by the individual as the approved adaptation to it, we make it difficult for ourselves to find and maintain authentic solutions. In the end, authentic solutions must be based on an identity which includes working with our trauma and its consequences.

We saw this sequence of trauma, denial, and permanent sacrifice in order to survive in Dr. Katona's family even before I was able to see it in my own. I saw her struggle with authentic identity as she worked with the consequences of Holocaust trauma before I saw a similar pattern in myself (non-Holocaust trauma). Dr. Katona's story was clear to me because she has been such a good friend for so long, and because she valued an emotional openness within the safety of that friendship, and because hers is part of a dramatic story of a generation of hidden Jews in Hungary after the Holocaust. As she shared pieces of this story with me, I could see how her parents had made the permanent sacrifice of cutting themselves off from their heritage in order to survive and how this solution by the older generation affected Dr. Katona's evolving identity. Here is her story.

Dr. Katona's Story

I was raised in a typical Hungarian Communist household. My parents were vigorous and loyal Communists holding positions of responsibility in the community. While I had been aware that contact with extended family from both father's and mother's side was nonexistent, I was not consciously aware of that situation particularly bothering me as a child. It seemed natural to me that I had no relatives other than my parents, sister, and brother. In fact it was an unstated taboo to speak about grandparents, uncles, aunts, or cousins, about any family links, in our home. A recurrent frightening dream that I was hiding in a dark, ill-defined place, about to be found and killed, made no sense to me; nor did I share it with anyone at the time. I was already thirteen years old before I learned, almost by mistake, that my mother was a hidden Jew. Until then I knew nothing of my roots. This awakening occurred in the early 1960s when, in our atheist society, it was still not wise to acknowledge one's Jewish (or for that matter, Catholic) origin.

Gradually, after learning of my mother's Jewish origins, I was able to collect from various sources the necessary pieces to put together my parents' silence, my own background, into a still incomplete mosaic. So powerful has my parents' silence been that even to this day they have never broken it. And for all the power of my evolving inner experience as I became a Jew, I could never really share it with my most immediate family members. For my parents had completely denied their past.

My father was one of nine children from a very religious Roman Catholic family. His mother died from cancer while he was a small child, and his father had raised the children in a cold, strict, very disciplined, religious, and puritanical manner. Father fell in love with his Jewish girlfriend in the bloody years of the early 1940s, when anti-Semitism was already at its height. In Hungary, anti-Jewish laws then in effect included statutes punishing people who hid Jews, lived with Jews, or married Jews. Statutes forced Jews into ghettos, transported them to concentration camps. Clearly father's relationship with a Jewish girl whom he married in 1943 was a capital sin. He hid her for months in order to keep her from Nazi hands. My father procured false papers for her through a notary. Then he found a room for her in a village northeast of the city. Budapest was frequently being bombed in 1944, and the practice of placing "soldier-wives" in the country for safety was common. My mother was pregnant with my sister at the time. She later told me she was in great fear of being recognized. My father's family expelled him for these deeds and never forgave him.

It is important to note that although he saved my mother from the camps by hiding her identity and marrying her, my father could not help my mother's family. All were deported to Auschwitz. Fortunately, two sisters and one brother survived; but all the rest of my family perished in the Holocaust.

So there they were, my parents: these two people whose only remaining family was each other. They both believed in a better future, including a nonreligious common world, for religion only meant pain and death for them. So they hid their past from their children in order to raise them safely. But how could they deal with their own personal losses and grief? To their utmost, they chose to isolate themselves from their past, making themselves impermeable to memories.

At least this is what I knew until our safe Communist world suddenly changed. As the political situation became more open, I began to fill in the blank background with the living features of my Jewish relatives and warm feelings towards those whom I had lost. Pride, disappointment, hatred, and anger swirled in me as I confronted my denied heritage. I fought hard with these emotions. I admired my father for his heroism in saving my mother, but I could not understand why his family had never forgiven him for marrying my Jewish mother. I could not accept mother's having denied her religion and her culture, even while living with the pain of her losses and grief. Beyond this, even though my parents had suffered so much, I could not accept the reality that they still chose to deny who they were. They still chose to live a secret. They had no contact with my mother's relatives who survived in Europe; they restricted themselves from keeping in touch with mother's relatives who emigrated to Israel.

My newly emerging identification processes were emotionally based. I refused the unforgiving, distance-keeping Christian side of the family, identifying rather with the persecuted Jewish side. My old dream of hiding as a child in the dark place and awakening frightened to death and perspiring, returned. Now I could locate the dream with clarity. It was Auschwitz, the concentration camp where mother's family had been taken, and where mother feared she too would go. It represented the most powerful identification with a part of my mother that she had tried to cut off from herself. But how could I integrate my new rather Jewish self with my past identity. I felt a discontinuity in my own personality development. I felt I could never speak of this with mother or father. I noted that I was unconsciously choosing friends who belonged to the same "secret-Jewish generation." They, like me, never spoke of our Jewish roots openly, never crossed the intergenerational silence. I began an extensive study of

Judaism, its religion and its culture, and, of course, anti-Semitism. I wanted to understand my people. Gradually, while I remained irreligious (in the sense of following ritual), I now considered myself Jewish.

Ironically, as an adult I unconsciously repeated one of mother's experiences. She married a man from a religious Christian family which, she later learned, never accepted her. Ten years after my divorce it became clear that my former husband's family considered me a "dirty Jew." My children from that marriage, whom I raised by myself, have emigrated to Israel.

Dr. Katona feels, and so do I, that these more recent events represent an important milestone in her own story. She has turned much of her energy and activity to dealing with minority groups.

Clinical Setting:
Our Work at the Crisis Unit at Koranyi Hospital

The clinical setting in which we see psychiatric patients is the Budapest Crisis Intervention Department. I work mainly with people in crisis, especially those in danger of suicide. This is the main function of our service. The crisis unit at Karanyi Hospital serves both outpatients and inpatients who live in a large sector of Budapest. Of special interest to us clinically is identifying and treating those who present in crisis and are in danger of suicide. Since Hungary has a history of having the highest suicide rate in Europe, it has been possible to obtain government support both to recognize this as a real medical problem and to develop programs to reduce the rate of suicide through treatment at units such as our crisis clinic, as well as to carry out research on factors influencing the incidence of suicide.

At the clinic, I am head of the suicide prevention/crisis department; I am also secretary of the Hungarian Psychiatric Association. Dr. Katona is research consultant.

Among the patients we see at the Karanyi Hospital Crisis Clinic are those whose pathology reflects the impact of changed political, social, and economic truths, truths which affect our very identity. Some patients had prestige in the previous regime, but in this transitional phase they experience both a great loss and a crisis in their values. Their world-view is shattered. What was of value ten years ago is not of value anymore and vice versa. They present with depression, narcissistic injury, and loss of prestige. Of these persons some exhibit serious mental disorders such as major depression and paranoid psychosis. For example, one client, formerly highly placed in the party, became psychotic with a persecution complex. Other patients in our clinic, of course, represent the usual distribution of neurotic, psychotic, and borderline conditions in which suicidal danger might be expected. They are exhibiting extreme consequences of individual as well as collective traumatization.

When Dr. Katona and I met in response to the letters from America, we sketched out the background of our presentation. But we had difficulty in settling on the right case and had deferred that decision repeatedly until the day she arrived at my office unexpectedly, with airplane tickets in her hand. Clearly there could be no further delay in selecting and working up our case. She set the tickets next to the stone on my desk.

Considering the many obstacles to our participation in the meetings set off in me both excitement and ambivalence. How would our work appear to an international forum? Would our treatment methods be seen as sufficiently psychoanalytic? Were we knowledgeable enough about PTSD? How would we approach the language problem? At what level would we find the intersection between psychopathology and history? As we spoke, the two objects in front of us came into focus: the flight tickets and the small stone. We looked at them and at each other. We had the right case in front of us. It would be Mr. E.

MR. E

Mr. E. first came to me indirectly, as his suffering was neither acute enough nor severe enough to warrant his being seen as a patient in the crisis clinic. Mr. E. felt plagued by the twenty-five-year-old statement on his medical record that he suffers from paranoid psychosis. For years he had wanted his record wiped clean; for many months he thought carefully about how he would seek a "letter of rehabilitation." In its origianl Marxist-Leninist form, "rehabilitation" for Mr. E. would have meant correction of deviant behavior against the state, in this case based on the diagnosis, paranoid psychosis. According to this definition, the rehabilitated person was one who once had been at fault—a designation Mr. E. rejected categorically. In its current form (during perestroika and after), rehabilitation would mean having his medical record wiped clean of his psychiatric diagnosis, or implicitly as close as he would ever get to the state recognizing it may have made a mistake.

When his neighbor became ill and needed psychiatric hospitalization, he volunteered to help her, seizing the opportunity to present his request for rehabilitation to the head of the clinic at the same time. It was in this context that we first met. This plain but distinguished-looking, gray-haired, seventy-seven-year-old man explained that about twenty-five years ago he had been hospitalized against his will at this same psychiatric unit at Karanyi Hospital, that he had suffered greatly because doctors at that time had found him mentally ill, and that this stigma had remained on his record ever since. Respectfully but insistently, he pressed to see me personally and to take up the issue with me. So it was that I began seeing Mr. E. in a psychiatric consultation which lasted for nine visits. After the professional relationship was finished, I had occasion for several follow-up visits. They confirmed that the encounters had affected both of our lives.

In seeking me out in order to have a psychiatric diagnosis removed from his record, Mr. E. explained that his diagnosis and hospitalization all those years ago had caused his scientific work to be dismissed as the ravings of a madman, and his reputation within the world of archeology to be shattered. Mr. E. explained that at the time he had been exploring ancient stones in a nearby neighborhood as part of his interest in archaeology and had come upon some stones which indicated the site of a medieval forge. Bureaucrats had already planned to build apartments on the site, and official archaeologists quickly dismissed his contentions as unfounded. He said that as public interest in the controversy grew, he was seen as advocating the rescue of the archaeological record of a Hungary which preceded the Communist era and, therefore, as being against the official line of socialist progress. He explained that the State saw his "deviant behavior" as an embarrassment and so sought an official psychiatric sanction to dismiss his claims. In order for the State to obliterate his claims, he was diagnosed with paranoid psychosis. Now, twenty-five years later, his health record still retained that permanent label. With the new climate in Hungary, he believed it was time to clear his name, to remove the diagnosis from his record, to obtain a new certificate of sanity.

Clinical Diagnosis: Paranoia in the Person or in the State

Mr. E. was tall, a very slim and spry gentleman looking younger than his age. He appeared animated as he explained that as a young man, before World War II, he had a hobby of collecting ancient stones and researching them. He was matter-of-fact as he described how he had taught himself about archeology, conducted his own research, and published what he found. He appeared adversarial as he discussed his rivalry with professional archaeologists, especially regarding the "rich archaeological area" he had discovered at a site where officials wanted to build a new settlement. He was adamant as he remembered his published statements that the apartment should not be built because to do so would destroy rich ruins of a medieval foundry. He appeared quietly indignant as he described the officials' decision to construct the new apartment complex in this area anyway. He seemed to be muting his rage as he explained that he was in their way, that the consequence of this debate with the authorities about the new settlement would result in his being taken to this very psychiatric department where psychiatrists confirmed the idea that only a grandiose paranoiac would have such ideas. They said he was a paranoid person and they kept him there against his will. His diagnosis then of paranoid psychosis effectively discredited his archaeological claims. He seemed cut off from feeling as he explained that his wife subsequently divorced him because his public controversy with government officials had placed great strain on the family. His family thought he had chosen to pursue a course of public integrity instead of taking care of his family and building up a good relationship with his children, and both they and he felt isolated.

Despite his hints at strong emotions, Mr E. remained self-controlled throughout his story. Especially when speaking of relationships, he was emotionless, almost like cold steel. What should we make of this initial presentation? On one hand, his claims about the false diagnosis might have been justified. On the other hand, he could have had a transient psychosis or at least appeared psychotic transiently. Of course such psychiatric abuses and personal humiliations did occur twenty-five years ago. But some people with legitimate psychoses did present with pretentious and grandiose claims, irritability, and paranoid reactions. Looking back, how could one reasonably be clear about a diagnosis?

Of course, it is impossible to reconstruct with certainty today the precise clinical state which Mr. E. presented so many years ago. We can only approximate. It is possible that Mr. E.'s archaeological claims could have appeared delusional and megalomanic to the examining doctor. After all, the authorities said he was fabricating his story. Could his psychomotor activity have appeared agitated over the harassment and charges? Might his mood have been labile? Could he have become uncooperative with staff? A decision to medicate him would have subdued his irascibility and clouded his senses. But might forced medications have convinced him further that he was being persecuted, and make his agitation grow worse? Yes, under the circumstances diagnosing—or misdiagnosing—a paranoid psychosis might have been possible.

Earlier records might have enlightened us, but then again earlier records might have been falsified at the request of the state police. Anyway, they are now lost . . . or have they been destroyed? And if there was a paranoid psychosis, to whom did it belong? It could have been Mr. E.'s, or it could have been our country's: a paranoid fear of connecting ourselves with our real past, a paranoid fear lest we doubt the benefits of this new order and fail to recognize the superior value of mass high rise living quarters to the dubious possibility of the existence of ruins of a past we must forget.

Because of the several diagnostic possibilities, I explored the surrounding circumstances in more detail. Mr. E. was already twenty-five years old when he became a soldier in World War II at a time when Hungary was allied with Nazi Germany. During the collapse of the Eastern front, he was captured by the Russians and taken prisoner for three months. Later, but still during the war, he lost three fingers of his right hand in an explosion. Since prior to the war he had been trained as a mechanic, the mutilation of his hand was a particularly harsh blow, leaving him disabled from traumatic injury while still in his twenties. While his prisoner of war experience and his disabling injury were the first two traumas chronologically, he did not begin his story of persecution with these events. They were traumatic, yes; but he did not feel singled out for such bad treatment. They were the risks of war.

Rather, Mr. E. began his story of persecution several years later, when, after the war, he was denied entrance to the university because in 1949 one of his brothers, a highly ranked officer in the Hungarian army, had defected to the West. His brother's departure from the newly Communist country placed the family under suspicion of Western influences. This was when the State started to persecute the family and especially Mr. E. Therefore, this is when he considers his serious troubles started, the date he was rejected by the university, the date his story of State harassment began.

What he described next was characteristic of the Hungarian situation at the end of the war and the beginning of the new regime. He was thirty when all his family's assets were taken into public ownership—when their land, house, clothes, books, everything was confiscated. At the same time, Mr. E.'s family was declared a class enemy (quite a common designation). The family didn't have a big piece of land, but they were obliged to give all that they planted and produced free to the public; failure to do so, to hide something for the family itself to eat, was termed sabotage. Mr. E. was accused of this crime, of holding something back from the public to feed his own family.

With everything taken from him, he had to start a new life in unfamiliar and further traumatizing circumstances. He left his town and went to Budapest, the capital of Hungary, but living conditions there were also very difficult. Since housing was in short supply, several families were assigned to each apartment, a whole family to each room. He lived in an apartment of three rooms with two other families. During this period, twelve children might be in the kitchen at one time. To complicate matters, the two other families were ex-aristocrats who treated him like a serf. Mr. E. found it especially difficult when others in the apartment looked down on him, regarding him as a servant because he was a simple man rather than a former aristocrat.

But life was not secure even at this level. In the 1950s those who had an emigrant relative were deported to another part of the country, a fate

Mr. E. escaped only by moving from place to place. He went back to his home town only to hear rumors that the whole family would be taken to another part of the country. In one year he moved to three different cities, trying to escape.

Later, in 1956, he participated in the failed Hungarian revolution (called a counter-revolution by the regime), but his only involvement was to make Molotov cocktails with his neighbors, who were university students. Despite the relatively minor nature of his revolutionary activities, the authorities wanted to sentence him to prison. He circumvented that by injuring himself seriously enough to require hospitalization. At that time, he worked in a factory, where he intentionally dropped a very heavy transformer on his foot, fracturing the bones. The long recuperation allowed Mr. E. to avoid prison. In 1957 he took a job at an electronics company, and the harassment began again. Now he and his colleagues were falsely accused of producing illegal radio signals, and state police came to search his house repeatedly, even though they never found anything.

In the mid-1960s, in his new career as an art teacher, he was once again harassed. It didn't matter that he was a very good teacher, popular with his students and his colleagues. This time the accusation was that he had assigned his students to read a pornographic story. According to Mr. E., it was a love story between young people and not at all obscene, but the government started a campaign against him in the media, insisting that he knew this book was pornographic and that he had knowingly participated in distributing it to young people. Because this period following the failed revolution was heavily reactionary in Hungary, conservative feelings ran high. Many of Mr. E.'s colleagues and many others in his community turned against him.

With this history, the context was set for him to be defamed in the controversy over the archaeological site, and for him to receive a psychiatric label. Indeed, Mr. E.'s claims of being persecuted by the State were beginning to hold together.

Later I filled in some of his earlier history. Mr. E. is one of twelve children. His father was a shoemaker who later became a clerk at a rail company; his mother stayed at home with the children. Both parents raised him in a religious (Roman Catholic) manner. His late adolescent and adult life was very colorful, punctuated by turbulent adventures. His work history was quite versatile; for example, he received vocational schooling as an educated mechanic; then he became a pilot educator. Later he earned qualifications as a miller. During hard times he also worked as a day laborer. In later years he became a school teacher. Although he didn't have a formal education in art, he gained enough knowledge on his own to teach art in school at the secondary and primary levels. He was a competent self-made man. Mr. E. married once and then later remarried the same person. Together they had a daughter and a son. Currently retired, he remains an active and respected person in his little town near the Austrian border. In his community, he is the "old, wise person."

Reviewing his life span we note many of the traumas which characterize Hungarian history of the period: war, invasion, occupation, purges, secret police harassment, marginalization. Perhaps only one of those traumas might be sufficient to set chronic PTSD in place for life; Mr. E. collected thirteen traumas. Sadly, we must acknowledge that they represent a very typical life course. Our emphasis here is not on the posttrauma stress disorder but on an exploration of how Mr. E. escaped exhibiting the disorder and what kind of activities he used to try to adapt.

Clinical Discussion

Upon completion of the psychiatric evaluation, we concluded that Mr. E. possessed remarkable ego strengths and resiliency in the face of trauma. Despite his taciturn ways he was a rather appealing person. Indeed his success in enduring these stressful life experiences and traumas might be better understood within a paradigm of the suffering of the Hungarian people rather than a diagnostic label such as paranoia.

Now, we reflect. There are so many facets to Mr. E.'s story: What inner strengths does he contain so that even a lifetime of traumatic experiences does not disable him from PTSD? Where does his drive to be recognized as archaeologist originate? Is it the blocked wish of adolescence? Is it the drive to connect with our collective past? Does he review his life with me in order to confirm his wish for integrity or in order to combat fear of despair? Why is his tenacious character aimed only at social truth? Why did he choose that calling when it drove him and his family apart? How does a society provide the forces to label a dissident's behavior as psychotic, so that medicine serves the dictates of the State rather than the meaningful needs of the individual? We shall pause briefly on each of these points, but our further narrative (Dr. Csiszer's Story, below) will pick up on yet another facet of the case: my countertransference reaction. For Mr. E.'s story set off a powerful reaction in me, forcing me to confront painful aspects of my own life, especially my relationship with my father.

First of all, considering Mr. E.'s personality development under the influence of his serial traumas, one is impressed at how resilient, colorful, and understanding a person he was. Mr. E. seemed to maintain a continuity of self throughout his entire life. Certain values, such as the demand for justice, remained central for him; he fought for this with all his strength. Perhaps more than others, he had the skills to represent the community's or individuals' interests and choose to do this despite costs to his family: his wife divorced him because his social activities endangered the family and interfered with his responsibilities to them. He failed to establish a fruitful relationship with his daughter and son. During the formal part of my interviews with him, which took nine hours, he never revealed emotions regarding family relationships. He did not talk about his emotional life or needs, his sexual life, his attachment to anything but his archeological stones and to rational abstract ideas.

In considering his character, I believe the defense of sublimation plays a dominant role. Consistent with this he showed empathy towards helpless individuals such as the woman he accompanied to the psychiatric hospital. He had a special mixture of creatively original and obsessively precise thinking. Basic to his character is the suppression of emotions, instincts, and temper, while intellectual activity and productivity are dominant. In his world-view, harsh experiences, even traumas and difficulties, enrich the personality. But in his interpersonal relationships, he does not primarily seek deep love. Rather he strives for acceptance. Moreover, he is willing to go to extremes to gain this acceptance, as illustrated by this endeavor to have his record wiped clean of mental illness. He strives for acceptance by the community and, as we shall learn later, also by his family. I felt that this fight became the essence of his life, and the energy he poured into it seemed to extend his youth. Perhaps he compensates for poor interpersonal skills and an arrest in the area of intimacy by his social commitment. Yet he pays a great price for his permanent search for justice, with its unlimited and uncontrolled intensity. He was unable to recognize the side effects of this commitment, his hurting his son and daughter, and his lack of consideration for family and, to some extent, his colleagues. I found myself irritable with him, even angry with him, especially for ignoring his family in the pursuit of his ambitions and ideals. We shall take up this important negative countertransference in the next section of this chapter.

The Process of the Psychotherapy

While it may not be immediately clear from the above narrative, I was having considerable difficulty listening to Mr. E.'s story: My feelings were intense and paradoxical. I admired his life, truly I did, but I found myself unwilling to understand and/or forgive the fact that he had turned away from his wife and daughter in pursuit of his truth. I believe I was controlling these feelings sufficiently to have our work proceed, but I was troubled. And so, as is my habit in such situations, I turned to Eva Katona, much as she did with me, to discuss the case. In our brand of peer supervision, we pursued the countertransference source of my anger and reluctance to forgive Mr. E.

We soon had reframed the treatment transaction between Mr. E. and me in the following light. Mr. E. presented wanting a special certificate clearing him from false accusations from a woman (myself). There was something quite alive in the interpersonal field of the therapeutic engagement in both his manifest request and his unconscious request to me for absolution. He was looking to me for something specific, a piece of paper certifying that he is not now and never was ill. I was to remove the past label which stained his image and left a stigma on his family. Officially, as the secretary of the Hungarian Psychiatric Association, I listened carefully to his story. I gave advice on how to go through the process to become rehabilitated. Those desiring rehabilitation must see a legal counselor and go to court, where there is a legal procedure they must follow. But also, I said, I'm not the law, I can't write this certificate of sanity, even though as the secretary of the psychiatric association I can explain how to pursue this aim.

In the meantime something powerful on another level was happening in the engagement. He asked me to review his life with him, and we did, and as we did, I began to respond. I, a woman doctor the age of his daughter, found myself angry with him, a man the age of my father. I identified unconsciously with the daughter who held him accountable for the domestic harm that paralleled his political courage. One of the reasons he sought "rehabilitation" is that he hoped I would accept the decisions he made; he hoped I would forgive him for the guilt he felt because those decisions had severed his relation with his daughter. As he pursued his life review, he unconsciously placed me in the transference role of daughter/judge. In the countertransference, I both admired Mr. E. and, despite his stiffness, gradually found him capable of an endearing kindness. But because my own father also left me to pursue social justice, I was reluctant to forgive him for all the pain of my personal journey without a father. Working out the countertransference reactions became the central feature of this case.

The Countertransference: Dr. Csiszer's Story

It was Dr. Katona's respect and collegiality, yet her insistent prodding for truth which highlighted many similarities in these two father–daughter relationships and helped the following story to emerge from within me.

My father was an engineer, a very active, colorful, versatile person, but I did not really know or remember him. As an adult I retained only bits and pieces I had heard as a child, mostly from my mother. After my parents divorced, when I was six years old, my father seemed to fade from my life. Even his name disappeared when my mother and I took my stepfather's name, the name I now carry. I knew that my father was the kind of person who took risks to help other people, including those in danger. In fact, this is why my mother divorced him: She felt that since his first instinct was not to protect or take care of his family, we were better off without him.

My father's activity was mainly political. He was in prison three times, first during the era of the Nazis, then during the Rakosi dictatorship, and finally in the revolution of 1956. The first time was in 1944, during the Nazi persecution of the Jews, when Budapest had a big ghetto. At considerable risk to himself, my father took food to some Jewish friends. But one time he slipped up and was caught by the Hungarian Nazis (the Arrow Cross). They put him in jail and, according to my mother, he was lucky they didn't kill him. They terrified him, but they let him go.

As an antifascist resistance fighter, he began to move from place to place. At first when he was assigned to a town, the whole family followed him. My mother gave up her interests and took us, the children, to join him. We were constantly traveling around the country and couldn't settle down. At the same time, he was very busy with his activities and didn't see us often or take sufficient care of us. This went on until, in the 1950s, he was overheard having a political debate. He was accused of saying something against the leadership and imprisoned again. At this point, my mother divorced him and remarried.

Before his third imprisonment, my father, who remained a respected person in his little Hungarian town, was elected to the workers' council. Then he became the regional head of the democratic movement (labeled "counterrevolutionary" by the regime). In fact he didn't do anything during the 1956 "revolution." No one on his town's council did anything, but after 1956 he was imprisoned a third time merely because he had been a member of this group. I learned later that during this imprisonment, he was tortured and badly injured. When he was released, he said that he would stay away from political life, and he kept his word. Nevertheless, he remained helpful to the local community and he was still known for having been an important fighter against the totalitarian leadership, but now he occupied himself by collecting antique cars rather than by engaging in political activities.

When the 1990s brought political change, people wanted him to get involved once more. But he refused because, by this time, he had concluded that any kind of power is corrupt. In fact, when nationalist leaders wanted to award him for his past services to the country, he refused that too. During the past several years, he described the overwhelming shift to materialistic values in the world as making him sick to his stomach. He thought people were changing in disappointing ways. They were losing sight of altruistic goals and becoming hypocritical. Now they sought only self-interest. My father resisted these changes until he died with stomach cancer in 1991. This is the story of his life as I recreated it from fragments I had been told.

I should add one more important detail: that I was not initially accepted at the university because of my father's record—his arrests and imprisonments, especially in 1956. Being denied entrance was a blow for me, but later I did get accepted and I started medical school soon thereafter.

My anger towards my father was real because he turned against the family and he left us. I thought that this image of my father as bad and cold to us would never warm up and would never disappear. But while listening to Mr. E., I not only recalled these fragments of my father's life but I also recovered some warmth from earlier memories of him which had been previously hidden. I remembered that when my mother died in 1958, my father came up to me and introduced himself after the burial. I was sixteen at the time, and very ambivalent about getting acquainted with him. I was already being pushed away by the second "father" in my life: my stepfather made it clear that he didn't want to take care of me anymore, and I moved out of his house when he remarried. At the same time, it is possible that my father also was ambivalent, even if he was somewhat sad that we had never had a relationship.

Dr. Katona and I found many similarities in the history of Mr. E. and my father's life story. Both men exhibited a significant pattern of commitment to social values and altruism, integrity in the face of totalitarian corruption, and courage and defiance which courted imprisonment and near death. Each displayed strength amidst humiliation, but also a weakness—a failure to get close to his daughter, a fear, perhaps a dread lest closeness cause too much pain; and hence each left his daughter with a pain, void, and coldness which she thought could never be warmed. Perhaps the greatest value to Mr. E. of our encounter was my authentic interest in his life, something he never received from his own daughter. It is certainly not of minor importance that I am the same age as Mr. E.'s daughter, nor that Mr. E. is the same age my father would be if he were alive. Access to my own life story permitted a deeper understanding of Mr. E., but it simultaneously brought me pain: The other side of my ambivalence is that it was very hard being a daughter of such a man. Hence my negative countertransference.

Final Reflections

Besides the nine counseling sessions, I have seen Mr. E. for several follow-up visits. During our meetings, he has offered me little presents, which he never gave to his daughter and that I never received from my father.

For one of our meetings I decided to go to a place which is very near to where Mr. E. lives. We took the opportunity to visit in his home town. He planned the whole visit. When we met and after we had been talking for some time, I saw how respected he was in his community. I found real warmth in myself for him. I found I really liked him.

Before parting after this follow-up visit, Mr. E. showed me a small shop where he stored and worked on artifacts from his many archaeological digs. He handled each stone fragment with care and tenderness as he spoke about them. This stiff man's tender side now showed itself to me more clearly than at any other point. He carefully selected a stone and, tearing slightly, he asked if I would please take it as a gift from him. I held the stone in my hand and turned it gently. I felt the ragged edge where it had been broken. I noted how as the sunlight streamed through the window it sparkled with different colors—red, brown, black, and yellow. I noted its layers; I said thank you.

Being aware of my own story helped me to understand Mr. E. better, especially the facet of his wish to have the forgiveness and respect of his children. But what has enriched my life is that I now know many of the things about Mr. E. that I wish I knew about my father. My real father can never fully tell his own story, and Mr. E.'s own daughter, estranged since childhood, may never know his.

Chapter Highlights

1. Those who suffered from psychiatric misdiagnosis for political purposes and their families are at risk for significant psychological sequelae such as alienation, depression, and disconnection between the generations. It is necessary to develop appropriate interventions when survivors or their family members ask for them. Psychiatry itself must come to grips with its complicity in the trauma and aftermath of marginalizing people by false diagnosis.
2. Serial trauma, where a single individual endures multiple sequential traumata, is a frequent condition in the trauma of political oppression. Cases need to be understood in terms of each of the traumatizing events, their cumulative effect, the hardiness of the survivor, and the evolution of the protean self.
3. A critical point in this psychotherapy was Dr. Csiszer's recognizing a complementary countertransference (Racker, 1968; Wilson & Lindy, 1994). It was surprising to her that she found herself reacting internally with blame and anger at him despite his heroic background. Being aware that the patient was feeling guilt and loss for abandoning his daughter, and was seeking her forgiveness and acceptance which

she felt loathe to give, led her to think in terms of countertransference and to seek supervision. This enabled the therapist to understand the complex attachments, disappointments, and yearnings that existed inside herself (the daughter of the father who abandoned her for political reasons) and inside him (the father who lost his daughter because he had to defend his political integrity). We shall return to these clinical themes in Chapter 9.

4. Dr. Csiszer values the piece of archaeological stone which Mr. E. gave her after the therapy. And Hungarians, as the following historical sketch underscores, value their connection to a Roman and Western past which even forty years of domination by the Soviet Union could not erase.

Historical Sketch: Hungary in the Twentieth Century

Robert M. Jenkins

Hungary began the 20th century as part of an empire tracing its roots to medieval times; it ended this century as a democracy reclaiming a place within the European Community. In the interregnum, Hungary experienced a range of social and political periods: war, Communist revolution, conservative reaction, flirtation with Nazism, fascism, war again, reconstruction, nationalization, Communist dictatorship, anti-Communist revolution, and reformist Communism. In every period there were both supporters and opponents among the Hungarian population and those who sustained physical and mental trauma like Dr. Csiszer's patient, Mr. E. As a result of this variety and conflict, a weary Hungarian population is easily divided in its estimation of the meaning of events.

The Hungarian state was created in the aftermath of World War I. Demonstrating that the Austro-Hungarian Empire had lost the war, the ethnically mixed territories of Hungary were lost to its neighbors. Millions of Hungarians became subjects of Czechoslovakia, Romania, and Yugoslavia. It was also in the aftermath of World War I that Hungarian Communism first showed its potential in the brief but powerful revolutionary impulse of Spring 1919.

As the old Hapsburg order tried to transit into the modern era during the inter-war period, many intellectuals sought to find a place between Western capitalism and Eastern Bolshevism. The rise of the Nazis presented an opportunity for the Faustian bargain that would restore the lost lands. Hungarian support for the German war effort led to involvement on the losing side a second time. Late in World War II Hungary tried to switch sides. The domestic version of the Nazis, the Arrow Cross, staged a coup and pushed the country into the most vicious forms of anti-Semitism.

For many in Hungary, Communism came to symbolize the force of resistance to Nazism. With support from the Soviet Red Army, the Hungarian Communist Party moved during the immediate post-war years to eliminate political rivals. By 1949, the one-party state had solidified and nationalization of property was complete. Over the following three years, show trials and purges, the characteristic elements of Stalinist political theater, came to Hungary. With Stalin's death in 1953, these excesses were reversed and the forces of reform, led by the Communist Imre Nagy, became locked in struggle with the hard-liners. This struggle turned into battle in the streets during October 1956. Only Soviet invasion brought an end to the revolutionary conflict. Though numbers are imprecise, the cost has been estimated in thousands of lives lost and countless more injured and imprisoned. Equally important, resulting scars remained in both public and private lives.

A final amnesty in 1963 cleared the way for Hungary's move towards reform. A radical economic reform program was developed during the mid-1960s and initiated in 1968. Full implementation of this market socialism was repeatedly blocked by political resistance but the changes were sufficient to lead the world to view Hungary as unique within the Communist bloc. During the 1970s and 1980s, many Hungarians had the opportunity to travel abroad and undertake limited private economic initiatives. At the same time, those who openly opposed the Communist regime found themselves subject to police harassment, loss of jobs, and occasional imprisonment. It was only in 1988 and 1989 that the democratic reforms first gained strength and presented the possibility of real change in the Communist system. The transformation was sealed with free Parliamentary elections in the Spring of 1990.

It is in this broader context that Mr. E.'s search for truth and rehabilitation and his therapist's simultaneous attempt to situate her relationship to her father should be seen as part of the larger collective effort to evaluate the meaning of the Communist era. The efforts of these two individuals are not universal, nor are they likely even representative, yet they are highly symbolic of the complex legacy of history in the lives of Hungarians today. Opportunity and limitation have varied with an individual's location in the variety of collective experience. What remains universal is the weight of this varied history for those who have lived it.

4
CHAPTER

German Democratic Republic

Editors' Note

Dr. Heike Bernhardt, a psychiatrist for children and adolescents, worked as a psychotherapist within the former East German state, the German Democratic Republic (GDR) in the 1980s. She also carried out research about psychiatry during the years of National Socialism. Later, shortly after the Berlin Wall fell, she helped to develop and then evaluate a counseling project for East Germans experiencing psychosocial crisis following reunification with West Germany.

During Dr. Bernhardt's education she acquired a vocabulary to value the internal world of her patients, not from her medical teachers but from dissident literary figures such as Christa Wolf (1970). In fact, her efforts as a young physician to find copies of Sigmund Freud's works in German libraries were all unsuccessful, as the works were only available for official critics of his thinking. Instead, she was offered the work of German analysts who had betrayed Freud, and was among the first to endorse the work of Pavlov whose stimulus response schema better fit German efforts to form the new Communist man.

In banning Freud, she argues, psychiatrists and educators of the GDR for many years also abandoned the developmental model of early childhood, replacing the atmosphere of empathy and phase specificity of learning, with expectations of conformity, duty, and guilt. As a doctor for children, she is an advocate of the reintroduction of developmental principles into the lives of children of the former German Democratic Republic.

In her chapter Dr. Bernhardt highlights some intrapsychic consequences of the totalitarian culture in which she grew up: the impact of premature separations from mothers, excessive state control of education and childrearing along with externalized values and prohibitions. She also discusses the impact of day-to-day life in a country in which security police are omnipresent. In her first case she examines the interaction between culture and individuals regarding work. She highlights the lack of preparation for reunification with the West and the dread in which autonomy and freedom are seen by certain East German youths. In this case she follows carefully her patient's clinical regressions to a dungeon-like protective state of mind in response to his anxiety over freedom and autonomy. In her second case she illustrates how the guilt of those who enforce the oppressive system of informing, the sins of the fathers, is split off by one generation and projected onto and absorbed by vulnerable individuals in the next. Because it interfered with her empathy with the family of her patient, Dr. Bernhardt must acknowledge her own feelings when she learned that mentors had spied on her, reporting their distortions to the Stasi. Transmission of guilt as a result of projective identification can be an adaptive ego state capable of forming in any of us. In both of her cases, radical discontinuities in social and psychological circumstances prompt expectations of individuals and society, making a seamless transition rather than working through traumatic change. People, individually and collectively, attempt to manage massive breaks in their lives as though there were no transition allowing for grief and mourning.

Finally, she includes among the trauma-specific legacy of her culture, the impact of the Nazi doctors murdering mentally impaired children during the Third Reich.

The chapter lends itself to further discussions of the day-to-day implications of growing up in a post-Stalinist world, and the intrapsychic barriers to integration with the West. Dr. Bernhardt identifies those who have been spied upon and those who have spied as populations suffering from the effects of totalitarian rule. In this chapter she focuses on the impact of early childhood on the personality development of her patients, herself, and her generation.

East Germany:
Absorbing the Sins of the Fathers

Heike Bernhardt

Introductory Reflections

It is sometimes difficult to convey to Western readers the more subtle forms of constraint which affect those of us raised in authoritarian regimes like the German Democratic Republic (GDR). Perhaps my impressions of two scenes which I encountered when I was traveling in the United States for the first time will help.

The first occurred in Manhattan in Central Park. There I saw boys and girls of different races and ethnic backgrounds dancing to music while on roller blades. The skating was energetic and rhythmic, it was very full of life, it was graceful and beautiful, spontaneous and creative. How proud they were of their dancing. I thought to myself, this scene must be typical of children raised in a free society. They exhibit themselves with pride and security. How different this scene is from my memories of childhood in the GDR.

The second scene occurred when I was visiting the Empire State Building. I had to queue for a long time to buy a ticket. Then I had to wait to get in the elevator. Finally after much waiting I got to the top. There I found many people, and a rope indicating that visitors should not go near the windows. I had traveled to the Empire State Building from far away because I wanted to see the panorama of New York and now I stood with all these people who also had waited a long time, but we were standing behind a rope. No one could really see the view. It was not difficult to go to the window; one simply had to walk there. I thought, well, if this is a free society I shall experiment. So I stepped past the rope; I went to the window and looked out over the city. I thought, this conformity is what people make of it. In the GDR we conformed, yet our limitations even there were to some extent what we made of them. In the GDR one said no, and all complied, but perhaps it would have been easy to do what we felt, or at least easier than we assumed.

Background to the German Democratic Republic and Reunification

I believe the truth of this matter has two sides: Forty years of the GDR certainly deformed the psychic life of its people, but during this time we the people allowed ourselves to be deformed. In this chapter, I would like to delve further into the question of the fear of freedom or the inability to be free—that is, the inability to lead a self-determined life in which one is accountable to oneself. I also want to examine the historical roots of this question and its impact on my patients and on me.

My discussion of the possible intrapsychic consequences which make freedom so difficult for the East Germans follows three major headings: 1) the conditions of childrearing and early education in the GDR, 2) the denial of history and the police state, and 3) the radical, sudden reunification with West Germany.

Childrearing Practices and Early Education in the German Democratic Republic

In the years before the re-unification (late 1980s), more than 95% of the country's women were employed, a figure made possible through comprehensive, state-funded child care. In 1988, 80% of all one- to three-year-olds were cared for in day nurseries (*krippen*), 95% of all three- to six-year-olds attended all-day kindergarten and 80% of the six- to ten-year-old school children attended after-school day care centers (*kinderhorte*). Yet we should not be misled by these figures. The high percentage of children in day care, coupled with one of the highest divorce rates in the world (43% in 1988) point to problems, especially in the early stages of socialization. Statistisches Arnt der DDR (1990), Statistisches Jahrbuch der DDR, Berlin, Statistisches Bundesant (1991), Statistisches Jahrbuch fur das rereinte Deutscheland, Weisbaden. [Bureau of Statistics for the DDR (1990), Statistical Yearbook for East Germany, Berlin] [Bureau of Federal Statistics (1991), Statistical Yearbook for the United Germany, Weisbaden]

Regardless of the culture in which one grows up, one requires a strong ego, a stable inward orientation, and a sense of autonomy in order to lead a free, self-determined, and responsible life. The development of autonomy is closely related to sufficiently good experiences with one's mother or other stable person. This relationship allows the child to internalize "good objects" (positive role models). Many of those who grew up in the GDR, however, display not autonomy but a great willingness to conform accompanied by emotional deficiencies that include a lack of constancy in relationships, difficulties with intimacy, existential angst, loneliness, and aggressive outbursts. In the *Krippen*, conformity was a matter of survival. The child with the greatest chance of being "adopted" by the nurses and female teachers had well-developed group skills and was neat, orderly, and disciplined—in short, the child who didn't make any trouble. This conformity, however, provided an insufficient basis for emotional growth. Unable to express inner drives, these children developed false, prematurely closed egos. Lacking sufficient maturity, the child internalized external constraints not through identification but though conformism. The false ego these children developed depended on external structures to provide not only regulation and control but also a sense of security. Such children suppressed their aggressiveness and their sexuality; as a result, they lived with a broken or never-developed sense of self-worth and an overpowering need for love and security (Israel, 1992).

A patient of mine, a little boy, brought his school notebook with him to a session. The figures on its cover explained that the highest goals of the education system are order, discipline, and cleanliness. The notebook cover showed the picture of a child in school and, in the next frame, the same boy continuing life in the army. I think the implicit pedagogy connotes subtle daily traumatization.

Of course what was ultimately decisive for each child's development was the reaction of that child's parents to this repressive education. By means of emotional involvement, therefore, the family had the potential to revitalize or compensate for the child's experiences. Unfortunately, parents and grandparents (who often helped) frequently lacked knowledge and, more important, intuition regarding the needs of their children. Faced with the State's dictum about what age children should be separated from their parents, what they should be taught, and how they should be disciplined, most adults simply acquiesced, handing over decisions about childrearing to the "experts," the authorities.

In that climate, those of us wishing to promote a developmental perspective found it difficult to have any impact on the country's childrearing practices. We knew that nothing would change unless teachers and parents worked together with similar assumptions, but in the GDR there had been no common ground regarding the phase appropriateness of emotional learning. Teachers, grandparents, and parents assumed that what they were taught in school (e.g., order, discipline, cleanliness) was right for today's children too.

For me, these childrearing practices are not simply abstract ideas but are very concrete experiences because they are the lessons I learned too: I learned not to shout; I learned to be dependent; I learned to be anxious every time I did something spontaneously, or something which did not exactly follow the regulations. I remember my yearning to gain my teacher's approval by behaving at all times in a dutiful, disciplined, and controlled manner. I remember feeling stifled by the regulations but feeling shame at my wish to be different. The pain of being different was very real.

Once when I was ten (1967) I had some papers from church in my school bag. My teacher, who controlled the schoolchildren, and gave us grades for orderliness, rifled through the papers and saw the note regarding church. She not only scolded me but gave me the lowest grade possible. I thought of myself as a good child and was humiliated at being scolded in front of my classmates for violating rules I did not understand. She said I was not allowed ever again to bring papers from church to school. I decided that my parents had put me in an impossible situation: I thought I would never go to church again.

Now, when I compare my experiences with those of colleagues who went to school in West Germany, I realize how really sad I was. I ask the older generation in the GDR why it happened. Why did our parents and our teachers do those things to us?

History and Its Denial in the Authoritarian State

In comparison to other European nations, Germany did not achieve nationhood until 1871. This belated development impeded the process of democratization, which did not assert itself until after World War I, with the founding of the first German Republic in 1919. Despite the new political system, however, large segments of the population remained oriented towards state authority and, as a result, they tended to support authoritarian solutions to both political and economic crises.

Following World War II, Germany was divided into two countries, the Federal Republic of Germany (or West Germany), and the German Democratic Republic (East Germany).

The Communists, who came to power with the support of the Soviet Union, found their legitimacy in their antifascism. They had suffered greatly under the cruelty of the Nazis who persecuted them and killed many of their friends and comrades. But instead of confronting the many psychological dimensions of their own injury such as cruelty and loss, the antifascists repressed the high cost of survival, unconsciously passing on to the next generation their own fixed images of friend and foe. Now the West would become the source of ongoing threat, harm, and injury.

The young generation that rebuilt a destroyed land had grown up during the period of National Socialism (Naziism). For East Germany, the change of political system from fascism to communism meant an unbroken tradition of life under a totalitarian regime that blindly followed the vision of a "better future." This post-war generation of East Germans is often referred to as the "HJ-FDJ generation" (Hitler Youth-Free German Youth), a label describing the seamless transition from one system to the other. Up until 1989, this generation decisively influenced the development of the GDR (Wierling, 1993a) and inculcated the next generation—mine—with the lessons of conformity and subordination and the fear of being different.

In this climate, ferreting out enemies of the State became an obsession. It was the task not only of the Stasi, an elaborate secret police, but also of ordinary citizens to report even the slightest deviancy to the authorities. In the GDR the Stasi came to have an extraordinary presence. When we add the massive network of informers, it becomes clear that the effects of Stasi activities were literally all-pervasive.

In such a situation, I believe, the distortions which arise in an individual's internal psychological structure contribute not only to a nearly universal paranoia but, even more important, to the simultaneous view of oneself as both persecutor/informer and victim, a theme I shall develop further in a case presentation.

The three most recent East German generations have grown up under authoritarian systems, each of which lacked checks and balances, each of which had little respect for its citizens, and each of which set up large-scale secret police/informer networks that persecuted many of us. At the same time, I must acknowledge the significant qualitative difference between Hitler's National Socialism and the socialist system. The legacy of the heinous crimes of National Socialism was an unbearable guilt that, with the division of Germany at the end of World War II, Eastern European consciousness handled by denial: by pushing it off onto the West. The reunification of Germany has made this splitting impossible. For example, "the wall" was called by the GDR government the Antifascist Protecting Rampart (*Antifaschistischer Schutzwall*). We again are face-to-face with a terrible realization.

History of Psychotherapy in Germany and East Germany

Reform efforts in the fields of pedagogy, psychiatry, and psychotherapy gained significant ground during the Weimar Republic, but were only partially successful. With the assumption of power by the National Socialists and their racist ideology in 1933, however, reform efforts in all three areas were discontinued. In particular the important tradition of psychoanalysis was truncated when most of the (often Jewish) psychoanalysts were expelled from Germany, beginning in 1933, and from Austria, beginning in 1938. This break with humanistic tradition made way for the implementation of organic and eugenic theories that viewed mental illness as a genetic deficiency. Remaining split off from its humanistic tradition, and blindly adherent to a racist philosophy, psychiatry in Germany permitted the murder of some 100,000 mentally ill patients.

With the transition to a Communist state after World War II, the field of psychoanalysis again fell under ideological censorship beginning in the 1950s and lasting into the 1980s. As in the Soviet Union, Pavlov's behavioral theories gained increasing favor because, with their emphasis on reflexes, they seemed best suited to a narrow, materialistic worldview. Self-hypnosis and group therapy became the only ideologically acceptable methods of psychotherapeutic practice. Patients were not allowed to organize into self-help groups. Thus the social structure prevented therapists an important avenue in gauging their patients' subjective experience of their illnesses and their treatment.

In fact the Communist system interpreted all expressions of individual initiative as a threat, even the spontaneous views of hospitalized psychiatric patients. For example, in the early 1980s after being asked to assist psychiatric in-patients to produce a patient newspaper, I was told that the project had been suddenly terminated with no explanation. After reunification I read the following account of this incident as a Stasi informer had reported it in my Stasi file: *Die Zeitung sollte als Plattform fuer die Verbreitung oppositionellen Gedankengutes dienen* ("This newspaper is intended to serve the propagation of oppositional ideas").

Above all, the form of psychiatry taught and practiced in the GDR was defined and determined from the outside. The high degree of conformity to (and resulting from) the socialist system led to a narrow definition of what was considered "normal." Here one must note that, like educators, therapists were agents of the social system. In the "real-existing" socialism of the GDR, the balance in the socially defined relation between individual freedom and government-sponsored health care fell in favor of the latter.

Further, a self-imposed isolation, symbolized by the Berlin Wall, effectively cut the GDR off from developments in Western Europe and the United States, for example in the areas of social psychiatry, psychoanalysis, developmental psychology, and the range of normal behaviors.

The Stasi (Secret Police) within Psychiatry and in Everyday Life

An important chapter in East German history is the political dimension of psychology, psychotherapy, and psychiatry and their misuse by the secret police. In numerous cases, doctors and psychologists placed themselves in the service of the Stasi—either officially, as employees, or unofficially, as informants. Their duties extended from educating other secret-service employees in the field of psychology (Plog, 1993) to betraying patients and their coworkers in the health profession. An estimated three percent of East German doctors worked for the secret service (Schrüter, 1994). Not infrequently, excerpts from patients' medical files turned up in their Stasi files; and the state police often collected information about therapists who took part in self-analysis groups with the intention of using it against them. It is important to note that in the GDR there was no protected space in which patients and their therapists could feel safe from state intervention (Simon, 1994). Reading my own Stasi file after reunification (1989) revealed that I, too, had been reported on.

Did they report on me because I was an especially dangerous person to the State? Somehow I do not think so. While I certainly supported peace and such humanitarian organizations as the Physicians Against Nuclear Proliferation, mine were hardly the views of a founder of an opposition party. No, I think my experience was more typical than not. In a country where literally hundreds of thousands of agents, both official and unofficial, are spying, it is probable that many would have a Stasi file with entries in it from their "friends."

Looking back on the G.D.R., I remember the degradation of the political system most acutely in two situations: when I saw the wall that divided Germany and locked us in to our part of it, and when we "elected" the "people's representatives." Those in power claimed that almost 100 percent of the population voted in these elections, and that their mandate came from those votes. Yet voters could only accept or reject the candidates presented to them. There was never a real choice involved. Students, too, were required to vote but in an election office that had been established solely for them. When as a student I voted for the first time, I had decided to cast a "no" vote. Those sitting inside the office, professors and students, all knew me. There was no booth to protect our privacy. Rather, we were expected to cast our "yes" votes openly. (Whoever voted "no" was considered an enemy of the State; whoever decided not to vote faced public repression.) Having difficulty locating the precise voting space, I asked where I could find it. Someone pointed to a podium standing in the middle of the room. As if I were going to make a speech, I stood there in plain sight of the very professors on whom I depended. The gazes of the "voting assistants" bore through me. I began to cross through the names on the voting list because, unless the voter marked through every individual name, the ballot counted as an invalid vote rather than a "no" vote. A great fear began to well up in me and I was overwhelmed with a sense of weakness. I began to shake and left the election office bathed in sweat. Although later I experienced far more dangerous situations, I have never since experienced the fear I did then.

Impact of Reunification/ Die Wiedervereinigung

Although these changes were felt throughout the "Ostblock," (Eastern Europe's Communist states) nowhere else but in East Germany did they occur literally overnight. Because of the timing of our fusion with West Germany, we experienced virtually no period of transition.

Prior to reunification many sociological indicators pointed to differences between East and West Germany. East Germans married younger than West Germans; they gave birth to their children at a younger age; their divorce rates were higher. When the wall was built these differences became more pronounced. Then, with unification came new dramatic changes: the birth rate in East Germany declined drastically, falling by two-thirds (such a decrease in a single year is quite striking and possibly unique); stress-related illness rose; right-wing radicalism and xenophobia broke out; and resignation and just plain complaining grew common.

It is true that the unification of the two German states was desired by a majority of GDR citizens whose expectancy of freedom and prosperity was strong. Many people experienced the new system as genuine liberation. Yet it is also true that many individuals found their life experiences, dreams, and goals of striving for an ideal socialist society suddenly devalued. Formerly accepted projections and images of foes were no longer valid. Moreover, there was no time and no real chance to find a GDR-specific solution to the country's problems. Many people of the GDR experienced social change as directed from the outside

My Medical and Psychiatric Experience

Medical School

As a rule, the only persons permitted to study medicine in the GDR were those young women and men who had gained recognition in school through their "political reliability" and their conformity to the system. Their parents were also expected to fulfill the same criteria. In addition, male students had to serve thirty-six months in the army rather than the eighteen required of all young men in the GDR. Only a very few who didn't fulfill these requirements were admitted to university. In my class of around 200 students, there were only two women who had not been involved in the socialist youth organization and very few men who had served only eighteen months in the military. I, too, had been active in the youth organization during my school years.

I studied at a small university in the north of the GDR. University life did not require us to be creative; we had to learn much by rote and we strove to be able to repeat the teachings of our professors word for word.

The university was run by men. Its structures and hierarchies were authoritarian; a professor generally held a great deal of power. I often felt powerless, at the mercy of this situation. Patients too were subjected to these power structures and this sense of impotence. Granted, there were doctors who respected their patients and there were clinics that enabled them to do so. Here, however, I would like to describe those experiences during my studies that today continue to be an emotional burden for me, experiences that I view as an expression of a totalitarian system.

We attended lectures in gynecology, for example, held by a professor who claimed over and over again that rats were the animals that women most closely resembled. Afraid of him, ourselves cowards, not one of the 200 students in the lecture dared to contradict his misogynist views. I am most ashamed, however, that I never protested when, one day, he brought a woman under anesthesia into the lecture hall and performed a curettage of the uterus in front of 200 people completely unknown to her. Sitting in the first row, I saw a lot of blood and this woman, in an undignified position, at the mercy of us all. I felt ill, as if my own insides were about to burst. I am convinced that this woman never learned what had happened to her while she was under anesthesia.

Pediatrics

Following my university studies, I began to work in pediatrics. This field enabled me to observe East German children in various stages of development, as well as their parents. I enjoyed the work, but I was constantly running up against occupational barriers. For example, I saw many children with spastic bronchitis that later developed into asthma. The clinic responded to their illnesses with organic diagnoses and various medicines. I often asked myself what it was that didn't allow these children to breathe. What pressures did they have to bear? In most cases, both parents worked and there was little time for the children, but we had only our instruments and pills to offer. I sensed that something was missing and, often, I myself had the feeling I couldn't breathe. It seemed that East German doctors had lost their understanding of psychic well-being. They diagnosed the picture presented to them without placing it the context of the patient's history or environment or family. We cared for many children and families of children with cancer, but we never dared voice our questions about pollution and the nearby nuclear power plant. As a result of these experiences, I began to search for a field of work where I would be allowed to ask questions about the whole patient and where those questions were indeed being asked. For political reasons, my then-husband was prohibited from working in the city where we lived. We were expected to move to a sparsely populated area with a shortage of doctors. During this time, we considered long and hard whether we should accept this humiliation or move to West Germany. In the end, our friends, and perhaps also our fear of the unknown behind the wall, kept us in the GDR. I took advantage of the move to change my area of specialization. In the field of psychiatry, I hoped to be able to work differently, to gain a different access to and understanding of people.

Psychiatry and Psychotherapy in the GDR

The field of psychiatry and psychotherapy which I was about to enter had been cut off in East Germany from its own humanistic tradition for most of the preceding thirty years.

Our training in, even our access to, significant mental health concepts long accepted in the West was virtually nonexistent. Even as late as 1980 I was refused a book by Freud at the University library. The library authorities said "This is bourgeois literature." I was not allowed even to wait for it. It was writers of the GDR, writers like Franz Fuehmann and Christa Wolf, from whom I learned about humanistic ideas compatible with psychoanalysis. They had a profound influence on me and I hoped to pursue them in my new specialty area.

I found a large hospital where the head doctor had been trying for years to release long-term patients and to find places and situations in which they could live. He was also working to reestablish psychotherapy as a valid component within the realm of psychiatry. Both concerns were important to me and I thought I would easily fit into this environment. In my first days at the hospital I was happy to find a workshop on xenophobia and psychological explanations for concepts of friends and enemies. In East Germany, these topics were highly politicized and considered taboo, so the workshop led me to think that a degree of political involvement might be possible in this hospital.

All that remains of this time, however, is the sense of being part of an arcane game whose rules I didn't understand. I grew increasingly wary of the head doctor who, at the beginning, had seemed so desirous of change. I felt as if he was using me like a figure on a chess board. Sometimes I was pushed forward, sometimes moved back. Only after the fact did my Stasi files help me to clarify the rules of the seemingly incomprehensible game. My feelings hadn't deceived me. The head doctor had been a spy for the state police and we had indeed been manipulated like marionettes. There had been a plan, according to which the head doctor and three other informants from amongst my colleagues had been assigned the task of destabilizing not only my professional and family life but also my very psyche.

This hospital boasted two modern, well-functioning stations for patients who had acute psychiatric illnesses or who were being treated for neurotic or neurological illnesses. For those patients in the same hospital who suffered from chronic illnesses or who were severely physically or mentally disabled, however, there was neither the space nor the conditions that would have helped their development and healing process. They were housed and treated in such a demeaning manner that their most elementary human rights were violated. As I asked disturbing questions about the history of this place, I learned that the very walls of this hospital contained the unwritten stories of children killed in Nazi Germany's euthanasia program. I was deeply moved by those who continued to bear the impact of those crimes and I shall return to a personal perspective on the research I carried out uncovering the documents of this euthanasia in the epilogue to this chapter.

Reunification/Die Wiedervereinigung Clinic

Meanwhile, events of enormous proportions were occurring on the world scene and in our country. Witnessing the impact of the changes that were occurring so dramatically with the fall of the Berlin wall and the move toward reunification, my colleagues, East German physicians and psychologists, and I witnessed a dramatic impact on our patients and on ourselves. Growing out of our clinical work and personal experiences, we decided to offer a clinic for people who were having emotional difficulties with the social changes after 1989. We set out to open a dialogue with the past and to ask questions regarding former and new-found identities, questions about the victim–perpetrator dichotomy, political repression, problems with work and unemployment, new gender identities, and familial and childrearing difficulties.

The people we were seeing often experienced an existential threat. Their angst included: (a) loss of identity with failure and unwillingness to search for new identity; (b) disappearance of external state care and economic stabilization and associated uncertainty; (c) loss of child day-care as a right and restrictions on the entry of mothers in the work force; (d) decreased availability of social services through bureaucratization; (e) loss of external definition of self as coping with newly found freedom causing demands for greater individual responsibility; (f) loss of work through destabilizing, widespread unemployment for those whose work was their only lifeline; (g) increased pressure to compete and consume; (h) reduced solidarity with the socially disadvantaged, and the subsequent growth of social differences; and (i) changes in previously valued norms and ideals.

Based on these observations, we decided to offer group sessions centering around questions of personal identity in this period of rapid change and personal uncertainty. Group meetings would include open sections dealing with personal experiences and also didactic seminars. We hoped our effort could serve as a pilot project that would inspire similar endeavors in other parts of the country.

Despite aggressive advertising, our offerings were greeted with only lukewarm interest, as our groups were poorly attended. As a result, we soon lost our funding and were unable to continue our project.

Reflecting later on our lack of success we considered a number of factors: (a) During this period of acute social crisis, perhaps other priorities such as economic necessity took precedence over psycho-social counseling. While neurotic decompensation seemed to disappear during such phases of social stress, perhaps it would be followed later by increases in numbers of cases; (b) Perhaps people were falling back on the historical experiences of 1945. At that time, rather than working through past trauma the population uncompromisingly and industriously oriented itself towards the future. In fact, the past became a taboo subject. As a result, East Germans have never learned that confronting one's past history can be a liberating experience; (c) The media's constant and sometimes distorted attention to the GDR's past made people defensive and reluctant to come to the clinic; (d) Rather than seeing the clinic as an opportunity for growth, perhaps people were afraid of what they would find there, afraid of having a moral judgment passed on them; (e) Ordinary citizens did not expect to encounter understanding from mental health professionals. This fear probably stemmed from historical experience, relating to our own complicitous past as psychiatrists and psychotherapists in the GDR; (f) As under the old regime, "real existing socialism," this new free market system rewarded—now materially— those who could conform the most quickly. Sadly, the new system created by merging with the West, like the old GDR itself, was more interested in conforming with the new order than in free, critical evaluation of the present and the past.

Other possibilities struck us as well. Perhaps the directness of our project was not in tune with the times. Such confrontation so early may have frightened people more than it encouraged them. Finally, because we ourselves, as therapists, had been involved in the old GDR system, we had our own great insecurities about whether or not we could cope with the changes. Perhaps for this reason our own adaptation to the new system was incomplete, so we were not yet in a position to offer the needed distance and support.

Whatever the underlying causes, the support group folded because of lack of funding after having existed for only one year. This failure pointed to our own inability to function within the new system: We had oriented ourselves towards the goals we wanted to achieve without concerning ourselves with the practical aspects of running the project. Products of a system in which the framework for action was always provided, we had never seen logistic matters as our concern, and, in the case of the clinic, we acted according to outdated models.

Finding Work in the West

After the demise of our project, I joined many others in the search for work. At that time, a secure job was a valuable commodity and unemployment was greatly feared. I did find work in West Berlin at a therapeutic practice for addicts and mentally ill criminals. It was the first time that I had worked outside the territory of the former GDR. In this practice in which patients and staff from East and West Berlin found themselves thrown together, questions arose regarding the degree to which similarities and differences in socialization in both countries would contribute to trust or distrust (see case of Karl on the next page).

We worked there with delinquents with addiction problems, many of whom had been ordered to stay in the hospital as part of their legal penalty. Many patients from the East, like Karl, below, were frightened by the opportunities and challenges which faced them in their new world. Individual cases allowed us insights into these people's struggles with autonomy, identity, life goals, wishes, and fantasies.

Returning to a Psychiatric Clinic in the East

Because of my previous experience, I hoped to find work in child and adolescent psychiatry and in psychotherapy. After a long search, the chance to realize this wish presented itself in a clinic for child and adolescent psychiatry in East Berlin, a practice with a strong psychoanalytic emphasis. The head doctor had been active in psychotherapy since the time of the GDR and I was happy to discover that she was open to different branches of the field. Even though, officially, the GDR distanced itself from psychoanalysis, here and there there was a niche where psychoanalytic knowledge and practice could exist and develop.

For four years I had also been participating in programs sponsored by a training institute for child and adolescent psychotherapy and analysis founded after the collapse of the GDR by psychotherapists from East and West Berlin. My experiences there have been liberating and enriching. I have had the chance to speak openly on topics that are new to so many of us and to hear therapists from diverse schools of psychotherapy. The clinic where I now work sets the high standard of dealing with every family member and every child as an individual. My work has never been as enjoyable, satisfying, and exciting as it presently is. This clinic has a limited capacity for outpatients, however, and most of our work is with inpatients. They are often deeply disturbed, coming to us out of crisis situations. We generally work with these inpatients in a one-on-one setting, but with the most severe cases, such as psychoses, we often work as a group. We also offer group therapy to adolescents, especially to those who have encountered identity crises with the onset of puberty. In every case, the work with parents and families is of utmost importance, and some of my colleagues are trained in family therapy. Of the two in-depth case studies which follow, the first case comes from my previous work in West Berlin; the second case comes from my current work in the former East Berlin.

Karl

Karl is a twenty-eight-year-old single man, delinquent, and alcohol-dependent, whose most recent arrest was for setting a fire in front of a neighbor's apartment. His alcoholism was severe and progressive, leading to episodes of pancreatitis. The judge had probated Karl to this hospital pending the outcome of his legal proceedings. I learned even before he was assigned to me that Karl was afraid of coming to a hospital in West Berlin. He wanted to stay in East Berlin where he felt more secure.

He told me that he was born in a little town of the GDR. His father left when his mother was still pregnant with him, so in his infancy he and his mother lived alone. When he was two years old his mother remarried and sent Karl to live with his grandparents. His mother and stepfather had a second child, a half-brother, whom, Karl explained, they liked more than him. During Karl's childhood, his mother remarried and changed her name two more times. Each time the marriage broke down and his mother was alone, she sent for him; each time she found a new man, she sent Karl away to the grandmother.

He recalls that as a little boy, he suffered from enuresis, a symptom which recurred when he was about twenty. In school when he saw other pupils, he thought, "I'm alone; nobody likes me." When he was living with his grandparents, he told me, "They gave me too much; they spoiled me."

At thirteen, Karl went alone to look for his own father, but he was disappointed to find that his father was alcoholic and unable to help or guide him.

When Karl finished the eighth grade, he was told he would need to learn a trade. At the same time, his mother was moving to Berlin and said "You have to come with me." Karl objected; he wanted to stay with his grandmother, but his mother's will overrode his objections, so he went to Berlin. The experience was terrible for him because "Berlin was such a big town," too big for him. He began to drink alcohol; by the time he was 16 he had become delinquent.

Karl's delinquent activities were quite varied, not repetitive like many other patients. The arson incident was the fourth charge to bring him to prison. First he stole and drove a car without a license. Then he was drunk and insulted the Communist Party. Then he broke into a flat and stole something.

As I listened to this history and sensed his aloneness, I thought this man had lost the most important experience of early childhood: to feel lovable because he has been loved. Instead his experience was: "I must not be lovable since my parents so easily discard me."

I tried to translate his delinquent behavior in terms of that theme— that is, as an expression of rage at a world that wants him only for its own purposes, then discards him. I was also aware of a second theme—his frustrated search for a father figure—and imagined that it would play some role as the treatment unfolded.

In terms of the focus of this chapter, it is interesting to review how Karl responded to opportunities to be free of his current surroundings, to travel, and to explore the world, especially once the door to the West became open.

He was twenty-four when the Berlin Wall fell. He reminded me of other patients I had from East Berlin who went into the West when the wall fell and wished "to begin a new life in the West now, but couldn't." Karl traveled to Giessen where there were big camps for the many people from the GDR going to the West, but he was drunk all the time, he said. So after six months he returned to East Berlin. Later he and a friend traveled to Paris together, but again he said he couldn't see anything be-cause he drank too much alcohol. On a third trip, he went to Italy with his mother. She had booked the trip, and he stayed in the same room with her. In each of these instances, he responded to opportunities for autonomy with regression, numbing, and alcohol.

The Process of Psychotherapy

When I first saw Karl, he looked pale and downcast. He avoided my eyes, although he did look tentatively around the room. There was a quality in him like a very sad little boy. I introduced myself as his therapist, saying that I had heard of his fear of West Berlin. I explained to him that there were other persons from East Berlin in the hospital as well. He seemed relieved by our first encounter.

Despite his interpersonal timidity, Karl was eager for therapy. Characteristically he knocked at the door five minutes early for his indi-vidual and group sessions.

In the first hour, as I was asking his life story, he volunteered a dream, perhaps both as a gift and a warning: "I saw many snakes and the snake heads were cut and these cut heads were sold." I elected not to ask for his associations to the dream at that time as I thought it more important to try to build on our rather fragile alliance. But it did strike me that he immediately sought to engage me on a powerfully symbolic level.

Karl told me about the pet rats he had at home. As other people might have a little dog, a rabbit, or a duck, Karl kept rats in his flat. He said, "I need to have them with me. I told my girlfriend, 'You must decide, you must take me with my rats or you may not have me.'" When I asked about the rats, about their color and whether they had names, he showed me, gesturing: "This is the white rat and its name is Nina, and this is the gray rat and its name is Lena." I could imagine the rats he was "showing" me in the room, and the space they occupied between him and me. I thought, he places the rats between us, keeping us apart, yet paradoxically he introduces me to them like a sexual offer.

The first weeks and months of this treatment were not so difficult for me. While I was not secure in it, I did think we two had a beginning alliance. One tension in our relationship was that we both knew eventually I would expect him to work, which he had not done for three or four years, and it was a necessary part of the treatment plan. I thought it would be important for the recovery of his socialization skills for him to work in the hospital, where the duties are not so hard. Our plan was that he would work three months in the hospital; and after that, if the work had gone well, he could look for work out of the hospital. In general I think that going to work is a step in which the patient takes responsibility for himself, but it is often very difficult. Patients frequently regress and act out in protest before they overcome resistance to work. Karl was no different. When I said the time had come, "You must work in this hospital," he grew very angry, refusing to do so and insisting that he had to wait for the court papers. I saw that it would be an especially difficult task for him to take responsibility for himself. In his imagery Karl summarized his protest about work: "I want to have a very big castle," he said, "I want to live in this very big castle, and there no one can come to me. I will have very big walls around me and nobody will come to me. That is a fine idea for my life."

As a condition of his probation, Karl had no freedom. I thought it must be terrible for him to live there with so little possibility of freedom, but he said he was very glad. If I were to say to him, "You can leave the hospital for eight hours," he would say he wouldn't go.

A second tension in the relationship with me centered on the failure of his girlfriend to visit him in the hospital. For this, he blamed his girlfriend's mother, saying that she didn't like him. It was clear that I also became involved in his projection when he said to me, "You don't want me to go with my girlfriend." So now we had two transference problems: In one I was in the cruel paternal role of wanting or expecting him to work; in the other I was in the engulfing maternal role of keeping him too close to me in a regressed position. As we continued to explore his feelings about work, he explained that in the past, "in the GDR prison, it was a nice time for me because I worked there as a crane driver." He also said that if he had refused to work in the GDR prison "they would lock me into a dark room, actually a dark cellar." I thought that he projected onto me the image of sadistic warden: If I would threaten him with a dark cellar he would go to work.

He said his time in prison was a good period in his life because the threat of the dark cellar motivated him, but I thought it was terrible that the motivation needed to be displaced onto this sadistic, authoritarian structure. It was very difficult for me to find the right distance in our relationship. I knew that he needed both distance and relationship, but I had trouble finding the optimal level between the distance he could tolerate and the one he could not stand. He needed his rats for distance from me, and he needed walls for distance from his own autonomy.

My countertransference reactions to working with Karl reflect themes similar to my reaction to other East German youths in similar circumstances. While I felt a strong wish to help, and while I was able, despite considerable difficulty, to form a good bond with him, I also felt helpless, as if I were swimming with no land in sight. I was hesitant; these youths evoked in me the wish to be very firm with them and to give strong advice as to what they must do to meet my approval. I felt this excessive direction- and limit-setting was stern, even harsh, like the bad teacher who had struck me as a child.

Perhaps when I told him to go to work, there was such a harshness to my voice that he felt my words were sending him away from me, reviving the traumatic separations from his mother in childhood. He became angry with me when I tried to suggest that he could take care of himself. Still one more displaced reason for not going to work was that his girlfriend was losing interest in him. She didn't even come to the court hearing. I thought this was really difficult for him because he was so sensitive to her reacting to his dependence upon her.

Transference/Countertransference

I believe Karl experienced me in many ways in this treatment. I was a steady and hopeful person who sat together with him, like his accepting grandmother. But at times he felt that I, like his mother, would take over his world for myself and send his girlfriend away. At other times he wished me to be the stern father or teacher who would punish him.

Many of these transference roles I find tolerable, but not that of the harsh teacher. Being cast in that role stirs in me a countertransference anger and, ironically, a wish to punish him for seeing me that way. For me, the freedom to take on social responsibility is a central human challenge. Karl reversed this, denying his own responsibility and trying to provoke me into sending him further into his regressive dungeon. In these moments, we recreated the persecutor/victim split which we were trying to put behind us.

My psychotherapy with Karl was incomplete. We do not yet know how things will turn out for him. I think that for many East German youth like him it will take a long time to risk leaving the walled-in castle in their minds.

Hans

Hans was fifteen years old when I first saw him, following a near-fatal suicide attempt. He was unconscious and hooked up to a respirator when I first met his parents. I sat with them during some of those early difficult hours when his physical condition was critical. I could sense their desperate search for explanations as to why their quiet, well-behaved son would suddenly try to kill himself, even as the family seemed to be recovering from so much recent loss. Hans' father broke the silence, uncharacteristically wiping tears from his eyes: "But we were (respected) functionaries (in the old regime), we were in the party, I worked in the ministries. We believed in socialism and helped to build it." As I watched this remarkable breakthrough of emotion from this otherwise silent man, I wondered whether the two factors were related: the son's wish for death and the emotional impact on him of the political past of his parents. When and how did this family, this boy, begin to suffer?

When he began therapy, Hans sat hunched over in a chair, his head down so that I couldn't see his eyes. He answered me in brief phrases, his voice without feeling. Although he was tall and lean, he looked like a little boy, not like a fifteen-year-old. He was, in short, a grown-up, very small child whose smile tried to tell me: It isn't as bad as you think. He made me feel maternal.

During our conversations I could only guess what his reactions were. His hair became a curtain between us. He seemed sad, lonely, turned inward with little hope. Soon, however, he put on a different face, one that gave me a greater cause for alarm. He flashed a wide smile that I couldn't see behind. I thought Hans must spend a lot of energy trying to maintain his mask as though everything was just fine.

In addition to depression, Hans' symptoms included 1) an eating disorder: apparent anorexia with obsessive monitoring of his diet and particular avoidance of protein; 2) aesthetic character traits: he isolated himself in his room, carried out an elaborate calisthenics program four times daily, and was preoccupied with philosophical poets; 3) a hand-washing compulsion; and 4) impaired peer relationships. As I watched his behavior, struggled to make contact with him, and read his poetry characterized by sharply contrasting moods, and the theme of good and evil, I feared he was close to a psychotic break.

In the GDR, Hans' parents were well known. His mother had been a teacher, his father a high-ranking official in the utilities. Both were long-time party members and part of the privileged class. Hans was raised in this privileged environment, and this status resulted in privileges and expectations for him. It was understood that he would be a member of the youth organization and take on leadership functions in his school. His was a family that never overtly doubted the existing system. They appeared happy to live in the GDR and functioned well under its conditions.

In interviews with his mother we learned that following World War II, her family fled East Prussia. In old pictures of these refugees, one sees hunched-over figures, freezing and starving, creeping along the street in the dead of winter, carrying what little they owned. Hans' mother was the first *Friedenskind* in the family, the first child born under conditions of peace. Through land reform, the family received a plot and worked hard to get by on a day-to-day basis. As in so many families, the war and the guilt and suffering associated with it were never discussed. Instead, the family worked hard and successfully to build a new existence. They carried the added burden of being forced to be, but also wanting to be, a part of it all. As refugees, they were foreigners, and as former adherents of National Socialist (Nazi) ideology, they suddenly found themselves in a socialist country: they therefore experienced a double break in their identity. The members of the mother's family told themselves that, if they worked hard and achieved a lot, no one would ask about their past; they would belong, would no longer be seen as foreign. For that reason work and achievement became the meaning of life for Hans' mother. She viewed integration of the past as a threat.

Hans' father's family had also been loyal to Hitler, but because of his important bureaucratic role in the municipal government he was able to make an easy transition to the new Communist State. He, too, chose to ignore rather than to integrate his past.

In a breakthrough of emotion from these otherwise hardened people, I learned that following the *Wiedervereinigung* (change), Hans' mother lost her job because her previously hidden role as Stasi informer had been exposed by the Gauck Commission, the special group appointed after re-unification to investigate the GDR's secret police files. His father, too, had lost his job when the ministry closed. Shame, guilt, and loss of careers struck as a triple blow following on the heels of the unexpected collapse of the social order in which they had held such high status.

In our first meeting, the mother explained that she had been a teacher and had just lost her job. Full of hate, she concluded with the sentence: *"Ich bin gegauckt worden, wie man das jetzt so schoen sagt"* ("I have been 'gaucked,' as we say nowadays"). That is to say that she had lost her job and her status because it had been discovered that she had secretly passed information on to the state police. Within this context, it was significant that her language was so full of hate and that, without hesitating, she placed herself in the role of victim. She felt she had been wronged, never asking whether her actions had harmed others. Despite the blow of losing their position and status by being *gegaukt*, Hans' parents used the same determined focus on work and action which had allowed their parents' families to survive the harsh years of 1945–48. The result was that, at least on the surface, they recovered quickly, and both had found new positions as managers within the newly developing business enterprises that West Berliners were opening up in the East.

But were either the current "successes" or the earlier "happiness" in the GDR really true, especially for Hans?

A closer look reveals puzzling factors already evident in Hans' early life. Hans was born at a particularly difficult time for both of his parents' careers and both had been ambivalent about raising a child in those difficult circumstances. He had been quiet, perhaps too quiet as a baby.

Like other children in the GDR, Hans was only six months old when his parents first sent him to the *Krippe*. There, he fell silent. His mother described how he had lain in a corner of the play room, hardly moving, for three months. When as a toddler Hans had to go to the hospital for a tonsillectomy and then an appendectomy, he responded to these abrupt separations in the same way: by breaking off communication with his environment. He didn't protest loudly, he didn't cry, but rather he drew back into himself. In such situations he seemed to become like stone. At that time, no one understood his withdrawal, nor was it viewed as cause for alarm. Later, Hans underwent no period of defiance, no "terrible twos." He maintained this pattern into the early years of school: He didn't cause any problems; he did what was expected of him. Although his parents claimed he had contact with children of his own age, he tended to be reserved. Perhaps he was using his inconspicuousness during this phase as a means of getting attention; perhaps this regressive withdrawal was more of a problem than his parents or teachers realized.

Things became difficult for Hans when he entered adolescence, a time that coincided with East Germany's falling apart. Adolescence seemed to take him by surprise, as if he hadn't had the necessary previous experiences to prepare him for it. During this time, he was often left to himself. His parents were concerned about their own problems: They had lost not only their jobs but also the social recognition that had accompanied those positions. For his parents, this meant a loss of identity and a previously unknown existential angst. During this time, Hans' symptoms grew worse. He ate less, particularly food prepared by his mother; he exercised continuously, although never outdoors; and he withdrew even more. We know that a suicide attempt is generally the last step in a long journey: When Hans' cries for help went unheard, he swallowed pills. This was his last chance to draw attention to his need.

When the treatment began and he and I were finally able to make contact, Hans told me of a dream of a tall plant in springtime with no leaves, only a fiery red ball in the earth without roots. The image of the fiery red ball led me to think of a tightly held, blocked feeling of anger. I explained that therapy would be a search for old and new roots, a search for a new sense of security.

In the beginning of our work we didn't allow Hans' parents to see him. Although they had difficulty dealing with this separation, Hans experienced it with a sense of relief. Only the hospital could provide the security he required. He showed me some of the poetry he was reading, and I found it striking, especially the phrase "exalting to heaven, saddened to death" in a poem divided into two parts, expressing a great, radical change in mood. I thought about our divided, unified country, that for so long had been spanned by a deadly wall. The sense of being divided, of breaks without transitions, of the inability to speak, of the fear of death; these were themes in the poetry and in our discussions over and over again.

When the parents finally admitted to having been functionaries in the Communist regime, I sensed this as a revelation, a clue to the puzzle of Hans' life. But this breakthrough also brought out powerful and contradictory feelings in me. I thought: "Back then, you didn't want the public to know that there were people suffering under the system," and I felt the countertransference desire for revenge: "It is about time that *you* are the ones who are suffering." Right away, with such anger at my patient's parents, I thought I didn't have enough distance from the situation to continue on the case. In this situation I was understandably identifying with revenge-seeking victims of informers. On the other hand, I thought: Perhaps the parents are also experiencing the desire for revenge, revenge because they have lost their self-esteem, their position in society, their power. How deep does the suffering of the parents lie when they can only speak about their disgrace, if at all, with tears? To what extent were the parents implicated in the old system and how great is the burden they bear? In this second situation I was identifying with their own loss and sadness in their role as victims.

Yet throughout the work it was only rarely that I was able to detect strong feelings coming from them. Most often their expressions were like wood. I noticed that in these situations it was I who bore the intense feelings, feelings not only of loss and revenge but intense feelings of guilt. I could trace this to several instances in which Hans' mother spoke abusively to me by telephone, accusing me of things for which I was not responsible. Yet I noticed that I sometimes felt this guilt just being in her presence while she was seemingly calm. If I was feeling such guilt now, then who was being forced to feel such guilt in the family? Were Hans' parents, particularly his mother, unconsciously forcing him to carry their burden from the old regime? In a projective test, Hans saw himself as a trash heap: Anyone could dump his crap on him. In this third situation I (along with Hans) was feeling his parents' projectively identified guilt which they had denied and split off.

The family never spoke with each other about the past, nor was it possible even in therapy to talk about the past with feeling. The parents defended themselves against confronting this topic by working manically in their new professions. They now held managerial positions, in careers upheld by the new system as some of the most successful. To me, however, managers are the "party functionaries" of modern capitalism. Looking back, I see the path taken by the parents as almost seamless. They were again functioning, were once again successful. It was only Hans who wouldn't and couldn't go on any longer.

Hans' therapy centered around questions about and the search for his identity. As I worked with him I noticed I developed an interesting countertransference symptom of severe bouts of hunger. As these struck me I remembered the image from his childhood which always shocked me: such a small child whom no one noticed. I thought to myself, so many individuals had been silenced. During that time, a heavy gray veil of cowardice, lethargy, and hopelessness hung over the whole country. Perhaps hunger was a hopeful sign that one was aware of one's own needs: hunger as a hopeful desire, as a cry of protest.

Now with my countertransference feelings of guilt, anger, and hunger better understood and with Hans' parents' experience more clearly in my mind, I could better understand the projected source of Hans' almost unbearable feelings of guilt, anger, and revenge. My thoughts returned to some of his other symptoms: As I watched him meticulously washing his hands, I saw and heard his mother, in an image that seemed superimposed, say, "Well, my hands are clean" (of guilt). As I watched him poke suspiciously at his food, I thought of his saying to himself, "Don't poison me with more of your hypocrisy." As I saw him shy away from other teenagers on the ward, I sensed his saying, "The badness I hold for my parents' deeds keeps me from being worthy of your genuine interest in me." As I read his poetry of divided fields and divided minds, I thought of our divided country and the enormous task we have to make bridges so that our two sides can truly communicate with each other.

Towards the end of his hospitalization, Hans expressed the wish to be moved. He criticized the conditions in our hospital, insisting that everything would be different in another one. He was impatient and angry. For the first time, I saw aggression in him, the red fiery ball of suppressed anger. Finally, Hans could express his anger and his frustration in an environment in which they were accepted; and he saw that, despite his behavior, we didn't punish him for his anger by sending him to another hospital.

Since Hans saw himself as a stabilizer for his parents he feared that his return home would place him back in this role, and he wished to live somewhere else. He wanted to move into a group home for adolescents and we supported this wish. Hans' family had experienced numerous breaks that they were unable to transform into transitions and thus couldn't integrate their past into the present. His parents could not speak about the past and therefore couldn't change themselves, but Hans had learned to speak about the past and was changing. This parting and new beginning, by being different, was an especially important and symbolic step in Hans' therapy. We discussed Hans' wish with his parents. They had the opportunity to express their fear that they had failed as parents, their sense of guilt, and their great sadness. They were finally able to grant Hans' wish and let go of him.

We worked on the transition to life in the group home in practical terms. He adapted well and seems to enjoy his life in the company of other adolescents—even though it is not without its problems. For the entire period he has remained free of his earlier symptoms. Improvement continues with six month follow-up visits.

Reflections

When I think about Hans and his family, I recall that Hans is only slightly older than my own children, his parents slightly younger than my parents. Their story is one of fractured lives and of the attempt to relocate and reintegrate those severed parts of one's history. It is a story which in part we all share.

Following the demise of the GDR, I, too, found myself questioning my personal history. In order to find myself anew and to orient myself with the new system, I was forced to explore both the extent of my guilt and its implications as well as my courage and positive traits. Even though I experienced the changes (*die Wiedervereinigung*) as liberating and even life-saving, I also saw that everything that had been was coming apart at the seams. The search for older, dependable roots as well as for new roots was beginning for me as well. Where did my path cross with Hans'? Did I, like Hans, fall silent in situations of separation anxiety and guilt? And why was it that no one seemed to understand this behavior?

Here, I arrive at a central question for myself and for all of us in medicine, psychiatry, and psychotherapy in the former GDR, regarding the role of perpetrator. We professionals (I was working in pediatrics at the time) failed to use our knowledge to resist the system. We cured symptoms without challenging their social causes. It was, for example, forbidden to inquire into the health effects of extreme conditions of pollution, so no one asked about them. It was forbidden to collect statistics on suicides after the rate had increased following the construction of the wall. How could the psychotherapists, psychiatrists, and pediatricians of a country allow themselves to be prevented from gathering statistics on suicides and suicide attempts, especially since such statistics should help to form the basis for preventing these attempts?

I have thought a great deal about Hans' "as if" face. Many individuals in the GDR led a uniquely double life. In public they acted as if everything were fine. The Socialist Unity Party always found enough people to vote for and laud it. At home or amongst friends, however, one spoke differently. This constant state of self-denial also meant the denial of one's feelings. Recalling the initial image in this chapter of the faces of the children in Central Park in New York gives me pause. If this double life was symptomatic of an entire population, how are children, the following generation, supposed to have open, honest faces?

I personally know of a number of situations in which I believed I had to deny myself. I recall, for example, my participation in a May Day demonstration. Increasingly, this became a day that those in power misused for laudatory self-affirmation. My participation was not voluntary. I felt as if my boss were pressuring me and I lacked the confidence to refuse to participate. In such situations I often felt as if I were turning to stone. Today, such memories are cloaked in shame and from today's perspective I find it difficult to understand the fear I had back then. At the same time I realize that my cowardice did not so much harm others as myself.

Laura

As I reflect on the clinical encounters in this chapter, I find myself remembering an important meeting with a woman of my parents' generation. While she was never a patient of mine, she influenced the path of my professional career. I owe her a great deal. I would have liked to have given this woman something for her way and I would like to conclude my chapter with her story. I shall call her Laura.

In 1938, two-year-old Laura entered the pediatrics ward of the psychiatric hospital where I began to work exactly fifty years later. She was admitted to the *Kinderfachabteilung*, or ward specializing in children, the name that doctors under National Socialism gave to those wards where they killed sick and disabled children. In fact, many children were murdered in this "specialized" ward; Laura was among the few who survived.

The reasons for her survival remain unclear. After the war, no one in the hospital ever mentioned these crimes and the perpetrators were never prosecuted. Even the victims sensed the taboo and maintained silence. Although she had no outward signs of psychiatric illness, Laura remained a patient in this hospital until she was twenty-six, and was never permitted to speak about what had happened. Even after she was released, the hospital psychiatrists maintained legal custody of her, effectively depriving her of her civil rights. As a patient she had worked in the hospital kitchen; after her release she received a small room on the premises and continued to work in the kitchen.

Some years later, she was given a small apartment not far from the hospital, and after years of legal incapacitation finally won back her civil rights. Nevertheless she continued to work in the kitchen, was paid little, and was allowed to take vacation only during the more dismal seasons of the year when others didn't want to take theirs. Fifty years had passed since 1938, since her hospitalization, since the murder of the children. Laura had grown into a lonely, withdrawn, shy woman.

I discovered this woman and her life story in 1988, when I was studying the files of former patients as part of my research on the history of the hospital. I wanted to ask her about what had happened, but she let me know that, while she certainly remembered the horror that was her past, she did not feel ready to tell me about it. I accepted Laura's decision, feeling sad that I had arrived so late in her life, and determined to write the history of the hospital without her eye-witness account. In the middle of this project, however, the GDR came to an end. Now there were new laws making it possible to compensate the victims of the psychiatric practices of National Socialism, at least financially. For the first time they could be officially recognized as victims of German fascism. When I asked Laura if I could help her to obtain this compensation and recognition, she agreed. I took care of the formalities; all she had to do was sign the appropriate documents. But she never provided that signature. Laura had lived for fifty years without making such a demand. She had of her own volition emancipated herself from the doctors at the hospital. Yet no one knows what was going on inside her during all of these years. By this time, she was no longer ready to divulge her story. She feared once again being marked as a victim of psychiatry, feared losing her hard-won emancipation. I felt ashamed for what the doctors had done to her, and I understood that, as a doctor within the field of German psychiatry, I had to bear part of this burden.

Laura helped me to understand how doctors and patients can pass by each other again and again over the period of a lifetime without ever really meeting. I came to understand the difference between the objectifying gaze that makes the patient into an other, one who has little to do with me personally, and the ability to meet the other as a fellow human being and as a subject. Laura's early traumas and life-threatening memories, all brought about by doctors, made a meeting between us impossible. In my experiencing Laura's silent story—the story of the murder of children at the hands of doctors— lay proof that we, the professional "children and grandchildren" of those doctors are haunted by the guilt they suppressed.

Chapter Highlights

1. Unemployed East German youth constitute a particular population at risk for depression, addictions, and violence towards the "other" in the period of rapid transition to a free economy. Special clinics for these youth (such as those set up by Dr. Bernhardt and her colleagues) provide one example of outreach to them.

   Their parents, having passed seamlessly through the trauma of two totalitarian systems, are also at risk, in that many have sealed themselves off psychologically from their own trauma and loss. We shall return to this group in Chapter 10.

   Citizens who read their secret police files, and learn that friends, family, and co-workers have been informers, become another population at risk for feelings of betrayal and breaking of important connections. Through the Gauck Commission, East Germans have been the first of the Eastern European countries to face problems of opening secret police files. Mental health workers struggle to make counseling available informally.

2. Dr. Bernhardt's clinical eye directs itself to the traumatic impact of totalitarian society itself on the developing personality. In the GDR, two omnipresent institutions—the police state, with its traumatic and omnipresent tentacles, and early childhood education with its focus on shame and conformity—affect personality. As a result, traits of fear and doubt and of distrust and betrayal penetrate across generations.

3. In a critical clinical moment in the case of Hans, Dr. Bernhardt recovered from a feeling of defeat and guilt when she was able to understand how these feelings were an identification with Hans' object world, in which he absorbed his mother's projection of blame. By understanding how the therapist, too, is susceptible to falling victim to the powerful person's projections she was better able to empathize with the patient as the repository of unconsciously projected guilt. In this way she could see more clearly how mother split off the emotional consequences of her behaviors, leaving her son to suffer. Splitting and projective identification of a parent's conflicts so that they seem to rest within the child, is not unique to the world of totalitarian Communism. In the West we are accustomed to think of these dynamics within the borderline picture of pathology. In this chapter we see how such dynamics affected a whole culture when leaders and followers consciously and unconsciously adopted these mechanisms for survival.

4. Dr. Bernhardt presents us with a sad and vivid image of her patient endlessly washing his hands to clean them of his parents' misdeeds. As the following historical sketch by Anette Schwarz indicates, the symptom expresses historical truth as well. One cannot quite grasp the challenge to today's former citizens of the GDR without grasping the struggle they have in facing or in not facing the "sins of the fathers."

Historical Sketch: East Germany

Anette Schwartz

The emotional euphoria surrounding the fall of the Berlin Wall in 1989 and the unification of the FRG and GDR in 1990 expressed for many Germans the joy about a long-sought-for and finally-achieved family re-union—a reunion, however, played out on the world stage and possessing an enormous historical significance. As if two siblings were finally reuniting after having endured a forced separation, many Germans shared the sentiment expressed by the ex-chancellor Willy Brandt that "what belongs together is now growing together" (Wierling, 1993b, p. 103). This sentiment and its celebratory tone, however, subsided very quickly and was replaced by the sobering effect of the tremendous task at hand, namely, how to reunify two Germanys that had in fact lost a "natural" feeling of belonging together and had grown more and more apart not only economically, politically, and culturally, but above all, as discussed in Dr. Bernhardt's chapter, psychologically. In short: the celebrations of newly achieved national unity ended when this unity revealed the "lack or at least the fissures of natural identity" (Geulen, 1995, p. 105). Thus the festivities closed with the erasure of the wall as the most visible line of division but also disclosed a deep split between East and West Germans that was not narrowing but widening with reunification. Indeed, Dr. Bernhardt's patients express sometimes severe emotional disturbances not only as a result of hardships in the old regime but in the context of tensions which arose at reunification.

The heated debate among intellectuals from the East and West that ensued with reunification and continues to this day brought the question of "national identity" into sharp focus. Attesting to the widespread igno-rance of politicians who considered national identity a fact given with the success of political unity, the intellectuals addressed the more realistic state of affairs: since the late 1940s two German states had existed not only with two different political but also national identities. The urgent chal-lenge which these debates issued was to reflect on the potential social-psychological conflicts arising within a newly reunified nation-state con-taining, however, two separate national identities. In addition, these debates reflected the complicated structure of interdependence that had characterized the construction of identities on both sides. Comparable to a dysfunctional family, the post-war generations on both sides had used and needed its "other" Germany in order to define themselves. Thus the West with its Western style capitalism could easily serve as a kind of bogeyman or Feindbild for the GDR while the FRG could easily discredit its leftist intellectuals for sympathizing with GDR socialism. Or, just as simplistically, the GDR could accuse its own intellectuals and literary writers of making alliances with the West because of the widespread publication and success of their works—a success that in turn could then be used by the West to criticize again those GDR intellectuals for their so-called "dissident bonus," which made them suspect as both victim and perpetrator of an opposed political system (Huyssen, 1991, 1993).

Reunification and its aftermath, instead of achieving one identity, only sharpened the contours of the "other." Equally surprised and overwhelmed by unanticipated historical events, both East and West Germans desperately sought to define the players: While the West undertook the financial, legal, and economic reconstruction of the East, the East Germans often felt "colonized" as second-rate citizens, resentful and lost. Although the East had voted for reunification, many activists of the "silent revolution" that dismantled the GDR system had hoped for a slower pace of events and the chance for major reforms within the socialist system. The mainstream Westerner, on the other hand, feared the financial burden of reunification and the huge influx of Easterners seeking employment. Insensitivities and ugly generalizations marked the tone on both sides. And it was in this climate of immense struggle with questions of "belonging" and identity after reunification that the "other" was often displaced onto the "foreigner." Thus the debates surrounding the East/West-identity crisis and the concept of nation empathically began to demand that the public focus laid on reforming the asylum laws in order to regulate the influx of foreigners should be shifted to a fundamental reassessment of Germany's stance toward questions of immigration and citizenship. As many critics in the current debates suggest, the linkage between questions of national identity and citizenship are of utmost importance for establishing "a democratic concept of nation" that "emphasizes negotiated heterogeneity" and not "fictional ethnic or cultural homogeneity" (Huyssen, 1993, p. 73).

Dr. Bernhardt's account of her experiences as both citizen and practicing psychiatrist in the GDR before and after reunification echoes the various sentiments expressed in the current debates. As a representative of the postwar generation in the East, she joins many others when critically reflecting on her own socialization in a political system that had spread a wide web of surveillance and censorship over its population. The release of thousands of Stasi files revealed to so many that both their private and professional life had been infiltrated by spies and thus contaminated by mistrust. She also emphasizes, however, that because or despite the system, life in the GDR was filled with special carved out spaces of freedom and imagination: spaces where a slower-paced style of living could be enjoyed and literature could achieve a significance incomparable to its status in the West, in fact a literature which influenced her humanistic work as a psychotherapist, as she says, as much or more than her formal medical training.

Reunification has been a catalyst for self-reflection on both sides. The postwar generations in the East and the West, despite their differences, are united in the attempt at reassessing their past and coming to terms with the divisions that marked their separate ways for over forty years. Nothing less is at stake but the critical re-evaluation of their roles as victims and perpetrators, critics and collaborators. It remains to be seen whether this new course of Vergangenheitsbewaltigung will achieve a sense of national identity, however fractured it might be.

CHAPTER 5

Romania

Editors' Note

Dr. Ion Cucliciu, a Romanian physician and psychiatric resident, was advocating for political change during the late 1980s and early 1990s. He lived in one of the harshest regimes in the Eastern bloc (Gilberg, 1990), Ceausescu's dictatorship. Politically induced stress was everywhere (Adler, Mueller, & Mohammed, 1993). Once change began Dr. Cucliciu advocated for psychiatry's examining its own role in totalitarian regimes. His interests in confronting the past took him to study survivors of one of the most horrendous thought-reform prisons in Romania—Piteshti.

In his chapter Dr. Cucliciu chronicles the experience of students, then in their twenties whose identity and beliefs were systematically assaulted in this prison. He shows how an ordinary person can be tortured into becoming a torturer, illustrating a central psychological principle in the Soviet state of mind, namely the fusion of tortured and torturer into the same being. He describes the implanting of false memories based at the primitive body ego level and shows how these may develop into a false self. Further he describes how a chief torturer can be imbued with supreme love as well as hate, fascination as well as dread, and how any of us is capable of becoming beholden to such a figure for our very life and in so doing lose who we are. Traumatized in such a way, the survivor develops, given sufficient exposure to a dangerous situation, a fluid ego adaptation into a false self necessary for survival. Accompanying the unwanted shift to this new indispensable psychological structure, the false self, is self-doubt, even loathing for having yielded. While those of us in the West may tend to shy away from this early example of Stalinist excess, it is important that Dr. Cucliciu does not. Rather he finds in his patient's fundamental metamorphosis, this yielding, the origin of thought reform in his country, and the dynamics of dissimulation which help him to explain what happened on a larger scale to the Romanian people under Communism and later Ceaucescu.

The intensity of the brain-washing experience of Piteshti vanished from people's conscious memory, yet it was preserved in the totalitarian structures of everyday life including the securitate (Romanian secret police), the distribution of food, shelter, and clothing. Yielding meant that the impact of these changes would be long-lasting, multigenerational, and ultimately would cause intrapsychic change. Dr. Cucliciu, through his examination of the Piteshti prison, examines how a people came to conform to a *weltanschauung* which was anathema to their history, their ideals, and their principles, and the techniques which the state used, including becoming the supplier of fundamental parental needs of its citizens. The new Communist man, having yielded to the State's philosophy, was to be a nonreflective agent in the new culture. This was the large-scale objective of the Soviet world, and the behavioral science of Pavlov became a useful tool to buttress the ideologues and practitioners of mind control, to convince them that their objective was feasible. Pavlovian-based mind control was then the basis on which large-scale brain-washing activities were carried out especially with political prisoners.

It led to the dispensing of an existence which is at the heart of ideological totalism (Lifton, 1961), and the remnants of these behaviors account for the extreme caution and ambivalence with which Romanians move towards and regress from a more democratic and responsible state.

Dr. Cucliciu's chapter underlines the importance today of designating former political prisoners as a population of traumatized survivors who deserve the best attention our mental health clinicians can provide. He underlines the reluctance these individuals have towards those who might offer help and the value of such assistance coming from within—by the spontaneous forming of self-help networks (such as the U.S. Vet Center Program for counseling Vietnam veterans, rather than being grafted on from outside by suspect governmental bureaucracies.

As these survivors grow older, the pressure of time makes it especially important for them and for us that their stories be transmitted in various forms (oral histories, case studies). As with Jewish Holocaust survivors, now is our last chance to engage them in meaningful dialogue and research.

Romania:
A Time of Yielding

Ion Cucliciu

The Eastern Bloc's Most Repressive Regime

On the eve of the revolutions in Eastern Europe, we in Romania still felt the grip of Communism's most repressive regime. Even as others were experiencing the effects of *glasnost* and *perestroika*, Romania's strong man, Ceausescu, was building massive edifices to himself in Bucharest. While initially promising liberal reform, he had evolved into a megalomanic and intrusive despot. His secret police, the Securitate, was infamous. For example, he turned its full force on discovering and punishing violators of his edict forbidding abortions, so that the secret police intruded literally into every corner of our personal lives. Romania's brand of Communist totalitarianism had always been harsh, as though something in the Romanian tradition constituted a particular affront or threat to Moscow. Perhaps this was because, even more than some other Eastern bloc countries, Romania had a strong pro-Western tradition, including a Romance rather than Slavic language; even the name of the country tied it to the Legions of Rome. Romania's transition from pro-Nazi rule to Stalinist rule had been rapid, with heavy reliance on the absolute rule of the Party and the all-pervasiveness of a brutal secret police. Further, Romania's repressive regimes did not thaw as much as those in other Eastern bloc countries, either in the late 1950s or again in the 1980s.

Nonetheless, during the last years of Communist rule in Romania, more people realized that the end was close and that something new but imprecise was about to begin. I watched with interest as this growing awareness of impending change freed many people—not only the intelligentsia but simple workers and peasants—to say publicly things which they had never dared to pronounce before. I waited as we prepared ourselves for the events to come: There was news of the overthrow of other Eastern bloc parties, then rallies in Timishoara and then in Bucharest, then the storming of government buildings, and finally the deaths of Nicolae and Elena Ceausescu. Immediately after the fall of Ceausescu's regime, December 1989, I joined with others as Romanians began to form political parties, to organize human rights groups, and to edit newspapers.

It seemed, at the beginning, that my hopes, like many people's hopes for true and fundamental change, would soon come true. But they didn't. Rather, a group of former Communist leaders under Iliescu were able to form a Union for National Salvation which surgically excised Ceausescu as though he were a cancer. They kept the bureaucracy intact, with the same suspect leaders—now known by a new Party name—in power. Some suspected even the overthrow was staged. What transpired was revolution with no cleansing, the introduction of the forms of democracy but not trust in the democratic process. We realized that, for us Romanians, the metamorphosis we wished for would have to come in excruciatingly small steps. Since then there have been many moments of despair and anger. It is in the context of this despair that I began my own search for the profound roots of this seemingly inexorable defeat of our dream.

How could people, after longing for so many years for *a* change, resist *the* change when it arrived? How could they refuse to admit obvious facts and evidence? At first I realized that only a minority was capable of opposing the difficulties because only a minority was capable of sustaining for over forty years an inner resistance to the totalitarian pressure. For the rest of the people, the enormous, ubiquitous, and continuous assault against individuals made by a diffuse and yet very personalized power ended in confusion and in apparent identification of the victim with the oppressors.

The Piteshti Experiment

My search for answers regarding the staying power of this totalitarian legacy took me to the critical period in Romanian history between 1945 and the early 1950s, when the first fearful wave of Communist totalitarian order swept through the country and into people's very minds. Under the direct control of Stalinist Russia, Romania carried out massive purges of elements in the society thought to be opposed to the new way. These included all remnants of noble birth, the bourgeois middle class, pro-Western intelligentsia, even peasants who refused to give up their land for collectivization. Especially dangerous to the new regime, and therefore particularly important for thought reform, were students, leaders of the future, especially those who had expressed views in opposition to the new Communist leadership. In addition to the purges, there were other elements in these political processes—such as dependence on the State for the basic necessities of life, a spy system demanding adherence to random and punitive rules, and complete acceptance of a single, yet ever-shifting, ideology—that foreshadowed the general transformation which was to take place in Romania over the subsequent forty years. Today we must deal with the dreadful legacy of this political system, and, ironically, a reluctance to part with it.

Naturally, in the first years of the Communist regime the terror was at its height: The stronger the opposition, the stronger the oppression. But why did this extreme form of repression, of which I shall speak, take hold in Romania and not in other newly Communist countries?

When I first heard people speak of the Piteshti phenomenon and then read about it, I intuitively thought that this seemingly accidental event in the post-war history of Romania deserved more careful attention, and might offer a key to the general state of mind around me. Then the world of negativism and terror I entered as I uncovered the facts made me see that the phenomena were indeed more general than they seemed at first. Ultimately I recognized features of the same syndromes in people who appeared not to be contaminated—and even within myself. For, in a larger sense, we are all survivors of the Piteshti regime.

The Piteshti experiment, which took place between 1949 and 1951, was the most extreme form of the Communist totalitarian repression which swept the country. With the exception, perhaps, of similar "experiments" conducted in the USSR, the harshness of the "re-education" carried out in the Piteshti prison seems to the best of our knowledge to be unique in Eastern Europe. It occurred in the first years of the Communist regime, when the terror was at its height, and was designed for students "tainted" by Western influences and for members of anti-Communist organizations, as these young people were seen as the biggest long-term threat to the new regime.

The Piteshti prisoners, whose average age was twenty-two or twenty-three, all had above-average intelligence. They had belonged to or at least sympathized with political organizations that were, from the Communist point of view, the most oppositional. Thousands of students were arrested, mainly in 1948. After their trials, which were a travesty of justice, many of them were taken to Piteshti prison towards the end of 1949.

The prisoners had been tortured prior to their trials, largely to obtain the names of additional suspect students. So they were pleased with what they initially encountered at Piteshti: a normal prison life without torture. At first, they were left with their fellow prisoners in large rooms and were not harassed During these weeks or months, they knew nothing about their future; they passed the time with old friends, trying to make plans—"What are our friends doing who are still free?" "When will the Americans come?" "What will we do thereafter?"—and trying to keep their mental abilities awake by teaching each other geometry, philosophy, foreign languages, etc.

From time to time, however, and without any warning, small groups of prisoners were taken away and put into another special large and isolated room, where another group was waiting for them. At first, the newcomers were glad to see still more friends and to meet presumably sympathetic people they had not known before. Yet, they noticed, some of these people behaved strangely.

Before long, a signal was given and a reign of terror ensued. To their horror, the newcomers discovered that their old friends had hidden clubs or belts and now began to beat them. When all of them were lying on the floor, the leader of the torturers made a speech: "You are nothing but garbage, bandits, dirty plotters against the glorious working class and the USSR . . . " Then he laid out the rules.

The prisoners were ordered to sit on a common bed with their backs against the wall and their hands either in their pockets or on their knees. They could look only at the floor at their feet and had to remain absolutely still; with any movement, even a sideward glance, they were beaten. For weeks or months they had to maintain the same position. There were only two exceptions to this rule. The first involved the daily trip to the lavatory, where each man had thirty to sixty seconds to eliminate; he was pulled out after this short time whether he had defecated or not. The second exception was the meal, when each prisoner had to put his bowl on the bed or on the floor and eat without using his hands, like an animal. The chief torturer himself distributed the food, and sometimes the torturers pushed the prisoner's face into the hot soup. At night they had to lie down flat on their backs with their hands outside the covers. If they moved while sleeping, they were beaten. During the day, friends were ordered to slap each other. Sometimes prisoners were forced to eat their own excrement. Many other means of humiliation were employed, and each prisoner could be beaten, even throttled to the point of death, at any moment, with or without a reason, at any time. Besides these repeated individual beatings, there was a collective beating almost every day.

After several weeks or months of this treatment, an "external unmasking" began. The prisoners were first asked to write down everything they knew about their "criminal activities." This included all relationships and conversations with any potential political overtones, including seemingly innocent comments made under any circumstances, even those within the prison. No detail was too minute for the re-educators. Such facts as a neighbor telling a joke about the Russians was considered politically important. If someone concealed something, it was very likely that another prisoner would speak up about it. Imagine the punishment of the "insincere bandit." (While the prisoners were addressing the torturers as "sir," they had to term themselves "bandits" when speaking or writing documents: This was their official name during the Piteshti experiment.)

The survivors say that during their pretrial torture, they were able to protect many friends who had not been arrested; they say that they revealed roughly ten percent of what they knew during the earlier torture. But the Piteshti experience was much worse. Prisoners were sometimes killed while being beaten, but of course nothing happened to the murderer. Committing suicide was impossible. The prisoners were submitted to this special regimen until they told almost one hundred percent of the information they had.

The next segment of the re-education was officially termed the "internal unmasking." This was a cleansing process, required, according to the leader of the torturers, because "you are all rotten from tip to toe; all this rottenness must be purged away, or else the working class will crush you." During this "internal unmasking," the prisoners were convinced by the torturers that similar processes were developing in other prisons and in the whole country, another tactic designed to convince them to adapt.

To reverse the prisoners' inner values, each one was asked in turn to speak of his family, education, moral and religious upbringing, etc. Each one had to declare that his father was a rogue, his mother a whore, that studying philosophy or going to church was a foul crime against the interest of the working class, and so on. Furthermore, they had to say all those things with so-called "sincerity" in the presence of the other prisoners in the room. If the attack against the family was successful, the other values were easier to weaken. Generally, after family, the order was religion, moral values, patriotic feelings, political values. This was the most unbearable period of their imprisonment. And if their unmasking seemed "incomplete," they were beaten to the point of death. The same thing happened if they were perceived to be "misleading." For example, one prisoner, pressed to reveal his actions, spoke of the sexual intercourse he had during his childhood with all the animals in his parents' farm. When he could not explain how and when he performed each act, he was accused of trying to fool the re-education committee. At a later stage, the prisoners were asked to tell their dreams. If they said they did not dream, they were beaten (because it is impossible not to dream); if they said they had dreamed about a "foul" practice or desire (such as going to church, or being a bourgeois prime minister and putting all the Communists into jail), they were beaten because the dream's content was against the State; if they said they dreamt of the sun representing the final victory of the working class, they were beaten for trying to cheat the re-educators.

After all of this external and internal unmasking was carried out, the re-educators declared that words were insufficient; they needed deeds. This was the critical moment when the prisoners could survive only by becoming torturers themselves. (In fact, the staff of the prison never did get involved directly in the process, as the chief torturers were always political prisoners themselves.*)

These chief torturers, especially those who had accepted this new role from the beginning, expected big rewards. But in 1952 the Party scapegoated them for the reign of terror. They were brought to Bucharest for another trial; some were sentenced to life in jail, while others were condemned to death. Charged with plotting against the State, they were said to have organized the terror in Romanian prisons in order to compromise the Communist regime. The argument was that a conspiracy had been planned by fascist organizations in the West.

After the Piteshti experiment proper ended, similar phenomena took place in other prisons throughout the country, where prisoners already re-educated at Piteshti were purposefully transferred. Generally, those examples of the Piteshti model were not as Draconian as the original. Besides this model, other much milder methods of changing thoughts were tried during the 1950s in almost all Romanian political prisons. In 1964 all the Piteshti survivors were set free.

In addition to thought reform, Romania also embraced classic repression, in which tens of thousands of people were imprisoned in the late 1940s and early 1950s, when the terror was at its height. Other tens of thousands were deported. Property was seized, people were arrested and imprisoned without trials, and armed attacks were organized—in miniature wars behind the Iron Curtain—against entire "rebellious" villages which would not submit otherwise.

But the Piteshti experiment was totally different, representing the dramatic beginning of the transformation of enemies into tools.

Initially Romanian resistance to the new Communist regime took many forms, ranging from listening together to foreign radio programs to forming armed guerilla groups in the mountains. But in time only the milder forms of resistance remained possible. All organized groups, whether armed or not, were eliminated. Individuals felt more and more in danger and could hardly protect themselves because of the arbitrary nature of the general threat—for example, the case of one former prisoner who explained that he was arrested and imprisoned for almost two years because he refused to give one of his dogs to a policeman who had decided

---

* There has been only one exception to this rule, when at the very beginning jailers had to intervene in order to assist the initial small group of torturers when they were about to be defeated.

to "requisition" the dog. He underwent no trial, and for the whole period of his imprisonment, his family did not know anything about him. Anyone could be arrested and imprisoned for years without any legal procedure at all, and even without knowing why. Private property disappeared in a "legal" nationalization, but an arbitrary nationalization was also very much present. Moreover, spies were everywhere, including very old friends transformed into collaborators.

Many people were killed. Others ceased to resist after years of special torture and brain-washing regimes. For many others, the rumor that some neighbor had been arrested overnight by the political police because he had made a joke with a political subject, or for no reason at all, was sufficiently threatening to cause them to abandon any hope of resistance.

Living in the Shadow of Deceit:
Psychiatry and the Former Political Prisoner

In the context of the tasks facing Romanian mental health professionals today, the needs of a special high-risk population of traumatized former political prisoners should have high priority. Their continued suffering is apparent: many show both numbing and hypervigilant features of PTSD as well as posttraumatic decline. They are confused by a paradoxical shift in their status: On the one hand, pro-democracy for us portrays them as newly discovered heroes; on the other hand, old-guard media attack them anew with a range of charges from "reactionary" to "fascist," an eerie repeat of accusations they heard when their troubles first began. Further, general feelings of guilt within the whole society tend to reject and deny their suffering, and split off the value of their experience.

But reaching out as psychiatrists to the former political prisoners is not such an easy matter. First, Romanian psychiatry over these forty years has lost its connections to psychotherapy and the humanistic tradition, so our intentions may be suspect. Second, Romanian psychiatry is only beginning to come to grips with its own guilt and complicity in the abuse of individuals on behalf of the State, so especially when political issues are involved, we cannot assume trust from our patients. Further, those of us in the profession actively working to bring true democratic reform and to value individual rights and growth find that we are not politically neutral. Quite the contrary: for us having been active politically in oppositions to the old regime or its remnants is an indispensable part of being a psychiatrist even though such involvement creates potential empathic barriers between us and our patients who yearn for the old ways.

At a time of incomplete and revolutionary change, as is going on now in Romania, subtle divisions among the parties promoting change and those who oppose it are everywhere. For me as a psychiatrist, the differences intrude unexpectedly and almost daily in my alliance with patients. A choice of words, a tone of voice, or an attitude suddenly breaks what was a growing empathic tie. A father in a delayed grief reaction for his son suddenly, in ultranationalist frenzy, shouts that he wants to kill all Hungarians to avenge his son. A distrustful woman suddenly attacks the leader of the party with which I am sympathetic. A patient brings into the office the newspaper of the former secret police (Securitate), saying an article interested her and she wonders what my attitude is on this subject. A daughter of a former secret police official longs wistfully for a romantic interlude in her life linked in memory to the words of the former State poet, but these same words evoke in me the very essence of selling out one's talents to the lies and cruelty of the State.

Yet I find upon reflection that the division between those of us who promote change and those who oppose it is an artificial one: Both exist within the self; both exist within myself. But this realization is only a small achievement as compared with the difficulties I had to overcome in order to give way to real empathy in my work with the former political prisoners.

Thus, the general orientation of our field, living in the shadow of deceit, and the limitation of all kinds of resources and experiences was making very difficult the beginning of such a project.

I had to act on my own. At first I went to the medical office of the Former Political Prisoners' Association. I asked my colleagues there (former political prisoners themselves, although they had fought against the Stalinist transformation of Romania) to become a link between me and the people I would interview. This first approach was unsuccessful, and I understood thereafter that general suspiciousness towards newcomers did not allow anyone to take the risk of introducing unknown persons.

After renouncing this approach, I fortunately learned of an independent multifunctional group which was also working as a self-help group within the Association. There I met for the first time people who really wanted to speak and to share their experience.

I began my work in March 1993, when I interviewed for the first time a former political prisoner from the Piteshti Prison. I saw five former political prisoners during a several-month period. As a psychiatrist, I assisted them in bearing witness to their experience, but not in a traditional doctor–patient relationship. Each former political prisoner introduced me to others and I visited each of them at his home, without exchange of money.

At first it was very difficult to overcome their suspiciousness. It took almost six months for a therapeutic alliance to develop and to allow for the real story of the internal unmasking. It took another six months for an understanding to develop and to allow me—finally—to listen. In my section on counter-transference, I shall explore in more detail the factors at work within me which both compelled me to pursue this work while also interfering with my listening, but first I should like to present some further details of one of the cases.

Mihai

Mihai was one of the Piteshti survivors with whom I worked most, a person whose energy and resilience were quite different from the others. This amazingly lively elderly man had a strong desire to speak about and to work through his experiences. When I met him he had already finished a narrative of all his penitentiary experiences (not yet published). In addition, he often spoke about them publicly and was participating in organizing his former fellows. But the relationships among these people were rather tense. Always in their minds were hard questions: Who was guilty and who was not? Who was more and who was less responsible? Moreover, it was difficult for Mihai and for his former fellows to psychologically integrate the central elements of their experiences.

Mihai told me many times about a discussion he had with one of his best friends (who had also endured the Piteshti regime) after the Piteshti experiment ceased. Both of them were transferred to another prison and put by chance in the same cell. They spent their time asking themselves how to make their experience known, but could not find an answer at that time. And now those same questions remained, no less puzzling as then. "I am not guilty, and yet I need to justify myself. I am the same person I ever was, and yet I need to recover myself. Why do I feel this way?" Mihai never actually formulated these questions, but this is how I understood and put into words his fundamental dilemma.

Before World War II he had been a student. During the war he was recruited. He resumed his studies after 1945 and, until his arrest in 1948, was very active in the resistance against the Communist government. During the interrogation, knowing he would be imprisoned, he declared that he was a student, hoping that the treatment he would be given in prison would be better. Ironically, had he concealed he was a student, he would never have known Piteshti prison.

I wish here to capture some of his more poignant words as he gradually revealed his experience of political imprisonment and thought reform.

The Idea of Death at Piteshti

Because he had been a member of a resistance group, Mihai had come to peace with the idea that he might die. But Mihai says: "[Before Piteshti] we thought that we would finally either survive or die, and that the death would take two or three or four hours. We thought we would die bravely. We never imagined death as a year-long fight. . . . In Piteshti prison they made us see that death is not as easy as that." There death would occur, if at all, only after violent, brutal, or extremely long continuous torture, and, where suicide was impossible, when the torturer, not the prisoner, wanted it to happen.

Death was omnipresent in Piteshti. If prisoners died during torture, the torturer might say, as he hit the dead body, "The bandit! He died too easily. You others, we don't want to keep you alive, but you don't deserve to have a death as easy as that."

But killing a prisoner was seen within the prison regime primarily as a technical error. Even deprived of all basic rights and liberties (as indeed they were), the prisoners could still feel free to the extent that death was always possible as a last and redeeming escape. In order to eliminate this fundamental liberty, it was not enough for the torturers to prevent suicide; they chose rather to demonstrate that for the prisoner even suicide was in the torturer's hands.

At Piteshti, each prisoner was several times tortured to the point of death. And for Mihai this time it was the *real* death, not the death one imagines: "There have been tortures when I regretted that I was dying. Within a moment the image of my mother, my family . . . came to my mind."

Real death, when close, was sometimes strongly wished for: "I was satisfied, and as soon as possible I wanted to reach that threshold of not existing any more, of dying. There was in me the idea and the awareness of being very close to the moment when I would escape suffering, and at the same time of succeeding in saving myself, that is, not giving the torturers the satisfaction of saying . . . " And yet, this desire to die was invariably terribly feared after it passed:

"But everything stops after having enjoyed this desperate hope of disappearing. When you come back to life, after having reached the point of death, from then on you know what the imminence of death means, and when you are tortured again—the first time you did not know—now you *know*—you realize that it may be more than that and you are terribly frightened."

He then described the effect: "It was the moment in which, I think, most prisoners yielded to a new way of thinking and living." Being willing to live now meant being willing to live in another manner, or even in any manner. Thus the mind was now really open for re-education.

Lessons in Marxism-Leninism: The Practical Over the Ideal

Mihai narrated many times during our work the chief torturer's method of playing with life and death to illustrate points of Marxist-Leninist doctrine, such as the differences between the ideal and the practical.

"I was lying on the floor after being tortured when Turcanu, the chief torturer, asked me, 'How about your former speeches on death? Die now! Why don't you die?' I answered, 'I was at that time in the theory stage (the ideal); now I am practical.'" While that statement might sound like the blackest humor to a Western ear, it was in fact just the opposite. It was the moment in which Mihai was renouncing the possibility of a brave, free death and it coincided with his being compelled to use the concepts of the new ideology: the relation of theory to practice, in which practice prevails.

But Mihai's actual position, and that of the others, was of constantly wishing to die in order to escape re-education, and at the same time of wishing to live, but only on the former moral grounds.

By this time the prisoner was no longer the owner of his own death. The act he had thought of as a last way of defending his freedom was no longer possible. It follows that, at this point, the "inner content" of the prisoner no longer belonged totally to him.

The Power of the Chief Torturer

The chief torturer began to have extraordinary power on the minds of the prisoners. For example, Mihai described him as always being able to see the so-called "guilt" he tried to hide.

When I asked Mihai how he felt when Turcanu was looking at him, he replied, "I had the impression that he always caught me in the act (. . .) like a cat at the cream bowl when its master has seen it (. . .) and this act was the very content (of my mind) within myself."

Mihai frequently used the word "emptying" to describe this phenomenon in which some hidden content of his mind was discovered. In fact he listed this word in a separate column in the series of epithets which he used to make concrete and to condense the prisoner's experience at Piteshti (namely, "being rendered bestial"). It was the final and separate idea. Emptying occurred I believe at a time when prisoners were aware of the fragmenting of their own self. As Mihai returned again and again to this moment, he held out to me his separate fingers each identifying a fragmented part of his mind and body: the forefinger was his thought, the next his feelings, then his behavior, etc. When listening to Mihai return to that moment of fragmentation, I felt he was torn between two states which I did not yet understand. But after listening to many prisoners I concluded that there existed in each of them at a certain moment simultaneously a pressure to yield together with the ever-present will to resist.

As his emptying progressed, Mihai unconsciously found Turcanu a fixating point for both addictive fascination and terror.

Mihai asked, "I did not understand, or I didn't try, how does this happen, they say, a woman is fascinated when she sees the serpent. What is going on? How does she become so fascinated that when she is before a window with gold objects, she cannot move. I have experienced this phenomenon, did you? When I was in Paris I went to Royal Street. Inside the shop, sitting openly on the window sill were beautiful jewels. Arranged, but with electronic alarms to protect them. When I saw there a little wrist watch for ladies, for example, which cost 2,700,000 FF., such prices! While I was looking I couldn't tear myself away, I, I was in ecstasy, but this ecstasy is . . . how should I put it . . . a beneficent ecstasy, it satisfies you, while the other was totally, how should I say, a dreadful ecstasy.

I responded " . . . this glitter, isn't it true that anyone may become lost in it for a moment, when looking at gold—anyone, it is human—but on the other hand the horridness . . . it may also arrest you, look, these are the two poles of diabolic fascination."

Mihai pointed out that this man (Turcanu) was selected because of special qualities. They say Rasputin became famous in the same way. The son of the czar was ill; he was not smiling. They called for all kinds of doctors to help because he was growing up in a great sadness. At a *Te Deum* Rasputin made a funny face, and the child started to laugh. His mother, the Tsarina, asked the Czar to bring Rasputin to the palace, for the child's sake and salvation."

But Mihai fought against those feelings. Consciously he described Turcanu as a degenerate brute. All of the Pitesthi survivors I spoke with remember Mihai's direct confrontations with Turcanu as special and highly significant moments.

But they all felt a strong wish to communicate directly and privately with the torturer. Why? Mihai says, "Perhaps to speak as an honest man before an honest man: 'Sir, I admit the so-called "truth"; spare me the tortures.' But here, after admitting the truth you saw he was accusing you . . . I have lost the thread."

The prisoners perceived the regimen they were submitted to as totally arbitrary, as if its origins were to be found in the very person of the torturer. That's why they tried, at least in fantasy, to get close to him. But the more they did so, the more they lost the power to orient themselves, and the more they lost that power, the more they became dependent on their torturer.

From Resisting to False Confessions and False Memories

Each prisoner tried to resist, at least at the beginning, and Mihai seems to have been especially endowed with an ability to find arguments and stratagems in such peculiar and extreme situations. Yet even he declared that "denying was useless because he was dominating you . . . you couldn't resist him . . . when he said, isn't it so?" You agreed: "Yes, it is."

And so, in the end, any private strategy was finally useless. Often the victim was tortured without knowing the precise reason and with no explanation at all. This was the case especially during the internal unmasking, when the torturer was only asking the prisoners to speak: "Speak!" "What should I say?" "You know very well what you should speak of."

Mihai described the threat: "You don't know any more? You will see; I will make you know." In those moments, he said, "we realized that none of us dared to say, `I've told everything I know,' because of the certain reply: 'I will show you that you have many other things to say.' So we were trying to save ourselves by delaying the outcome, and we said, 'I can't remember,' or 'I can't remember now'. On the other hand, if the torturer was making you remember by torturing you, he would say thereafter, `So, you were saying you didn't remember. Why didn't you speak without being beaten?' and the torture would resume. That's why you learned to say, 'Sir, I have the willingness . . . but I can't remember now.'"

At those times, some kind of a gap in consciousness occurred, and the victim's mind became an almost complete blank. The prisoner could no longer use his conscious mind to invent answers. Hence the periods of torture, alternating with the unmasking posture, were breaking through his capacity to curb his fantasies. And the prisoner may now speak because his unconscious is set free. Using Mihai's term, it was a period of "dough rising." Then what I term a lyrical debacle began.

"So," says Mihai, "stories and poems may be created not only under inspiration's mastery but also under terror." And then he remembered a passage from a chronicle. A long time ago a prince of Moldavia threatened a noble with death if he did not compose at once some verses on an obscene matter, but the noble, who was also a poet, quickly invented some rhymes so bold as to surprise the prince, who spared and even congratulated him. "Terror and despair," concluded Mihai, "may have men make verses."

During the "internal unmasking" each prisoner was at first taken aside by the re-education committee in order to make a preliminary confession. Then he had to repeat it before the other prisoners in the room, then answer questions and demonstrate that everything was accurate. Finally, a collective insanity took hold, as newly deduced false memories came cascading from the prisoners' lips. Mihai says, "This waterfall-like stream of confessions created an atmosphere of collective insanity; hence, a man experienced more pain, fear, and dread of not being able to be a part of this stream, this waterfall. When the tortures began again, one's mind was mobilized, turned upside down and whirled round as in a washing machine."

Within this stream of false memories, the first and most important object was the mother, then the father and siblings. Stories about adulteries and incest were very frequent. Because of the unconscious mechanisms at work, it was paradoxically easier to speak about one's mother. Mihai explained that perhaps it was more difficult to make up something about the father because "as children we lived mostly with our mothers. Hence it was more difficult to know or to invent lies about our fathers who might be seen in the midst of the family carrying a bunch of flowers in order to mask his infringement or act."

Mihai demonstrated how the prisoner's reality testing was pierced in many points. For instance, he said that, when listening to a former friend describing the promiscuity within his family, one could think that "even if [this fellow] does not believe what he says, a coincidence is still possible, no one is perfect, all he says about his family may be true." And one could, at the same time, question his own family: "Is it possible that similar things happened in my family too? Was I blind?" When another prisoner was unmasking himself, one might think, is this the friend I used to trust? Moreover, the whole process of re-education could be looked at in the same way the re-educators explained and justified it. Mihai says that only later, during the 1952–54 inquiry, did he understand the whole political dynamics of the Piteshti experiment.

What Did the Torturers Achieve?

All these processes engendered very strong feelings of guilt in Mihai: "My lack of power to avoid what happened to me made me feel guilty, unworthy, deprived of any virtue, as if I would say to myself: How can I live while letting my mother (and her dignity) die, when I should have stretched out my arm towards the enemy to kill him, risking my own life in order to save her (dignity)."

Finally, what emerged from the thought reform was an altered self, one which, because it was tied to the most basic human images and fantasies of childhood, became intrinsic to the prisoner's being, his body ego, and more lasting than we might otherwise suppose. After the Piteshti trauma, the former prisoners tried to recover, but their feelings towards their own selves remained conflicted: "For a long time," said Mihai, "I have been convinced that they succeeded. They succeeded. But in time, some part of ourselves recovered. We reclaimed our inner selves. So, they did not succeed. Their purpose was to change our nature. What would have been the use of transitory changes?" At other times Mihai spoke of this differently: "They did not want to change my nature, not the intrinsic part, not this very deep part upon which man cannot intrude, but only the manifestation, the part that would behave and submit to their political system. Yes, this part was modified and became submissive to them."

Countertransference

It has not been easy to reach out personally to the Piteshti survivors, to listen to their stories, and to try to empathize with their experiences. At a number of points along the way I found myself numb, enraged, humiliated, and morally overwhelmed. At times, I felt blocked in the work.

When my initial efforts at contact were turned away, I was ashamed at my failing. Some time later, guilty lest my delving might cause the survivors harm when they opened up about this past, I found myself blocking out large parts of their suffering. When they explained how they were beaten and humiliated, I became angry, but when they spoke about prisoners turning on their brothers, I felt dismayed. And the awe with which they viewed their chief torturer surprised me. Each of the situations called upon my own self-reflection and painful self-awareness as a method of maintaining contact with my patient and allowing him to continue with his work.

I knew that certain parts of my own experience were both driving me and inhibiting me. I knew, for example, that the history of my family included several political prisoners. I had often heard family stories about people who had died before I was born, or when I was a little child. But one story struck me more than the others: One of my uncles had been imprisoned for political reasons in the late 1940s, when he was very young. After his release, he went to the High School (Gymnasium) of History in Bucharest. But when he was about to graduate from this school, the political chiefs of the university found out that he had been a political prisoner and excluded him because those who were not politically orthodox were not allowed to follow those kinds of studies. His colleagues, who valued his contributions to academic life, threatened to go on strike. My uncle tried to persuade them not to take such an action on his behalf, but it was too late. Because of the strike of his colleagues, my uncle was arrested again, this time for mutiny. Once more he was condemned as an enemy of the State. His second imprisonment was so difficult that he survived only six months after being released from it.

I was not yet able to understand properly the link between such figures in my background and my contradictory feelings about political prisoners. When the medical office of the Former Political Prisoners' Association, which I contacted first (as if I wanted to have a kind of intermediary), postponed again and again the green light I expected, I felt both frustrated and guilty at the same time. In January 1993 I went to the central headquarters of the organization of former political prisoners. I went first to their medical department and spoke to my colleagues there, explaining what I intended to do and showing them some materials in order to be more convincing, but they remained finally unresponsive. I asked twenty or thirty times when I should begin. Finally they said they would call me, a clear message that they never would. Then I learned of some former political prisoners who were organizing a self-help group. They invited me to speak with them openly about my purposes, and they were more receptive. Nevertheless, it took almost six months before a former prisoner told me about the internal unmasking. It took us a long time to develop trust. Suspicion was disappearing but almost always appeared again when entering new and deeper areas of our work. At those moments I was feeling afresh that I was doing something wrong. A diffuse guilt was hindering me, but fortunately it was never overwhelming; it was as if I knew that this work could precisely deliver me from it.

I wondered, upon reflection, if some of my contradictory feelings might relate to my own unresolved conflicts towards my family history and especially to my uncle who had been imprisoned two times. When I became aware of his history I saw him as a symbol of courage, but I was also chagrined at our actual attitudes and behavior which was not keeping abreast of this ideal. How would I have felt at such times? And what would he think now of my endeavors?

With this first insight in mind, namely my fears of my uncle's rejecting me, I returned to the clinical task ahead. My sense of guilt, shame, and rejection felt more understandable, while my conviction to proceed was even greater.

Once the former prisoners accepted me, I was surprised to see that many of them were very kind and wanted to speak of their experiences. Yet the first former Piteshti prisoner I met there, Andrei, seemed a little different. Although willing to speak, he did so painfully, shyly; for the most part, he rarely looked at me. What could I do, I wondered, to make him know I was not as far away from his experience as he thought?

Initially I avoided questioning myself, for example, about what I would have done if I had been one of the Piteshti prisoners. At that point, I was trying to understand the phenomenon as an exterior one. I was mainly angry at how the prisoners were beaten and humiliated, and dismayed at how someone could turn on his brothers. I could not imagine how such circumstances could be possible. I found myself avoiding the task of trying to empathize with such betrayal and cruelty. I blamed the torturers and, especially, the chief torturer. I was reluctant to imagine that the depth and power of the thought reform technique could evoke such hatred at the remnants of one's own most sacredly held values and relationships; I could not imagine that it would be actual merger with the chief torturer that would enable the prisoners to beat, nearly to death, the remnants of themselves which they projected on to the friends of their former world. Sometime later I had the first insight. It happened that I was very angry with one of my friends and I was also re-reading a book on the Piteshti phenomenon; suddenly I felt that in such a setting it really would be possible to strike a friend.

When I told this to Andrei, he began to speak freely and openly. He told me details about the way in which Turcanu, the chief torturer, had used him. On my way home I felt released; it was the first time I had got near to the survivors and their experiences. For a moment there was neither distance nor guilt. In this frame of mind I had the fantasy of a play in which Turcanu had the main part and demonstrated to the audience that everybody in the theater resembled him. At that time, I did not try to understand the meaning of this fantasy, but I would return to it.

The second person I met was Mihai. From the very beginning I asked him to speak of the image he had of the chief torturer, and of how he perceived him, but, to my surprise, I was unable to listen. During the third visit Mihai spoke of the point of death he experienced many times during the tortures. Again I found it difficult to listen. When, afterwards, I listened to the tapes, I was once again surprised by the discrepancy between many of my questions and interruptions and the content of Mihai's discourse.

Why was I responding like this, I asked myself. How would I continue this work? I realized that most troublesome to me was the ambiguity of the material I was listening to. It was as if something was drawing me towards this abyss, yet at the same time something was blocking my understanding in order to preserve the values I attributed to Mihai and to myself.

There were several components in my patient's description of the chief torturer which I found puzzling. He was conveying unconsciously strong paradoxical feelings of love and hatred: total fear, yet uncontrollable fascination, intoxication, ecstasy, and wishes to merge. My own feelings towards the chief torturer were initially quite the opposite; I found him repugnant, evil, intrusive, and corrupt. I wished to defeat him in a battle of wits, not to merge with him in ecstasy. As my own reactions grew more separate from my patient's, I realized that there was some danger to our alliance. My empathy would need to stretch to encompass his powerful contradictory experience. We were confronting together the forces at work in an overturning of one's mind; and I needed to be respectful of the power and potential universality of such forces. New endings to earlier fantasies began to take form as I imagined my own confronting of the chief torturer. I knew in my heart that he was gaining pleasure through his omnipotent power over me and that he manipulated that power to his own ends. At the core of him, there was deception. But when analyzing this fantasy I found that convincing the torturer could mean as well succumbing to merger. What if he would finally turn to me and say "so, we are one?"

In prison, according to Mihai, trying to resist was the rule: "I had this playful ability," said Mihai, "which allowed me to confuse them and to find at certain moments the opportunity for giving any reply and for getting out of trouble."

But resistance couldn't be neat: "None of us was persuaded to tell the truth, but all of us found somewhere in ourselves the instinct of preservation which made us say anything the enemy liked; and on rare occasions the disobedient and skillful prisoner used this method to save himself."

And: "It was difficult for me to renounce my dignity and my personality, but it was no longer possible to maintain them in the presence of the torturer, since I knew that would work to his advantage."

Thus, when Mihai narrated the moment when a prisoner yielded completely, I remember I felt some kind of relief. Yet I did not want to see or listen to any continuation of the narrative. In fact, at the time I couldn't stand it. Pure and unalloyed resistance was my ideal. Nevertheless, I needed relief and the yielding functioned as an end to this ambiguity of the psychological world I was facing in Mihai and within myself.

The same ambiguity was at the core of the transference–countertransference processes. I was sometimes the undoubtedly loyal comrade; but when Mihai spoke resentfully of the torturers or the political leaders of the time, I often felt as if his adverse feeling was directed towards me. For me, too, Mihai was many times a reassuring presence. Yet when I felt myself an object of his anger, it was as though he embodied the very persons of whom he was speaking of so hostily, and I feared him in much the same way I feared other figures in my past.

I was nevertheless reluctant to admit all that I felt and of which I had become aware. I was saying to myself: What would I have done in similar situations?

I understand how and why I couldn't have resisted.
But with understanding comes the possibility of change.
So I must resist, therefore I would have resisted.

This is the ambiguity I felt at that moment in our work.

Finally, my own memories as a student emerged.

When I was as young, around 1980, as the Piteshti prisoners, I entered a small secret group of students. We were trying to reach a way of thinking and acting that was totally free from contamination from the hypocrisy around us. But in the ideology of the group, "true Marxist values" in addition to classical philosophical ones played an important part, and the organization was very authoritarian. We found ourselves unconsciously trying to create a miniature version of an absolutely pure totalitarian life even as we thought we were strong opponents of the regime, the life-size, real, and impure totalitarianism. Before long, because of the contradictions within itself, the group ceased to exist. Nevertheless I felt guilty without knowing precisely why. Afterwards I was interrogated several times by the secret police. Although I was threatened with beating and with overnight prolongation of the questioning, I remember that I was not at all frightened by this, and determined not to give any information at all. But at a certain moment, an officer asked me if they needed me to, would I become a member of the Communist Party. I answered, "Yes," even though he knew perfectly well I was lying. In turn, I was also aware of the game we were playing—that he only wanted to be sure that I could dissimulate and to see how I went about it. I never became a member of the Party. But had I answered "no," the consequences might have been unpredictable, and I knew this.

The former prisoners had been submitted to extremely hard conditions in order to be taught to dissimulate. The next generations, born under the new rule, learned this trick as I did, smoothly and insidiously. By the time they entered school, little children were already organized politically. And the very first books from which we learned to read and to write were ideologically impregnated. My work with these former political prisoners brought back many such memories for me.

When I first began to understand the psychological mechanism at work within the Piteshti phenomenon, it was as if I had said to myself: "If their experience and their reactions are general, they may be mine too; but I could also be an exception." I accepted our commonalties after my memories came out. And that was the moment when I really began to show empathy with Mihai and with the others. I no longer put awkward questions to them; now I could listen, and at the end, we were friends, and I felt guilt no longer.

Discussion

In a setting such as the Piteshti prison a torturer may be seen as an ideal father, a complete father, precisely because he controls everything, where and what and how the prisoner eats, when and where he sleeps, even whether he moves his eyes. In families, each real father gives something, and each son is unsatisfied, at least in his unconscious. But giving something is giving little, while taking all away may turn out to be an absolute gift. A total torturer may become a total father.

Moreover, this total father, while trying to destroy the prisoners' intellectual and moral values, and their religious faith, plays himself the part of a preacher and of a god. He repeatedly harangues the prisoners with snatches of a frightfully naked philosophy. And, as if he were divine, he does not allow himself to be looked at. "If anyone tried to study him, he was punished terribly," says Mihai. Besides, the torturer announced often, "Don't think you die, but rather, you will die only when I want you to die," as if he had the supreme power, to take or to give life and death.

But the torturer could never be a total father without also replacing the prisoner's real mother. This is perhaps the milestone of the Piteshti regime. As the prisoner was asked to enact all his oedipal fantasies, the "incompleteness" of the real mother became more and more unbearable. Instead, in the process of transference, the torturer took on a maternal as well as a paternal character. Besides, he was using the prisoners in a somewhat maternal way. Prisoners were forced to lay on the bed except when they were tortured, and they were forced to eat and to eliminate in a way that stands comparison with the way a mother looks after her infant.

Ambivalence towards moral, religious, and patriotic values develops in the same way as the prisoners' feelings towards their parents. There was always the same intrusion of infantile, mainly sexual, desires into everything, for example, prisoners were compelled to mix blasphemy with pornography. A general assault from beneath, with the participation of the ego, tries to lessen the pressure from above.

Of course, the prisoner tries to devise stratagems in order to survive and to avoid being tortured. The reality testing is not completely destroyed. He knows he lies, and he may choose to make a certain "confession" or recite blasphemy only to avoid speaking of something else which could bring about much more suffering for himself or for his fellows. But when doing so, he may unexpectedly feel pleased.

And at a certain moment the prisoner can't stand any more of this fundamental ambiguity. One way out may appear to be to enter the world seemingly free from contradictions which is continuously offered by the torturer-father. But even if he takes this path, it turns out that his former values and links to his past are not entirely lost, and that he will continue to fight a losing and desperate battle against them. As his inner struggle continues, he must lash out against his former friends to get rid of his former self. Even jailers are not so cruel and inventive as the tortured self in its self-defeating efforts to find peace.

The prisoner who chooses to abandon his former self and to yield completely to the torturer-father will enter an absorbing realm. But the ending of the experiment and of the detention itself offers the prisoner who has abandoned his former self nothing but new traumata, almost as intense as the first ones.

I have thought of calling these phenomena a Molotov complex, after Molotov, for many years foreign minister of the former USSR under Stalin. How could the offspring of a noble Russian family destroy the class he was part of? In the Molotov complex there is a continuous symbolic murder of the real parents and the frantic destruction of all related values (or the continuous attempt to do this). It is as if a new superego is saying, "I am nothing but your darkest secret wishes."

Reflections

When Ceausescu took power in the 1960s, tough measures were no longer necessary, because from then on the seemingly light but continuous and ubiquitous pressure was more than sufficient to weaken the resistance of the general populace. The whole population living under totalitarian pressure had already gone through an experience analogous to the Piteshti prisoners', though at much lesser degrees.

First of all, there was economic pressure to accept the government. Goods and services were only given and received, not "earned" as such. For example, people received jobs and wages. There was no unemployment under Communism—unemployment and inflation were said to be features of the "rotten capitalist society." Moreover, there was no negotiation for wages, nor the slightest idea of it. Apartments were neither bought nor rented, but distributed by the employer or by the town authorities. When food began to be scarce in the markets, the verb "give" almost completely replaced the verbs "sell" or "buy." One would hear sentences like: "Go at once to the market; they just started to give cheese."

It is worth noting that before World War II, the Romanian population was mainly rural. The huge Communist industrialization brought into urban areas a majority of the village people. Thus a numerous working class began to function as a perfect receiver of the totalitarian gift.

Ideological pressure, as strong and continuous as the economic one, bombarded Romanians on every front. The media delivered overt propaganda but also impregnated with ideological links almost every apparently politically neutral bit of information. All institutions and enterprises had a strong political character, and the principle that "political fitness is much more important than professional skills" was fundamental to society. Each institute included a political organization, and each employee had to attend regular meetings. This "education" began at the age of four, when all kindergarten children had to join an organization called Homeland's Falcons.

It is impossible to belong to a Communist society and to avoid either feelings of guilt or an indifference to personal or general infringements of law, official regulations and standards, etc. In Romania, Communist rules and standards were far too complicated and comprehensive. No one could adhere to them. Thus a peculiar mixture of guilt (because one could never meet the theoretical standard) and antisocial behavior (because one needed to disregard regulations in order to survive) added to the economic and ideological pressure of daily life.

Yet a totalitarian regime cannot be effective without personalizing itself. The head of the State and of the Communist Party was seen as the source of everything, the one who controls even the most insignificant details of everyday life. Even now, years after he was deposed, one can hear people saying, "Ceausescu gave us housing" or "This road was made by Ceausescu." He was said to be the origin of the whole "ideological truth," or at least its main points. In fact, totalitarian power in Romania was personalized at all levels: Each county had a total prime-secretary, each enterprise or school or hospital had its total director. But these persons were only images of the primary, the only leader. The head of the State and of the Party was a composite mother, father, and god altogether.

The result of this personalized totalitarian pressure was a general process of identification with the oppressor. Even so, the Romanian citizen had to choose between a partial and a complete yielding, no matter who one was or whether one was aware one was making a choice. Even the person who made every effort to avoid compromise could not succeed. One cannot obey totalitarian rules, even for brief moments, without damaging one's inner balance, because even temporary obedience requires a very subtle and misleading kind of identification with the oppressor. Just as people could not completely resist, neither could they completely identify, even if doing so would avoid uncertainty or contradiction. In a totalitarian system, neither complete avoidance nor complete identification is possible.

This was the world in which we lived and the world that lived within us as we waited for the fall of the Iron Curtain, the world that faded from memory for a moment after 1989 but only for a moment because subsequent events taught us not to forget.

Chapter Highlights

1. Dr. Cucliciu identifies former political prisoners and their families as a population of trauma survivors in the wake of the Soviet era. Many suffer from PTSD and other long-term effects of assault on the core of their being. He enumerates the difficulties in reaching out to them, given the specifics of their traumatic experiences and problems around trust. Informal networks, such as the grass roots origins of the Vet Center project in the USA rather than official government programs may be more successful. The mental health task relates to their current stage in life and therefore relates to Erikson's stage of integrity versus despair.

2. Dr. Cucliciu describes how in a totalitarian state which uses brainwashing and torture, there can be generalized cross-generational preservation of a layering of the personality such that at an internalized obeisance to the State occurs as an unconscious ego mechanism. Yielding ceases to have its all-or-none dramatic quality on which an iden-

tity is formed; rather it becomes a character trait on which secret police can depend, and even self-reliant, seemingly autonomous citizens unconsciously comply.

3. The most striking clinical moment in the psychotherapy centers on the patient's self-condemnation for yielding and the corollary disidentification on the part of the therapist. Such yielding cannot be tolerated as part of the identify of the therapist. Thus, there is a temporary lack of empathy until the therapist is able to remember that moment in which he too yielded, and empathy is re-established.

4. In exploring the dynamics of the Piteshti prison, Dr. Cucliciu taps into the mysterious connection between victim and persecutor. Whether it be the hostage's fascination with the hostage-taker as in the Stockholm syndrome, or the complex blending of sadistic and masochistic responses in such commonplace situations as the battered wife syndrome (Walker, 1985), the victim feels attracted to understand the motives of the powerful figure and to remain trapped in the fascination of sadistic attack on the self.

For Romania, especially in the twentieth century, it has indeed been a time of yielding. The following historical sketch by Ivo Banac conveys a grim story of which Piteshti is only a part.

Historical Sketch: Romania

Ivo Banac

In the years after 1947 the newly empowered Stalinist Communist Party in Romania went on a terror binge, directing their wrath at leaders of the old "bourgeois" parties, at the churches, and all independent institutions and persons including students with "bourgeois" leanings. It was during this period that the thought-reform Piteshti experiment occurred, traumatically affecting the lives of young people like the student, Mihai, whom Dr. Cucliciu describes now many years later. Ultimately, the Communist leaders turned on their own, carrying out bloody purges that claimed many lives, including leaders of the Piteshti experiment itself who were later deemed enemies of the State.

Indeed, for much of the twentieth century Romania has remained in the hands of ruthless dictatorships. After some democratic advances in the years before 1938, and a brief monarchy under King Carol II (1938–40), Romania fell to the fascist Iron Guard (1940–41), and the axis collaborationist General Ion Antonescu (1941–44). These regimes exposed the country to partition (losses of territory to Hungary, USSR, and Bulgaria in 1940), war (participation in the war against the USSR in 1941, whereby Romania gained territory lost to the USSR and then some—all the way to Odessa), and anti-Semitism (participation in the Holocaust in a particularly vicious form).

To these dictatorships one must add another—Communist dictatorship whose effects were structurally most significant and, of course, long lasting (1944–1989). After the Red Army crossed into Romania in August 1944, the fate of the country—a strategic neighbor of the USSR—was preordained. King Michael, Romania's captive ruler, was obliged to abdicate by 1947, when the Communists, only 600 strong in 1944, dispensed with the pretense of acting within a coalition and proclaimed a people's republic. What followed was one of the harshest Stalinist regimes in Eastern Europe. The Communists started persecuting leaders of the old "bourgeois" parties, like the Peasant Party leader Iuliu Maniu, even before 1947. These were the years of the Piteshti prison's worse offenses. The principal Stalinist boss of Romania from the 1950s to 1965 was Gherghe Gheorghiu-Dej, a rare working-class prewar Communist of Romanian stock, who spent the war in Romania and not in Moscow. His ruthless-

ness was hardly mediated by his growing independence which became increasingly evident from the time of his resistance to Nikita Kruschev's de-Stalinization policies after 1956. For a while Dej regrouped with the shifts to harsh policies in Moscow, for example, after the invasion of Hungary in 1956. But on the whole he increasingly pursued an independent foreign policy, while at the same time giving no quarter to any potential domestic opposition. He warmed to Yugoslavia in the early 1960s and refused to attack China at the time of the Sino-Soviet split. He also rejected the Soviet diktat in economic policy by pursuing industrialization against the Soviet scheme whereby Romania would remain primarily agricultural within a "socialist division of labor." After his death in 1965, his successor Nicolae Ceausescu, maintained Dej's policies, only briefly giving a show of liberalization that included attacks on Dej.

Ceausescu, like Dej, rejected any diminution of Romania's sovereignty contrary to the views of Western countries, notably the United States. He raised, too, the issue of Romanian control of Bessarabia, the part of the Soviet republic of Moldavia, albeit more academically than in an attempt to correct the Soviet-Romanian border. All along he maintained good relations with China and Yugoslavia and, in 1968, backed the Czechoslovak reformers in their independent policy (not its domestic content). Romania did not participate in the Warsaw pact invasion of Czechoslovakia.

Nevertheless, after the mid-1970s, when Ceausescu consolidated all power within his most immediate retinue, the regime took a bizarre turn to Ceausescu's self-glorification, nepotism, and repression. Determined to eliminate the growing foreign debt, accumulated by generous Western norms, Ceausescu pursued a policy of belt tightening that brought most Romanians to the verge of starvation. Miners' strikes in the Jiu valley were put down by brute force, as was any sign of stirrings among the Hungarian nationality. For all that, the West kept backing Ceausescu as an obstacle to Moscow on which it could depend.

As crisis mounted and the country appeared to be reeling from Ceausescu's increasingly bizarre policies (his campaign against abortion with harsh penalties for violators, registration of typewriters in an attempt to impose total censorship), Ceausescu's opponents within the Communist regime started thinking of ways to remove him. They seized the time in the fall of 1989. As Communism started collapsing in most Eastern European countries, they prepared a coup that led to a bloody removal of Ceausescu in December 1989, events that are central to Dr. Cucliciu's experiences. Ceausescu and his wife were executed after a sum-

mary court-martial, many officials of the dreaded Securitate secret police being similarly liquidated.

The new regime of the National Salvation Front headed by Ion Iliescu, one-time associate of Ceausescu, was nominally non-Communist and certainly tried to dismantle the ideological house of Dej and Ceausescu. But it scrupulously protected the interests of the "old boys" in Communist apparatus, who were never in danger of being obliged to atone for their past deeds. The transition in Romania was therefore slower and more contradictory than in neighboring former Soviet bloc states, frequently giving credence to the newly unleashed rightist forces of the past. Although the worst features of Communism were certainly eliminated, the country's transition to a pluralist society has been slow. Scarcity and fear of repression have been prominent in the lives of Romanians, and characterize the period in which Dr. Cucliciu was seeing the former political prisoners who were his patients. Hopefulness began to appear with the elections of 1996.

CHAPTER

Russia

Editors' Note

Dr. Fyodor Konkov, a Russian psychologist, worked at a twenty-four-hour suicide prevention hotline in Moscow in the mid-1980s; he also consulted with Russian veterans of the war in Afghanistan and with survivors and rescue workers following the Armenian earthquake and the Chernobyl disaster. In August 1991 his veteran friends asked him to accompany them to the Russian White House which they were guarding as the pro-Yeltsin forces were barricaded there in protest against an attempted right wing coup. Dr. Konkov shared that experience with us shortly after the event itself. So, we encouraged him to set his chapter against the background of the assault on the Yeltsin White House, the prism through which we heard him.

In his work at the suicide hotline as in his work with trauma survivors, Dr. Konkov and his generation of therapists shared a contemporary bond with their Western colleagues before the fall of the Soviet Union despite the international boycott of Soviet psychiatry (Miller, 1985).

But Dr. Konkov and his Russian colleagues knew they were living and working amidst enormous contradiction and change. All was not well in the Soviet mental health system of which he was part. Since Brezhnev's time, psychiatry served the forensic role of agent in the punitive system of internment of political dissidents (Miller, 1998). By 1977, the World Psychiatric Association had expelled the USSR for these practices.

In his day-to-day work there were multiple contradictions. Authorities might view his patient as a potential dissident so the KGB could monitor the telephone. By attempting suicide, his patient could reflect badly on the social effectiveness of the Soviet system, so bureaucrats could cut off funding for the program. In describing the motives for his patient's suicidal behavior Dr. Konkov could not publicly formulate dynamic ones, as Freud's ideas were officially anathema to the State (Miller, 1998). He and his colleagues invented new terms which came close to the truth and did not violate the system. But on the whole Dr. Konkov was not so worried by these contradictions as we Westerners were. As he says, in the final years of the USSR the KGB had better things to do than to invade his treatment with his patients.

Just as his patient's family struggles to integrate hidden information regarding family members who have been politically murdered in a totalitarian state, so too Dr. Konkov struggles with previously hidden information regarding his own past. More immediately, both his patient and he struggle with the wish to understand not only what happened but how this lost parent was thinking and feeling about violent political events and why he chose the course of action he did. We can here "palpate that gap or emptiness in identity" which this younger generation feels and liken it to the missing piece in an adopted youth's knowledge of himself or herself (Lifton, 1994). One of the images around which these powerful psychological events turn is a hidden and crumpled piece of paper with indecipherable writing on it , a note as it were from son to father and father to son, first expressing itself as a symptom from childhood, a note perhaps intended to fill the gap between one generation and the next.

The chapter lends itself to discussions of the role of suicide prevention services in the expanding humanitarian activities for a new generation of psychotherapists who grew up behind the Iron Curtain; and of the significant role of a conspiracy of silence which hid a generation of children from knowledge of the actual events in which their parents and grandparents participated (Baker & Gippenreiter, 1998). We can also feel powerful barriers at work even on a societal level as a counterforce to forming new bridges between generations.

Russia: An Emptiness Within

Fyodor Konkov

Reflections on a Journey

I don't think I ever doubted what I would do that night in August 1991 when Yeltsin and the pro-democracy forces were holding vigil in the Moscow "White House." We had all come so far, those of us identified with reform in the Soviet Union. Now, suddenly, Gorbachev had been placed under house arrest while he was away on vacation. The hard-liners were asserting their control in a coup d'etat and Yeltsin, holding the banner of the reformers, was opposing the hard-liners in open conflict. I could not predict the outcome. We might live; we might die. In either case it was important to take a stand.

Yet what stands out today as I reflect on the struggle that was to culminate in Yeltsin's victory is not the presence or absence of physical courage but rather the internal journey I was on: a journey involving my own freedom and its constraints, my own connectedness with others and my estrangement from them. My generation and I continue to struggle with these issues.

This chapter is the narrative of one Russian psychotherapist's experience working with clients who carry with them the seventy-year legacy of a totalitarian Socialist State. It is also a brief chronicle of my inward journey to achieve continuity between the generations. Like my walk that night in August from my flat to the place where the democratic reformers had gathered, this chapter is a narrative of a journey, one that addresses missing bridges in myself and between my generation and its past. It is a journey that is not yet finished.

Communist Russia, Forever

I am really a very simple man, and my family is a very simple family. By the time of my childhood in the 1960s, I was already part of the third generation of Russians to know Communism as a way of life. As a Russian child, there was a stability to life that came not only from the surety that what is true in childhood will be true forever but also from the steady sameness of life during the Brezhnev years. Had I thought about it in those days I would have dismissed as impossible the notion that I would be part of the generation which would take a stand against and eventually defeat the dominant position of the Communist Party in Russia.

I was born in Magdeburg, East Germany, where my father was assigned to the Russian military. At age six, when his assignment changed, we moved to Lviv, Western Ukraine. This exposure to East German and Ukrainian life had its impact on me. I felt both the comfort of playing on old abandoned Nazi bunkers knowing that Russian tanks were not far away, and the discomfort or guilt of not wanting to be seen by the Ukrainians, as a *moskal*, an invader.

My more continuous memories start with the late 1970s, a period of apparent stability in the former Soviet Union. In those days, there was a routine to all aspects of Russian life which had been unchanged for decades, and the general understanding was that the present way of life would last forever. We believed that there was no force in the world powerful enough to change anything in this order. It was a period of the triumph of Soviet ideology. Most of those who did not sincerely believe in all this ideology nevertheless knew that they needed to follow Soviet rules. They needed to demonstrate that they were good and loyal citizens of this country. That there were groups of people who were in open opposition was generally perceived as something to be expected, that a fringe of society would inevitably be composed of deviants trying to do something against the State. Yet everyone knew that if they were to go too far, they would be persecuted. Dissidents were punished—a government response that was perceived as part of the order of life as well. The war in Afghanistan (1979–1989) offers a good example of the sweeping nature of Russian judgment. As usual the Russian political leaders were trying to convince the Russian people and the world that they knew better than anyone else how the Afghanistani people should be living.

By that time the Secretary General of the Party, Brezhnev, had been ruling for so many years that his personality was connected with the regime. The news of his death in 1982 led to confusion about the directions the next leader would take. But for most there remained the unspoken expectation of consistency: the new leader would take over power and the same regime would continue. When, therefore, *perestroika*—change—was declared in 1987 by Gorbachev, the society was shocked. And contrasting views of the Brezhnev years, seen as an era of stability by older people but as a period of stagnation by younger ones, served to separate the generations. The new perspective allowed openness and change—exciting possibilities for me as a young professional. But for others, the former stable and familiar attitudes were so firmly entrenched in their minds that it was too frightening to try something new. For that reason even the changes of *perestroika* failed to make the structure of the old order behave in a new way.

The End of an Era

By the end of the 1980s it was clear that the old order was crumbling. There were attempts from Gorbachev's government to encourage people to improve efficiency and productivity, but only by doing more of the same old things. People were promised that real changes would occur, that democracy was possible, and that freedom of speech was a new reality in Soviet life. But the expectations for better living conditions which Gorbachev and his government had raised in people's minds did not materialize. Opposition to the process of *perestroika* came from two directions. On one side, Communist conservative forces were still hopeful of keeping power. They felt they could still influence Gorbachev because even though he presented himself as a new-thinking Communist, he remained a Communist. Moreover, even though conservative Communists were afraid of losing control over the situation, they still controlled the apparatus of the economy, the military, the KGB, and many other aspects of society. The other flank of opposition was fueled by those who were impatient for radical political and economic reforms. For the reformers, things were not happening fast enough. For a few days after the coup attempt in August 1991, and when Gorbachev was removed from political office, these two forces battled each other for supremacy. Ultimately, the radical reformers won and Yeltsin, their leader, became the country's president.

The events leading up to and following the coup attempt in August 1991 continued to unleash divisive forces which had previously been suppressed and controlled. Conflicts erupted over such national issues as the struggle between Azerbiajan and Armenia (see also Chapter 8) and such social issues as the rights of returning Afghansi veterans. The government could not control open confrontations and military conflicts, nor was it able to deal competently with disasters such as the earthquake in Armenia and the nuclear meltdown in Chernobyl. Furthermore (although the government pretended otherwise), its inability to control their forces was becoming obvious.

In this difficult period, psychological stress to the ordinary citizen came from three sources. The first one was *lack of predictability* in a society so accustomed to stability. Where once Russians had known exactly what their futures held, now life was totally uncertain. People did not know what to expect tomorrow politically, economically, or socially, and their uncertainty produced significant stress. A second source was the *surfacing of previously suppressed trauma*. It was already common knowledge that abuse of power and trauma to innocent individuals had been part of the Stalin era, but those conditions were not confined to that period. By the early 1990s the trauma which had taken place throughout the history of the Soviet Union could no longer be denied. The truth was becoming more obvious as people were getting more information. Yet all this information assaulted old values, producing widespread anger and disillusionment. Together, uncertainty and disillusionment caused great stress in people's private lives. Third, there was *conflict between generations*. The young generation of which I am part was excited about what was going on under *perestroika* and the hope of radical reform. We felt it was a good thing for us to show the older generation that they were not right, that the old values they were trying to force on us were not good enough and were not working. It is this third stress, the stress between generations, which will be the clinical focus of this chapter.

Reflections on a Journey

I received a call from one of the veterans with whom I had been working on that August evening in 1991. He said that many people were gathering around the parliament building, the White House, to protect Yeltsin. He said the Afghanistan War vets would be defending the position. He said they regarded me as a supportive person who helped them share their thoughts and feelings. I was welcome to join them.

*As mental health professionals, it is not often that we are invited to participate directly in the political events of our time; it is not often that we are asked to put our lives on the line because our ideas are at stake.**

Moscow's Telephone Hot Line

Perestroika brought with it changes in how psychologists and psychiatrists were permitted to and chose to function. For years psychiatry, particu-

---

*Shevardnaze's open position that the USSR had done things that were wrong in the Afghanistan War, much like Carter's position on the Vietnam war, helped define the Afghansi veterans as a special group with the ability to address the past with integrity.

larly, was marred by its role as entry point to the gulag. Under Gorbachev, formal State psychiatry mounted a faltering effort to gain international respectability. At the same time, certain mental health service facilities provided a setting for the new generation of clinicians. Those of us who were part of this new development saw the expression of human conflict as part of our personal challenges, not as statements against the State. One of these progressive clinical programs was a twenty-four-hour telephone hot line in Moscow where I worked from 1986 to 1990.

The suicide prevention program, an illustration of early efforts to Westernize Soviet psychiatric services, was a large extended service with three interrelated facets: a twenty-four-hour telephone hot line, outpatient follow-up, and an in-patient unit.

When I was working there, we had six telephone lines in use at all times with an average of three calls per hour on each line. We also had fifteen outpatient clinics spread throughout Moscow, a city of more than ten million people. Finally, we had one inpatient unit for patients who would need inpatient treatment. Although patients who actually attempted suicide were generally placed on locked wards, ours was not. Those who would call the hot line and who needed some deeper therapy than is possible over the phone were referred to a therapist in the nearest outpatient clinic. Approximately ten or fifteen percent of those who were advised to see a therapist in an outpatient clinic followed through; the rest failed to show up for their outpatient visit despite real need. Often they would call back to the hot line trying to resolve their problems on the phone, but this was not always possible.

Rates of suicide were highest in big cities like Moscow and they were rising. Several types of patients commonly called the hot line. One group consisted largely of newcomers to Moscow. Because these were not permanent Moscow citizens, they needed to get special permission and to go through legal procedures, which were restrictive, discriminatory, and stressful. Often such people did not have a good emotional support network. Further, they were coming from some situations where they already felt stress and dissatisfaction. Another group of callers were people who had already talked to nonprofessionals about their problems, but had been unable to change anything about their situation. Typically these callers were suffering from dysfunctional relationships. Regardless of their reason for calling, patients tended to be open on the phone. They often felt safe enough to explain in an hour something that they might not tell in a month or two in treatment at a therapist's office. There was much less feeling of distance in these phone conversations despite some of the paradoxes we experienced regarding confidentiality (see below). Nevertheless the work was intense and emotionally draining, more draining for me, for example, than work with psychotic patients in an inpatient setting.

The hot-line service was started in the late 1970s during the Brezhnev era despite the fact that its very existence pointed to what the authorities saw as an oxymoron: a suicidal but sane Soviet citizen. From the point of view of Soviet psychiatry, no sane person, as a citizen of the Soviet Union, would even think about committing suicide because he or she was supposed to be very happy about living in the best country in the world. The State recognized no neurotic, antisocial, or other reasons for a sane person to attempt to take his or her life. On the other hand, according to Soviet psychiatry, if one were mentally ill, suicidal thinking was conceivable but it meant that the patient would need to be treated as severely mentally ill. Those of us who staffed the hot line therefore found that our first task was to find a loophole in this ideology. Towards that end, we arrived at the concept of the micro-social trauma—an interpersonal trauma not significant enough to concern the regime. A micro-social trauma concerns itself with people's relationships and might include unhappiness in love and in relationships with children and families. The theory was that with such inner trauma people could, by mistake, think about taking their lives. While their main destiny remained to continue to build Communism for future generations, being stressed by micro-social trauma meant that they could momentarily think about something like suicide. This theory allowed suicide prevention services to be accepted. I do not mean to suggest that mental health professionals were trained to believe in this concept. It was a concept devised for officials, for those authorities who otherwise would close the suicide prevention program; it was a concept for officials who had been taught to see stress only in socialistic terms and would therefore have no comprehension of subjective intrapsychic conflict. For them there could be only macro- or micro-social trauma.

The Party, the KGB, even *perestroika* itself provided a curious combination of contradictory forces affecting our ability to provide a confidential setting for our clients; they also contributed to an institutional transference which sometimes colored our work. Threats to our ability to maintain confidentiality came from the Party and frequent pressuring of our administration to provide an acceptable rationale for our work. Moreover, the KGB continued to ask us directly for information regarding whether or not the caller was dangerous to society. Historically, of course, Party control had seriously constrained confidentiality.

Because our callers didn't need to tell their names or addresses, they were anonymous, and from a psychological point of view their identity was protected. Yet, because telephone wire could be tapped, we were, from a political point of view, all vulnerable. We all understood that, whenever they chose to do so, the KGB could listen to phone conversations without permission of the staff or the authorities of the suicide prevention services. In balance, however, during the curious climate which was the Moscow of *perestroika* in the late 1980s, the forces of political repression were on the defensive and the likelihood of such intrusions were less threatening. Because *perestroika,* "change," was specifically designed to give people freedom of speech, people came to believe that such change was real, that open expression of frustration was now an acceptable phenomenon, and frankly, that the KGB had better things to do than to tap the wires of our clients.

In addition to the hot line, another area in which some Soviet psychiatrists and psychologists were taking on a more humanitarian role was in providing services for survivors of trauma: specifically victims of military natural, and technological disasters. It was in this context that I began to consult with Russian veterans of the war in Afghanistan, (Kindra & Turakhodzhaev, 1994) and which also later took me to Armenia to work with earthquake survivors (Kalayjian, 1999). As bridges to the West were being built in the late 1980s it was in this capacity that I first met with Jack Lindy and other therapists whose work appears in this book. It was also in that role as consultant to Afghansi veterans that led to a telephone call in August 1991.

Reflections on a Journey

Things felt ominous in Moscow that night. Watching television that evening, I saw sober-faced newscasters and listened to their expressionless voices and old-fashioned language—a peculiar use of the passive tense and other obscure matters of syntax. I felt the world of my childhood returning, a world in which all the changes we had worked so hard for would disappear. My mother called, warning me to be safe. Her manner on the telephone was superficially calm and reassuring, yet excessively firm, belying a tremulousness underneath. I thought to myself as I was walking to the White House to join my friends, how familiar that tone of voice was, how great the fear, how much in the old days we had lost from our parents in order to reassure them we would be safe. They must have asked themselves, "what is it which we must not say to each other so that those who spy, those who inform for the State, will not endanger our children? What must our children never know about themselves?" I remembered a number of the parents and their families whom I had seen in connection with the suicide prevention center and realized now that, as I had listened to the stories of others in pain, my mother's tremulous voice had already been a clue to me. It was a clue that instruction to be safe could interfere with growth, and that the tremulousness meant not only succumbing to the State's power but also losing one's own voice and one's own history. It was this tone of voice I had recognized in a caller to the hot line, a tone which helped me see a void in her son and an untold story by her mother.

Dmitri and His Family

Galena M. called the hot line after her twelve-year-old son, Dmitri (Dima), barricaded himself in his room threatening to hurt himself. Her voice trembled, "If grandmother, Antonina Nikolayevna forces her way in to his room, Dima will jump out of the window." Galena was frightened about her son's threats, but once on the telephone with me she calmed down. She explained that before she called the hot line, Dima had locked himself in his room and stated that he would kill himself if anyone tried to come in. Only after Galena told him that his grandmother had re-treated to bed saying she would have a heart attack, because of his be-havior, did he unlocked the door and let others in. As we talked, Galena began to reflect, was it possible that her son Dima's behavior was a pro-test against his grandmother's incessant efforts to control him rather than an acute suicidal danger. I was interested in the problems of Dima and his family and, once the crisis had settled down, I recommended follow-up psychotherapy at the outpatient clinic so we could understand more about the circumstances leading to this "micro-social trauma."

At first, Galena felt guilty and helpless, saw herself surrounded by forces and individuals she could not control, but was unwilling to consider that she played any role in Dima's problem.

I met with Galena and Dima separately and together. Galena explored her feelings about her mother, Antonina Nikolayevna, the boy's grand-mother. The grandmother was the source of much pressure for both of them; it was she who decided what was and was not permitted at home. I thought that one way of seeing Dima's protest was as an appeal to his mother, Galena, to defend herself and to define her own role as mother. Dima perceived himself as defenseless while connected with his mother's helpless stance. As he saw it, Dima enjoyed reading books, working on crafts, and listening to music, but grandmother would interrupt, saying, "It is Monday so you must read books from 2–4 p.m. and work on crafts from 4–6 p.m." Dima said he lost interest in activities once grandmother took control. Eventually, her list grew until he wasn't able to do anything independently, and he felt that he had no space or time of his own. When he went outside to play with other children, she controlled his actions there as well. Now he was starting to protest.

When I talked to grandmother, she told me she was very surprised that Dima became so nervous when she entered his room. From her point of view, this Russian child was very fortunate to have his own room. She remembered times when several families would live in the space that the three of them now occupied. But Dima didn't feel that he had his own room because, from his perspective, she did not allow him to retreat to it.

When I met with Galena alone, she explained that she had never seen her own father. She was born in 1941 when her father was in the military. Since early childhood her mother and her aunt repeated the family story that father had been a Red Army officer who died as a hero defending his Motherland. That was the only story she ever knew about her father. At school she was taught another story, that comrade Stalin was the kindest and most caring person in the world, that he was like a father to all the Soviet people, and that he cared so much that he did not even sleep at night. Stalin was always watching what was happening and thinking about ways to make people happier and to protect them from their enemies. Portraits of Stalin hung in every classroom. In contrast, Galena had access to no pictures of her real father. Her mother, Antonina, would explain to her that she did not like to show the few remaining pictures in the old family album to anyone, that she did not like to talk about her private life in those far away times. So Galena had little direct knowledge of her parents or their earlier lives. She heard Antonina talk of work, of coworkers, and of good times when, despite extreme hardships, people were better, harder working, and more dedicated. Those were the times of certainty. As her mother described them, things in the old days were black or white: The "bad guys" were always punished and this was the best reward and motivation for those who were good.

When Galena married and gave birth to Dima, her mother did not approve. During the four years of her marriage, Galena tried her best to win her mother's acceptance of him. Later, in one of her sessions with me, she explained, "Now I realize that my priority in the early years of the marriage was wrong. I should have been establishing privacy with my husband. We should have been accepting each other, not simply striving for my mother's acceptance. I never felt comfortable with him, and I seemed always to be blaming him. I was never able to understand what he wanted from our relationship. But I was sick and depressed for a long time after the divorce. Once my husband left, mother was very supportive. She took care of Dima. . . . I can't recall now how it happened that she did not allow my ex-husband to see Dima."

Clearly, this grandmother was a very strong personality. Even at her age, she continued to work and was well liked and respected there. At work everyone knew that she was in control and that if you needed something, she was the one who could help you if she wanted. To me, Galena's mother resembles many older people in Russia who carry the heritage of the Stalin years. They feel that those times were very hard, but that values were clear. Then, one always knew what should and should not be done. They prefer a sense of certainty to the lack of certainty in the current situation in which there is no strong leader. Now, one doesn't know what should be done. Perhaps Antonina Nikolayevna's personality is part of the twentieth-century experience of tragedy, hard work, and the melding of rural hardiness with the urbanization of the Stalinist era. Perhaps it is a part of a story of hardiness and aggression as being coping styles for women who survived in the harsh rural life of Russia since the middle ages.

I saw grandmother on three occasions, but I didn't have any illusions that I would be able to treat Antonina Nikolayevna directly. Indeed, she remained resistant to therapy. Grandmother came only because I explained that I needed her help. I had requested her participation in the therapy because she was the one who knew most about the family's history. (I knew that she would tell me also what I was supposed to do, and that I would listen.)

In the middle phase of therapy, I saw Galena alone. She expressed her dilemma in this way: "I am having a strange feeling (now in your office), as if my mother is here carefully listening to everything I'm telling you. It is as if she's reproaching me in her eyes, because by talking with you I am doing something wrong, something threatening to her and to myself, something to be ashamed or afraid of. Possibly, I have lived with this feeling of her physical presence intimidating me all my life. She tries to guard me, keeping me from being too trustful, too relaxed, too involved in relationships, too happy, always because she knows better. She knows I will regret giving in to such wishes. Yes, she always knows what is good and what is bad. And I am never able to understand or anticipate how she might control me. If I could understand this maybe I could begin to look after myself. She has been through a lot in her life, and she has survived. All of her friends and colleagues respect her. But, now as I am here, speaking with you, trying to figure what I can do to prevent my son from threatening to take his life, I feel she does not approve. It is as if my working in treatment, trying to save my son from his self-destructiveness offends her. I feel guilty. It's too much for me, I can't stand it any longer. . . . "

Galena and I came to an insight about why her mother behaved this way, but only after she learned more about her own wishes and fears. We had been working on trying to understand a troubling symptom of Galena's: attacks of severe anxiety when she feared a terrible accident would happen to her son when he was out of her sight, as, for example, on his way back from school. In the fantasy, Dima darts out onto the street and is run over by a truck. Her son behaves rashly and she is unable to save him. The more she felt helpless, the more her anxieties and fears got out of control. She was terrified by these pictures and experienced them as nearly real. I understood this as an expression of her frustration and ambivalence regarding trying so hard to protect her son. On the one hand, not constraining him might mean losing him. On the other hand, caring for Dima was so confining that Galena could not see any future for herself. This was a painful dilemma and she was terrified by her fantasies of her son dying. But appreciating it also allowed her to think differently about Antonina's behavior. Perhaps grandmother, like her, was controlling in what she intended to be a protective way, because of a fear that otherwise she would lose what she loved.

As Galena and I established a better relationship, she and her son also established a better relationship, one which was not under the pressure of the grandmother's dominance. Galena's insight into her mother's constant presence and control helped. She realized that her mother's actions may have been a defense against a fear of loss. This helped her feel less vulnerable to criticism, and less under her control. The fact that a male (the therapist) was now part of the family dynamics also helped her achieve some distance from her mother.

Another area of painful insight was related to Galena's absence of real knowledge about her father. There was something unclear in what had happened to him in the war. For a long time she believed in the "hero" story she had been told as a child, but she recalled that once, when her aunt was staying at their house, she overheard her mother and her aunt talking about her father's apparently well-known impulsive behavior, which they never mentioned in Galena's presence. In trying to put these pieces together, Galena came to the conclusion that her father had not died as a hero fighting the invaders, but that on the basis of some impulsive behavior during the war, he very likely was accused of some offense dangerous to the Communist regime, and died in a Siberian work camp, a victim of the *gulag*. Galena admitted that she always had mixed feelings about her mother's elaborate yet vague stories about him: She wanted to know the truth, but at the same time she was afraid to learn it.

My role in this therapy was listening empathically to Galena. She wanted to change her life, especially her relationship with her son. As she worked on her feelings, she was able to separate herself more from her mother and to be more assertive with Dima.

She realized she could create a future for herself and could see her life in a positive perspective, including the value of spending time with her son. Galena was able to give her son choices and make him feel reasonably responsible. That was a difficult but positive gain in the therapy.

From Dima's perspective, one improvement was when he began to see his mother as a separate person from grandmother, a live person in her own right. His acute self-destructiveness and self-restrictiveness eased. He was sensitive to his mother's relationship with grandmother, and to grandmother's strong tendency to violate the privacy of other family members. Fortunately, grandmother's job gave her an outlet for her need to control, and there she found people who valued her communication skills and her ability to help people.

There are many apt formulations in this case. One could emphasize the absence of male figures in Dima's life, and his phase-appropriate needs for privacy and autonomy. One could focus on the poor communication skills between the generations, or the characterologic dissonance between them. In my practical handling of the case, I utilized a family systems model, but I wish here to emphasize a psychohistorical element in the case: an emptiness, a void present in both Galena and Dima which represents a problem in multigenerational identity. In this case, children and grandchildren suspected but did not know the *true* stories of their own family. Moreover, they discerned from subtle forms of speech and tremulous tones that defects existed in the *fabricated* family stories.

It is important to note that some developmentally important information was missing. In her wish to protect the younger generation, Antonina Nikolayevna had filled a gap in the family's history with a fabrication. And because Galena had sensed for some time that Antonina had lied about her father, an emptiness resided within her. In the absence of truth between the generations, grandmother's persistent over-protectiveness, as a form of undoing, produced the opposite of what she intended: to make her family safe. Of course she could never bring her dead husband back from Siberia, nor could she protect Dima from what life has in store for him. In trying to hide the truth, however, she left her daughter and her grandson feeling less, not more, sure of their origins, less, not more, sure of themselves.

Clinical Discussion

I would like to speculate about this and similar cases in which a void exists in the emotional life of the younger generation because important facts and feelings were not shared between the generations. Often, parents hide facts because they don't want to endanger their children. They reason that ignorance of a parent who has been purged or marginalized will protect their children from having problems with the regime. But what I understand happens in such situations from the child's point of view is that an empty space, a void develops in their identity. Even though both the parents and the child try not to see it, the gap exists, leaving the child to feel that there is a missing link in who he or she is.

Perhaps an experience in another setting will illustrate the point. In December 1988 when I was in Armenia working with children who were orphaned in the earthquake, I learned that orphaned children were often not told the truth about their parents. On one occasion we were taking care of a child who refused to eat, didn't sleep, and had behavior problems. She had not yet been told that her mother had been killed; instead she was told that her mother was in a hospital. Faced with this situation, the family and community said to me, "You are the professional; you know how to tell her the truth." I felt pressure to comply with their wishes. I also remembered that in ancient Rome they killed the messenger who brought bad news. We can accept bad news, I thought, but we can't accept the one who brings it. Maybe the wish to avoid the role of dreadful messenger is universal. Perhaps that is why those close to the survivor commonly look outside themselves for someone to speak the tragic truth.

In my experience what actually happens in these situations is that survivors process the many nonverbal messages which transcend a messenger's ability to control information. In Armenia, I saw this phenomenon in action. This child, for example, had heard adults insist that her mother was in the hospital, but she had heard their unspoken messages too, messages that contradicted their spoken words. The result was that, unconsciously, this child knew that her mother was dead. To accept this fact, what she needed was to be together with those who were then close and would remain close to her, to be able to feel this closeness physically, and to express their joint grief together. Instead, the child was alone with her loss. Her family was adding to the trauma by hiding the truth, even though their motive was to help.

Maybe this is what happened to us in Russia, what happened to many of our parents as well—hiding trauma and loss with fabricated versions of truth. The parent thinks, if I deny that something bad has happened to us and I deny and prevent myself from showing the feelings I have about this trauma, I will save my child the pain of these feelings. But the surviving parent also prevents himself from the potential closeness with the child which comes from sharing the pain. By behaving in this manner, the parent trains the son to deny the clues he has already perceived. And the son, having no parent to affirm his inner life, grows to reject both his parent and his own inner feelings.

This is my understanding of what was happening in Dima's family. It is also my understanding of an intergenerational void that has characterized many families in my country. It was certainly the case during Stalin's purges and perhaps later as well.

Many factors in a totalitarian state contribute to this intergenerational silence. Where random interrogation by secret police is more likely than not, it may seem better to have no emotional ties to family. When the KGB, for example, wants you to confess or inform on someone, they do not come to you and say, "I'm going to kill you if you do not comply." They come to you and say, "If you do not do as I say, we will kill your wife, we will kill your children, we will torture your mother." They have found that these threats work better. To be safe, therefore, to protect yourself from this kind of control and manipulation you must have no children, no wife, no mother. Only then are you safe because then the only thing they can do to you is to kill you.

Reflections on a Journey

Shortly I would be inside the perimeter of tanks around the White House. I could feel my pace quicken. I was looking forward to feeling safe, at peace there, ironically, in the most dangerous spot in Russia that night in August 1991.

On the perimeter of the White House I found my friends who explained that they were concerned that someone might lose composure and act precipitously. I found myself making rounds, listening, for example, to a non-combat veteran youngster who joined us, finding myself soothing his agitation. Later I listened to a seasoned Afghansi, a veteran who commented how good it felt to be defending the moral side in a conflict. As I listened to myself during those tense hours I could feel my loyalty to the military men who stood on ethical grounds; I could feel myself as one with them, and yet even in this camaraderie I also felt separate from them, alone. I continued to feel the polarity between connectedness and void as the evening wore on.

I remembered that such feelings had also been stirred when I worked with my patients. During the vigil, there were moments of great tension as we learned that a column of tanks was heading towards us. Clearly the showdown would be soon. There were also lulls that night, when we simply waited. I remembered, and I tried to piece together the sense of void in myself with what I knew about my own past.

Countertransference: Dr. Konkov's Story

Like Dima and Galena, I have also felt a void, an emptiness in identity that comes from being denied access to my own past. And since I believe that I cannot deal adequately with my patients if I am not able to understand myself, I am driven to search for the meaning of the void in myself. My story starts with the fact that I come from a simple Communist family. My mother's father, my grandfather, who died when I was twelve, was an unpretentious, idealistic, and exemplary Communist. A teenage participant in the October Revolution in St. Petersburg in 1917, he later served in the military in the war with Finland in World War II and in the war in the Far East. He was a simple, true, yet practical Communist who lived responsibly and believed in Communism's ideals. Yet he understood Communism's dangerous side. He did not seek personal advantage and power, and he never held a top position in the Party. Furthermore, he never sought material possessions for himself. Two years after he received his country cottage, a dacha near Moscow, as a pension for his military career, he returned it as a gift to society. Giving it up was a sacrifice of basic human comforts, but he did so not only out of altruism but also to protect himself and his family's future: One could never predict or trust how the leadership would later define simplicity (having a dacha could be held against someone in the family in the future). He died at the age of 69, felled by a heart attack on his way home from a Party meeting. My father was also a simple Communist. He served in World War II from the first day until the last, and, like my mother's father, was a career military man. He, too, did an exemplary job and was always respected. To me he was a self-contained, restrictive man who always kept something of his emotional life away from me.

These are the family stories I heard growing up. Perhaps I had feelings about missing information but I cannot remember. The something that was missing, however, was not only in the past, before I was born, but existed in my emotional situation at home as a child. Something was missing in the confirmation of my inner feelings. I remember playing a game, perhaps to give me some relief, although at the time I didn't understand its meaning. First I would take a sheet of paper and I would make a drawing or a note on it; then I would crumple the paper. But then it was as though I *had* to save it, to restore it, to restore the drawing or the writing. I felt compelled to play this game over and over again: The purpose was to restore something previously destroyed, something hidden from me. The end of the game was the restoring of the piece of paper as well as I could. The game offered relief from tension.

I had one sibling, a brother, now a military lawyer, who is a year and a half older than I, and whom my parents treated very differently from me. I have been told that I was expected to be the girl in the family; in fact, I was treated like a girl until age two. I was my mother's child, while my brother was my father's child. As I grew up, I had a feeling that more expectations and responsibilities for the emotional well-being of the family fell on me than on my elder brother. I avoided certain expectations of boys and men such as proficiency in mechanics and controlling leadership. I was given the freedom to feel, the freedom to develop receptive capacities, and the freedom to see things in new and different ways.

My father did not reveal much of his emotional life to his family. His job was to provide for our living conditions. Because he was in the military, he would receive orders and then we would not see him for a week or two. It was obvious that he wasn't a person who belonged to himself. Indeed it was obvious that no men belonged to themselves. They belonged to something else, perhaps the Party or the country. To me my father seemed like a man who had lost something of himself as he had been absorbed into duties that may have been at variance with his character or ideals. Nevertheless this was the way men lived. Like our grandfather, our father was in the military, and we were supposed to follow in his footsteps. My brother became a cadet, and I spent a year in the military institute, studying languages there.

I would say that the greatest value of the family, from my father's point of view, was having children. He couldn't understand why, since I had two children, I would divorce my wife. It doesn't matter, he would say, what relationship you have with your wife. You have two children; this is more than enough reason to do anything you can to keep the family together. He did not show his feelings. Once he thought I was too emotional about something. He told me that there is no use to show your emotions to anyone, because no one cares about them. He gave an example that when his mother died, he did not cry. Only once after the funeral when he was alone, he did let himself cry a little bit, but that was it. After that, he said, he showed no emotions about anything.

I've always felt that, although he said it was fine to be free, I should not take his words at face value. When I was a student in the university, for example, he never wanted to see me smoking. He would grab the cigarette from me and throw it away. He wouldn't hurt me, but by stopping my objectionable behavior he would make the situation tolerable for himself. His manner of setting limits was paradoxical. He didn't forbid me my freedom, but he warned me ominously that I must not go too far. He was also uncomfortable about my studying psychology while he was in the military, as though through my circle of contacts I might damage him or me. I pointed out to him that like any university in the world, Moscow University was a setting for an exchange of ideas and confrontation between students and authorities. But he thought such confrontations were inherently dangerous.

For reasons unknown to me, I was accused of disseminating religious propaganda among university students. This was not true. I did have friends in the United States, and my friends and I would make calls to the United States from the university phone. One student was leaving to stay in the United States, and, for this reason, the authorities blacklisted him, stigmatizing him as someone who displayed behavior unworthy of the Soviet student. When I joined a number of students in a meeting in which we protested the authorities' action, my father became very angry with me. Afterwards he said he had been shown my KGB file and told I was in danger because of my activities. He was warned that I should stop. I became angry with him that he was not giving me room to live my own life. My mother blamed me for giving him a hard time when I knew he had heart problems. So I felt guilty about confronting him. He was trying to explain to me that he could use his influence to tell them not to prosecute me, but only to a certain extent. My KGB file also included the accusation that I was selling foreign currency, although while in Moscow I had never even seen anything but Russian currency. I tried to tell my father that the accusations were not true, and that I wasn't involved in religious propaganda either. An informant must have misunderstood and misinterpreted something I said as religious propaganda, but it was not true. My innocence was not my only point. I was also trying to tell my father that I was not going to quit living because of false accusations. At the same time, I could understand his fears for me because I remembered reading in newspapers from 1949 that people had been sent to prison for less dire charges than these.

I can't say my father was a prohibitive parent. He was trying to explain to me what I shouldn't do, but he understood that he was helpless to stop me. In such situations two parallel events occur. Because parents are answerable to the authorities for their children's behavior, they fear for themselves. That is why in such cultures the birth of a child is both very good and potentially threatening—because the child may be accused of actions that bring shame or punishment to the family. Inevitably, in such a situation, people feel responsible for those who are closely connected to them. In addition, there is the ever-present universal parental concern about what will happen to the child. This combination of self-preservative and altruistic motivations for withdrawal gives rise to defects in intimacy, in shared feelings, in shared information, even in shared reasoning. It is not hard to understand that children raised in this way experience gaps in their emotional life which affect their ability to make and keep intimate relationships. Many layers of understanding are missing. If a parent goes outside with his children and remains centered on the child's needs, he might allow his child to climb a tree, to run, to play noisily with other children. But, if the parent is centered on the fear of what people might say, such as, "Your son is doing something wrong, he shouldn't climb that tree, he shouldn't spill water on the flowers," the parent would forbid his child from doing all these things so that he would not be censured by representatives of society.

I remember when my children gave me a good lesson in this phenomenon, using as a text the daily nap. There is a rule in Russian families that children rest in the daytime. This is thought by adults to be very healthy and therefore something that should be done. On one occasion I was the one responsible for enforcing my children's nap time, but I was having little success. For thirty or forty minutes, I tried to keep the children quiet in their beds and to get them to go to sleep, all the while aware that my parents and my wife's parents were in an adjoining room and that they wouldn't like the fact that the children were not sleeping. Finally when they erupted into jumping and playing for what felt like the millionth time, I asked them, "Who needs you to sleep? Me or you?" and they cried, "You!" I realized they were right, and I told them to do anything they liked. I left the room and announced to the other adults that the children wouldn't be napping that day. My in-laws had an immediate and negative reaction; they said that I did not care about my children.

My own childhood, of course, had included no such flouting of the rules. Our simple Communist family was headed by my father, a man who tried his best to do everything that he was supposed to do to provide safety at home and in his career. I knew that he was a propaganda officer charged with convincing the enemy to stop fighting. During and after World War II, he was a specialist on the German National Army and was very well respected by his superiors.

I knew he was involved in these things, but I never knew what he really felt about them. After his death, when my mother asked me to go through his papers, I knew that she was inviting me to find something I might want to keep. If I discovered something, she implied, I should take it; if not, that was fine too. What I found in my father's papers was a glimpse of some of his thoughts, his personal opinions that he probably never shared with anyone. In with some material declaring that the German National Army had no future, there was also, as if set out for me to find, his objection to the Soviet policy of bisecting Germany, a statement that such a division might not be the right thing to do, that it would be artificial for a culture united by language and history. I had known that my father's first graduate degree was in German literature and that he was working on a book which was never finished, but I didn't realize until after his death that his understanding of and sympathy for German culture caused him so much conflict in the face of official Soviet policy. But my learning about my father did not stop there. When he died in 1986, I felt moved, for a reason I did not understand, to put a small cross into his pocket before the funeral began. So this is how he was buried, having this cross with him.

Five years after my father's death, I learned that his father, my paternal grandfather, had been an Orthodox priest in Southern Russia. He suddenly disappeared in the purges and was presumed by the family to have been killed in the early 1930s by Communists. There were nine children in the family, with my father being the youngest son. When I was told about this part of my history, I realized that I had never questioned who my other grandfather was. Military assignments and geography had separated us from that side of the family. It was always as if it was enough to have one grandfather. Now knowing that this traumatic loss happened to my father in his childhood, I am left with a nearly palpable sense of the gap in my family story, as well as a resentment that this was forbidden space between me and my father, and between me and my grandfather. Maybe this gap explains why I am so interested in the issues of not losing the nuances of what is true in emotional relationships especially between the generations, because I know that passing on this truth and the ways we cope with that truth is valuable. I also know the void when we lose it.

Reflections on a Journey

Something about the tanks drew me near to them. Oddly I felt comfortable. I re-membered being a child living in East Germany, playing by the tanks at the kasserne (military base). The tanks were Russian, they made me feel safe, and as the son of a Russian officer I felt at home around them. But the tanks also frightened and confused me. They also brought back the memory of walking at night in Armenia after a hard day's work with survivors, when a Russian tank stopped me and threatened me as though I were the enemy, a political criminal (for these were the days of revolutionary ideas as well as the earthquake). And now here were Rus-sian tanks around the White House to protect us and other Russian tanks which had come to destroy us. People were upset telling me what they had seen: three people smashed by a tank. By the time I had arrived, the bodies were gone. Now splattered blood marked where they had been and flowers rested next to the blood. It was over; the vigil was over and people were celebrating, yet I felt sadness. I did not quite feel fully part of the group. It was not truly my victory. It was as if I were ordained to be there, as though my presence, my witness to human struggles for dignity in the face of violence, might somehow protect against death, or as if my witness were the fulfillment of my parents and granparents' unconscious charge to me to say and feel finally what they were prohibited from saying and feeling dur-ing their lifetimes. Yet whatever I did or didn't do that night at the Yeltsin White House could not quite restore the crumpled paper of my childhood or bring a full sense of relief for myself.

As I continue to process what is it that consitutes my identity, I wonder if the legacy of my fahter's father, the Orthodox priest in central Russia doesn't some-where live in my soul . . . a part of my personal history I never knew . . . yet some-thing that paradoxically I always knew, if only as yet to be explained void inside me.

Chapter Highlights

1. For Russia, arrested grief is endemic. Millions of families lost a mem-ber (usually male) during the purges, and often, in order to adapt to the new order, a surviving parent erected fabricated stories of the lost family member's life and cause of death. In the years of awakening during *perestroika* and after, these fabrications came to light, and ques-tions about personal identity as well as cultural identity became wide-spread. The need to discuss these issues and to resume dialogue be-

tween generations exists within most Russian and many Eastern European families. Mental-health efforts must dovetail with widespread cultural awareness as through cinema, arts, and literature, to encourage this dialogue within the family.

2. Dr. Konkov describes a specific affective state, one of inner emptiness, which children experience during arrested grief, when they feel they have been lied to about the life and death of their parents or grandparents. This calls for reconstructing and integrating the real parent out of newly discovered fragments, and then mourning that newly discovered parent or grandparent for he or she, too, is no longer available. The task is similar to that which the adopted child might confront in the West.

3. Dr. Konkov discusses the day-to-day pressures on the psychotherapist to bend the integrity of the therapeutic frame: to violate confidentiality, to invent an acceptable context for seeing a suicidal patient, to distance oneself from the State's use of the therapist for its own means. We North American therapists struggle in a world of managed care to maintain balance and integrity when third parties try to control indications for hospitalization, length of treatment, the type of medication, etc. We feel powerless in the face of intrusions which endanger a viable therapeutic alliance. Yet such intrusions pale in comparison to the pressures of the KGB in the life of a Russian psychotherapist even as late as the late 1980s.

4. Dr. Konkov sets this chapter and the case of Dmitri against the backdrop of his journey to stand by fellow reformers in the face of tanks which could have been ordered to fire on them during the attempted right-wing coup of 1991. We, in the West, are brought up short as we see the mental health clinician participating with integrity in the revolution of his own times, a history sketched in more detail by Mark Steinberg, on the following pages.

Historical Sketch: Russia

Mark D. Steinberg

For those living through it, like Dr. Konkov and his patient's family, Russia's recent history has been both exhilarating and disturbing. Three decades of relative stability and security, as well as of persistent economic backwardness and rigid and often repressive political and cultural conservatism, gave way in the mid-1980s to unprecedented open debate, economic and political reform, social crisis, and an uncertain future. These have been contradictory times and they have elicited conflicting responses.

In August 1991, conservative Communists attempted to seize power by force in order to stop Mikhail Gorbachev's efforts to establish a freer relationship among the republics of the USSR and to reverse his continuing (if vacillating) promotion of freer civil discourse, competitive parliamentary elections, and market reforms. [It is his journey to the public rally in opposition to this brief coup and the events of that night which provides the backdrop for Dr. Konkov's narrative in this chapter.] In the wake of the coup's failure, the Communist Party was suspended, the Russian Federation and other republics and regions declared their independence from the Soviet Union (effectively ending its existence), and Gorbachev resigned. The most immediate effect of this collapse of traditional centers of authority was the radical, and increasingly uncontrolled, dismantling of Russia's planned economy, and the virtual disappearance of controlling State authority. The result has been a decade of economic upheaval and crisis, deep political and ideological conflict, disintegration of the social fabric, and a great deal of both widespread idealism and cynical corruption, but also much hope and determination to make democratic change real and permanent. The times have become only more contradictory.

The historical experiences themselves have had potent and often disturbing effects on people's lives. But these effects cannot be understood apart from a less dramatic, but no less consequential, process of historical transformation that had begun well before Gorbachev came to power. By the 1960s, Russia had become a predominantly urban society in which most people had at least a secondary education and many had a higher education. At the same time, with the passing of Stalinism, barriers to the larger world and restrictions on expression had weakened. In this changed setting, many Russians—especially urban, educated Russians—began thinking differently about themselves as individuals, about their place in society, and about their nation's past. It is fitting that Fyodor Konkov returns so often in this chapter to his and his patients' efforts to figure out how to orient their lives in an increasingly unstable present and to recover suppressed or hidden memories about the past.

Gorbachev and other Communist reformers spoke of these social and psychological changes when identifying the crisis that loomed behind the apparent face of stability and security of the Brezhnev years. Gorbachev identified as markers of this approaching crisis not only declining economic growth rates but a deeper and even more troubling erosion of ideological and moral values. Above all, he was troubled that people [were] losing interest in social affairs. This loss of civic enthusiasm and faith was widely acknowledged and documented. For some time Soviet sociologists had been describing a broad retreat by Soviet citizens from public life ("building socialism") into more private worlds of family, friends, and self. Among the young, this retreat was most extreme and often belligerent. It was evident even in the work of social science professionals, who articulated what amounted to an alternative ideology and morality, emphasizing the centrality of the individual in society and the necessity of paying greater attention to the psychological and moral needs of individuals.

Hoping to stimulate an enlightened return to civil life and thus to renew and invigorate socialist society, Gorbachev and other Communist reformers called for freer public discussion of social issues. The effects of this greater openness, however, were often disturbing; the Soviet press became filled with reports describing social problems whose existence had previously been hidden and denied: poverty, homelessness, malnutrition, child abuse, high infant mortality, prostitution, suicide, alcoholism, drug addiction, and violent crime. Reports on the long war in Afghanistan (the Soviet Army was fighting there from 1979 to 1989) revealed demoralized troops and traumatized veterans. Journalists and senior politicians alike spoke publicly about a slowing economy and shortages of food, housing, and consumer goods and services. And the past, especially the Stalin and Brezhnev years, was subjected to the same critical treatment. Public debunking of the myths and falsehoods that Soviet people had for so long been told about their past went so far that nationwide history exams had to be canceled at the end of the 1988 school year. The nation's past, like its present, was destabilized.

Gorbachev's reforms—both the successful opening of public debate and the far less successful efforts to reinvigorate the economy through limited market reforms—simultaneously fostered enthusiasm, disenchantment, and resistance. Many shared Gorbachev's vision of making socialism viable and humane. But many were confused, fearful, and angry as assumptions about the past and the present were undermined and challenged and as their country's problems were aired before the world. And many, especially among the young and the educated, were already too skeptical and disillusioned to believe in the possibility of renewing socialism or to be satisfied when, as they saw it, lies about the present and the past were replaced with only half-truths.

For all sides, memories of the Stalin years provided a political and personal touchstone. In reality, Stalinist Russia was a mixture of violent repression (purges, show trials, executions, labor camps) and heroic collective achievement (industrial construction, wartime solidarity and glory, great power status), of authoritarianism and resistance, and of the lack of political rights or freedom beside plenty of everyday pleasures. This contradictory reality yielded contradictory memories at best and, more often, one-sided and tendentious retellings. For Russians mainly unsettled and angered by the civil disorder and fragmentation, national weakness, decaying moralities, and uncertainties of the present (like Dmitri's grandmother in the case presentation), Stalin's era appeared in memory's reflection as a lost age of stability, community, discipline, national pride, and certainty about the future. For individuals determined to bring to Russia democratic rights, a market economy, and international partnership with the West, Stalin's time has evoked mainly hateful memories of repression, terror, forced labor, and xenophobic isolation. Historical truth, of course, is more mixed and complicated. But it is the immediate meanings *of the past which have been most at issue in these recollections, where past has functioned chiefly as a means to define political values and to make sense of one's own place in Russia's traumatic history and uncertain present.*

7
CHAPTER

Croatia

Editors' Note

Dr. Vasko Muacevic is professor of psychiatry at the University of Zagreb, Croatia. He was senior psychiatrist delivering mental health services to the Croatian military and to refugee camps. As Dr. Muacevic explains, his is the view of the clinician who has lived through five radically different regimes, who brings longevity to bear, and the necessity of an ethical centering point around which identity must form in order to survive psychologically in the post-totalitarian fever of nationalism in the countries of the former Yugoslavia.

Dr. Muacevic's cases highlight the fratricidal nature of civil wars in the Balkans as ethnicity intersects Communist and post-Communist forces (Kaplan, 1993). Here, the seasoned clinician, while dealing empathicly with ethnic passions, must move beyond ultranationalist leanings in order to hear the complex stories of patients faced as they are with contradiction and controversy (Klain & Pavic, 1999; Milivojevic, 1999). Unlike his East European colleagues, Dr. Muacevic, a Croat, survived the years of Communist totalitarian rule with ties with colleagues and relatives in the West intact, and has taught and practiced social psychiatry. The striking facet to his cases is the way in which contradiction and irony overlie tragedy in this war where mixing of ethnic traditions as well as separation of ethnic strands is so much a part of a common tradition.

Dr. Muacevic presents the case of Viktor, a veteran of the former Yugoslavian army whose dormant PTSD became exacerbated when soldiers

143

wearing the uniform of his former army turned on his new state, Croatia. The case raises questions about hardiness (McFarlane & Yehuda, 1996) and the specific stimuli capable of reactivating the PTSD syndrome thirty years later (Aarts & Op den Velde, 1996; Op den Velde et al., 1993). His second case is of a Slavonian Croat, Josip, whose stresses included fighting against the Serbian invasion of Vukovar, being captured and held in a detention camp, and finally becoming a refugee (Kozaric-Kovacic, Marusic, & Ljubin, 1999; Martic-Biocina, Spoljar-Vrzina, & Rudan, 1996, 1998). Josip's symptoms focus on the death of a best friend who chose to fight on the enemy side. Dr. Muacevic discusses the powerful feelings stirred by such cases and his role as advisor/mentor to those on the scene of battle.

While the traumas of this war and the psychological aftermath have much in common with other wars, the cultural dimensions to this post-Soviet-era conflict pitting ethnic groups who have lived with each other for centuries in mortal combat against each other appears especially frightening, contagious, and vengeful. We continue to see its effects in Bosnia and Kosovo.

The chapter lends itself to discussion of the problem of identity for post-totalitarian Eastern Europeans (Vanista-Kosuta & Kosuta, 1998), and to the strong countertransference emotions stirred in the therapist when confronting crimes against humanity, the inevitable accompaniment of "ethnic cleansing."

Croatia:
Old Scars, New Wounds

Vasko Muacevic

Personal Reflections

I was only a child when I first experienced the atrocities of war. I remember sensing my parents' fear of German and Italian fascism: I watched my Jewish friends leave Zagreb and I gazed in horror at the vision of dead people hanging from trees at the side of the road. Later, at the very end of the war in 1945, I witnessed large crowds of people running away towards the West to save themselves from the advancing partisans, intending to surrender to the Western allied forces. I heard rumors about advancing Soviet troops coming towards us from Hungary and Serbia, and I remember welcoming the end of the war with relief as we expected something better to come. What came was repressive totalitarian Communism.

I was still in high school when I decided to study medicine. Perhaps my choice was influenced by the very war atrocities I had seen, my encounters with people left mentally and physically disabled, my visions of those who were killed and massacred. I thought that someday as a physician I might be able to help the unfortunate survivors. And I refused to believe that such evil would ever be repeated.

I entered the Faculty of Medicine in Zagreb in 1947. I was happy to be allowed to do so, as I had not been, nor have I ever been, a member of the Communist Party, and I knew that in many Eastern European countries such a career choice was practically impossible at that time, especially for those belonging to middle-class families like mine.

University Clinic Under Circumstances of War

My chapter deals with psychological and psychiatric responses to war, war that has formed and scarred me just as it has formed and scarred my patients. My colleagues in Eastern European countries describe the psychological impact of Communist dictatorship and years of inhumane manipulation on their patients. I describe war victims. My patients' mental disturbance is the direct consequence of the destructive impact of war on their mental and physical health. Past trauma, both personal and political, is imbedded into the trauma of the present. These people and their identities are dominated by fear of what they have just passed through and what they fear they must continue to pass through.

I was working as a supervisor and as a psychotherapist in the Psychiatric Department of the Medical School of the University of Zagreb, within the Clinical Hospital Centre Rebro. In this setting my psychodynamically oriented colleagues and I used a combination of psychosocial interventions and psychopharmacology to help us in our work.

In circumstances of war, the matter of our identity as psychotherapists, including our capacity for empathy, is a central one. As therapists in Croatia, we have been exposed to the same war conditions as have our patients, and these conditions make it difficult for us to remain totally neutral and objective as we approach our work. We find it difficult to avoid our own subjectivity as we approach the problems of trauma and loss in our patients, conditions so severe in refugees and displaced persons that even those with a healthy childhood show mental difficulties as a result (Klain & Pavic, 1999).

While our therapeutic goals must more and more effectively connect biological, psychological, and social factors, I think our most important goal is and will continue to be to provide psychological support to our citizens. But the scope of that task is enormous. The number of therapists trained to provide that support in contrast to the number of people who need it is daunting, to say the least.

Since the beginning of the war we have been concerned with 1,500,000 refugees. While they are not all mentally ill, many of them do need both social and psychological assistance, and we do not begin to have enough psychotherapists to treat all those who should be treated. These days we see fewer so-called classic patients—those with typical forms of neuroses such as various phobias and obsessions. More and more we are dealing with people who are in the midst of life crises, people who need help relatively quickly. For these reasons, I see us as functioning over the next decade in a team, collaborating with our mental health colleagues who are psychologists, sociologists, social workers, and nurses to offer psychological support to the many, many people who need it.

Military Psychiatry

At the beginning of the war, we at the University Clinic were assigned to provide psychological and psychiatric help for the soldiers of the Croatian Army and for the threatened civilian population as well. The military, however, did not greet us with what could be called open arms. Sometimes we felt a certain distrust on their side. They considered themselves to be mentally sound, not in need of our services as psychiatrists. But their attitude shifted gradually; they learned from us and we learned from them.

Our new experiences taught us that the management of panic among younger soldiers is best handled as close to the soldier's natural support network as possible, for example, by an older individual whom the young soldier may have known in the past, such as a priest or an older family doctor. We also learned that a young psychiatrist is much more useful at a field hospital somewhere at the rear than on the line of battle.

With these and many other principles in mind, we devised a plan of education that would begin with command staff and would include offering psychological support to the soldiers on the first line of battle. The strategy of psychiatric service in war would, in that way, include the education of commanders, provide for aid to psychically imperiled soldiers, and ensure qualified psychological or psychiatric help to enable both groups to carry out their necessary tasks.

The Psychiatric Needs of Refugees

As the war developed we soon learned that it was not only soldiers who must be our priority; increasingly displaced persons, civilians enduring the hardship of this war, demanded our attention (Jukic, Dodig, Kenfelj, & DeZan, 1997). This is a very difficult war, a war of ethnic cleansing and destruction, a war of horror that has never been seen previously. Sometimes it elicits not so much the risk of death but perhaps more the fear of death. This war, as distinguished from many wars in the past, has not been directed to the killing of soldiers, but often more to the destruction of the civil population. In its destruction of civil and sacred objects, and its spreading of misinformation to reduce civilians' and soldiers' motivation to offer resistance, it has also been a psychological war. We have people fearing sudden attack living under great physical hardship in cities that are surrounded for many, many months. These people have gone through great physical suffering due to the lack of food and fuel and the destruction of property. In these circumstances, I think that the military are often in a better psychological situation than civilians because soldiers in war have a specific mission: they have guns, and they know how to use them. It is probably children who suffer most terribly under these circumstances. As Anna Freud noted in the case of English children in World War II (Freud & Burlingham, 1943), we find that children who are separated from their parents in order to be sent to safe ground become very anxious, and that boys have more difficulty with this separation than girls. We made these observations first hand as our clinic took on the task of the mental health of nearby refugee camps.

Onset of Symptoms

For more than half of our refugee patients this was their first experience seeking mental health care. All the refugees we saw reported traumatizing events in connection with the war and their dislocation. Over half had a significant latent period between these traumatizing events and their reporting of symptoms. The specific war stressors to have influenced our patients were those which surrounded their decision to leave home. When leaving their homes, they could see fights in and around their houses, and bombing and shell showering of their neighborhoods. By this time, all their homes have been demolished or burned down, so that a return to them is physically impossible. Some reported that they left home since the key individuals in their life were killed, often in their presence. Others were exposed to real and severe threats of murder and material loss, or watched as this occurred to neighbors. A large number were exposed to multiple traumatic stressors, such as the death or disappearance of loved ones, the wounding of others, the loss of property and assets, etc. They explained that they left primarily to save their lives and those of their loved ones from imminent danger.

Two Symptom Groups

All the refugees expressed fear of remembering the past but they also reported fear of the continuing danger to relatives who had not escaped and were still exposed. Their symptoms can be divided into two main groups: 1) those whose symptoms centered on fear, anxiety, and PTSD; and 2) those whose symptoms centered on somatization and depression.

Patients in the first group had actually encountered direct and close danger (bombing, artillery attack, or infantry armed conflict). They had lost close relatives and friends, and they had witnessed death, fire, and destruction to their own and their neighbors' homes. They were exposed to physical threats and they heard recurrent rumors that even the current circumstances were dangerous (indeed refugee villages were routinely shelled to keep such fears alive). These patients presented with disturbed sleep, traumatic nightmares, and constant remembering of traumatic events. Many had lost interest in their surroundings or, alternately, were hypervigilant. Their concentration was impaired, they grew suspicious and alienated, and they became socially phobic and agoraphobic, fearful of groups of people and open spaces (of every scene outside their own most familiar surroundings).

The second group responded to similar stressor events with a somatization of fear: disabling aches, pain, and weakness, along with the loss of appetite, sleep disturbance, and weight loss. These refugees appeared hopeless and helpless and fell into frequent attacks of weeping. Interestingly, in these patients we found no oscillation of affect, early wakening, or depressive delusions; theirs were reactive depressions, not endogenous ones.

In both groups of patients we felt secure in attributing their pathology to recent traumatic life events: previous psychiatric history was absent, traumatic stressors were clear, and symptom pictures were appropriate to their trauma and loss.

Psychosocial Factors in Refugee Trauma

Several social psychological features of the trauma to these refugees are important, not only for characterizing their pathology but also in devising treatment strategies. First, the loss of home and place, which for many may have taken hours or even minutes, induced negative psychosocial changes which would be quite long-lasting. They experienced changes in role(s), interruption of work (in agriculture or the home), and clear and objective differences in daily living circumstances. It is no surprise that trying to absorb all these sudden negative changes at once strained their adaptive capacity mightily. While positive and negative changes in these aspects of life also occur in peacetime, as with economic emigration, in the context of peace they tend to be more volitional, more predictable, more gradual, and less traumatic.

A second negative factor in war migrations involves the sudden disruption of the usual social support. In these circumstances, familiar environments literally disappear. The persons who filled many of the refugees' daily living functions disappeared as well, separated from them by war or by death. The result is that refugees, when coming to a new environment, feel abandoned by the social field to which they had adjusted.

Such social psychological considerations play an important part in how we think of our primary therapeutic interventions, which, in addition to the refugees, often involve the structure and function of the refugee camp itself. We listen to, empathize with, and change, when we can, negative aspects of their new living conditions which had deprived the refugees of old roles and meaning. We try also to improve their new social environment. By offering adequate psychosocial help, we try to restore their lost self-respect and give them the feeling that they are not abandoned and that someone will still take care of them. For example, the general practitioner's tending to bodily needs with appropriate care and medicines is part of that older order that we try to maintain.

Those who are then sent on to the hospital receive dynamic psychotherapy based on empathic understanding of their dilemmas. We use direct problem-solving techniques, and we add pharmacotherapy as indicated, primarily for anxiety and depression.

Reactions of Therapists

Our psychotherapists, whether treating soldiers or civilian refugees, run into many emotional obstacles which can adversely affect their functioning. There is often insufficient time for each patient and insufficient sessions for the treatment. Therapists must often send patients, both soldiers and refugees, back to places from which they came even though psychotherapy is not yet finished. Such decisions present a moral dilemma for the doctor.

Our therapists are most often open to two kinds of countertransference reactions. In the first they may over-identify with their patients, substituting their own feelings, for example of helplessness and fear, in place of their patients'. In these treatments, the unique distinguishing features of the patient's experience and his or her own emotional reactions are not explored. In the second kind of countertransference, the doctor may be horrified by the contents of a patient's trauma and unable to continue psychotherapy. That occurs when the therapist cannot suppress antipathy for what the patient has reported. This happens, for example, in the treatment of soldiers who report having been forced to shoot and kill not only enemy soldiers but also, in the context of the war, innocent victims. Listening to these stories I find myself experiencing a mixture of anxiety, fear, horror, blame, and guilt. These are extraordinarily difficult circumstances in which to work.

We must also deal with patients who sometimes have religious or ethical or political views that differ from our own, or who belong to other ethnic groups. Here the therapist must proceed strictly professionally as all other doctors do (surgeons, for instance, must operate equally conscientiously on their own and enemy soldiers). The therapist must restrain his or her negative feelings so that they do not interfere with treatment. In the special situation of war, these are very difficult issues for therapists. We all are human beings after all; we all have values and loyalties, and strong feelings about them, especially in the face of atrocities that remind us of the horrors of the Second World War. Yet despite our personally held, very strong views, it is not our role to have those views disrupt our empathy with our patients, even when we are confronted with very difficult moments, as illustrated in the case studies below.

Viktor

Viktor, a sixty-four-year-old disabled veteran living on a pension, came for psychiatric treatment in December of 1991, about four months after the beginning of the war in Croatia. He complained of restlessness, agitation, disturbed sleep, and apathy. A traumatic nightmare which had been dormant for many years was recurring. In it he was blindfolded, tied to a tree, and awaiting execution. He awakened from it startled, perspiring and terrified, and unable to resume sleep. It had been thirty years since he had last experienced PTSD in connection with his World War II experiences.

When Viktor was 16, his father was a Domobran, the home guard or national guard which was then in league with the Croatian forces collaborating with the Nazis. But Viktor, along with his uncle, protested the brutality of the occupation by joining the underground pro-Tito partisan forces, fighting with Communists and against Nazis in Croatia's civil war during World War II. In May 1943 he was lightly wounded and taken prisoner. His captors tortured him in their efforts to extract information about the partisan forces and their military positions. In the most physically painful part of his experience, his captors broke his fingers.

But it was another event during that capture which has remained with him all his life. Two days after the pro-Nazis broke his fingers, Viktor was told that he had been sentenced to death—that he would be shot the following day. He was taken to the barracks and, at the expected time, tied to a tree in the courtyard. He was already blindfolded when another soldier arrived, explaining that the execution had been postponed. On the following day, he was set free. Viktor to this day does not understand how his life was saved. He returned to his comrades, spending only two days in the hospital before rejoining his partisan unit. Three months later, he was wounded again, when a hidden mine exploded, killing fifteen partisans and wounding sixty others. After three months in the hospital, Viktor again returned to his unit and served there with no further injuries until the end of the war.

Although Viktor's first few post-war years passed without significant emotional difficulties, by the early 1950s he began to experience disturbing dreams, insomnia, tension, and a general weakness. At the time, Viktor, as a decorated war hero, had been assigned the job of lecturing schoolchildren about his role as a loyal Communist partisan in the war. It was this activity that reactivated his distressing memories, leaving him with black and depressing thoughts. He was treated for these and other symptoms (fear, pressure around the heart, depressing thoughts) by Dr. Steve Bettelheim, at the time Croatia's most prominent psychiatrist (and my teacher). When he went to Dr. Bettelheim for help, he could not concentrate and felt a general sense of inadequacy, especially in developing relationships with people around him. He had no ambition to work, no sense of the future. Viktor reported that his greatest problem was this same recurrent dream after which he awoke in fear, disturbed and wet with perspiration. In his dream, he was being blindfolded and was waiting to be shot—a traumatic repetition of the very situation he had lived through in the war. That dream proved most resistant to therapy, recurring until the early 1960s. Then it disappeared, not to return until his current episode of illness.

It was his seeing soldiers who were dressed in the uniform of his old Yugoslavian Army, now invading his home in Croatia at the beginning of the current war, that once again triggered Viktor's PTSD. He again grew nervous and unable to sleep, and again experienced the terrifying dream. Now his nightmares awakened him and left him unable to go back to sleep. In the mornings he was tired and in a bad temper; in the evenings he feared the night and the recurrent dream. He felt cheated and betrayed, depressed and apathetic. He felt especially bad when he looked at the army barracks near his house where he used to go to enjoy the friendship of many of the officers. Now he felt threatened by those same officers, and the prospect of spending time with them left him tense and sweaty. Viktor tried to fight his black thoughts but had little success.

As he tried to understand what was happening to him, Viktor declared that his difficulties did not stem from regret for the past or fear of the current non-Communist authorities. He had joined the new Croatian government long ago and continued to support it. But a review of his history shows that the shifts in his emotional affiliations—and, perhaps, in his mental health as well—were radically affected by the warring political entities in his country. Viktor grew up in a household supportive of the Croatian forces collaborating with the Nazis; his father was a Domobran. As a teenager, however, he turned away from his father's influence to join the partisans and embraced the Communist cause. After World War II, he took pride in becoming president and secretary of a Communist Yugoslavian organization for veterans (all of whose members were former partisans). He devoted much time and energy to the success of this group, which stood for the same principles he held and which shared his history. Now, seeing soldiers in that uniform attack his home, he felt betrayed and overwhelmed.

Clearly, Viktor was suffering from chronic recurrent PTSD for which I prescribed psychotherapy and antidepressant medication. I found myself very interested in Viktor's case for several reasons. First, here was a case of PTSD which had been dormant thirty years before exacerbation. Second, Viktor's history includes the dividing of father from son on different sides of a war. Torture and preparation for execution nearly enacted in reality the oedipal fantasy in which the son is punished by death for fighting against the father. Further the recurrent dream of being blindfolded and expecting execution seemed to have several layers of meaning: Was it guilt from long ago over opposing the father, or over harming friends? Was it panic at imminent death back then, when he was so full of life, and now, as war again loomed? Or was it the opposite—a wish for death in the present because his identity (as loyal disabled war veteran) had lost its meaning now that Yugoslavia had turned against itself?

Therapist's Reflections

The case of Viktor was also distressing to me personally. As I listened, I was very aware that I too had been a boy during the Second World War, a time of civil war as well as world war. I too understood the dividing of a single family on the basis of political attitudes. As I was considering Viktor's dilemma during the first years of the new Croatian State, I held the view that the establishment of democracy in Croatia might be able to resolve our many political and national differences.

Observing and living for many years through all the experiences about which I write, I think to myself that all of us need to have one autonomous point in our ego (Hartman, 1958), a center within us which cannot be touched by neurotic or psychotic processes. We have to maintain one point, an ethical point, to survive this complicated situation. I remember that in the Holocaust, most of us were anti-Nazis and hoped that after the war something better would come. But what came was communism, with its own oppressive character. One must have a strong private self to survive such ordeals, such unexpected disappointments. Finding and maintaining this identity was frankly my key for surviving these harsh regimes.

As I reflected on what was constant in my identity amidst such change and turmoil, I have come to appreciate Viktor's aspiration to be an organizer among veterans. Perhaps what was unique and constant about Viktor's character and loyalty was not that he was for Tito's cause or the Yugoslav Army, but rather that he understood what it was like for boys and young men to sacrifice their lives and limbs for a cause in which they believed. Perhaps it was less important that disabled veterans during World

War II were loyal to the Croatian Home Guardsmen (Domobrans) or the partisans than that they shared a common history as Croatians. Could all these elements come together in a new organization of disabled Croatian veterans, where the identity was Croatian rather than Croatians split against each other at some period of history? Viktor accepted that outcome as a possibility and continued his work with my support. With these thoughts in mind, I encouraged him to pursue his interests in participating in such developments. And, as he invested his energies in the new project, we observed that his symptoms abated.

My work with Viktor was supportive and empathic. I am not a psychoanalyst and I did not interpret the many layers of meaning suggested by his symptoms. I used medication (antidepressants) to reduce the symptoms and improve his mood. I acted primarily as a social psychiatrist and dynamically oriented psychotherapist assisting him in applying his considerable ego strengths to a new task: the building of the Croatian veterans' group. Perhaps at some level, both his work and mine on inner identity amidst rapid change contributed to the positive outcome.

Viktor works now in the newly formed Croatian Veterans' Association, a group comprising all Croatians who have served in the military, regardless of their political sympathies. In this group of Croatian veterans, only war criminals are excluded.

Josip

Josip, a forty-five-year-old Croatian from Vukovar, a Croatian border city with Serbia to the east, presented to our clinic with traumatic nightmares, intrusive images, and depression one year after the fall of his home city to the Serbs, and six months after his release from being held as prisoner of war under brutal conditions.

Past History

Josip grew up in a traditional patriarchal Roman Catholic home. After World War II, his father, a farmer, moved from Herzegovina, where he worked on a poor and rocky farm, to Slavonia, a rich agricultural lowland, the most eastern of the Croatian provinces. There Josip's father settled in a multiethnic environment in which Croats, Serbs, Hungarians, Ruthenians, Czechs, Germans, and others lived together. Josip stayed in Slavonia and settled in Vukovar. He worked hard on his own modest farm as well as for other, more prosperous farmers. Later, he found employment as an unskilled worker in a local factory. Josip describes his father as a diligent and honest man whose work meant that he was often away from home. During the last years of his life, Josip's father developed organic brain syndrome. During the recent war with the Serbs, father was exiled from Slavonia by the Serbs and fled to Zagreb, and his condition deteriorated dramatically. He died early in 1994, quite demented.

Josip described his mother as a traditional housewife who took charge of her children's education and worked on the family farm, primarily helping to raise cattle. Although she was devoted to the family and was always considerate of her husband and children, she was never openly affectionate, either verbally or physically. She died of heart disease in 1987, at age sixty-eight.

Josip, his older sister, and younger brother grew up in a poor family that valued hard work, honesty, determination, courage, and respect for one's elders. Josip talks about his childhood in positive terms. He mentions being disturbed by the family's poverty but doesn't dwell on that fact. Instead, he recalls his involvement in his religion (he attended church regularly and served as an altar boy), his success in school (he learned easily and finished the eighth grade with top marks despite his many time-consuming farm chores), and his friendly relationships with his schoolmates, who came from varied backgrounds. Indeed, the pleasant time he spent with them at the river came to be very important to him, leaving him with a life-long image of the river as a source of pleasure and peace of mind.

During secondary school, Josip's attentiveness to his studies was gradually replaced by involvement in football (soccer), dances, and parties. He became interested in girls and in spending time with older friends. He began to drink, sometimes to excess, and sometimes found himself in drunken fights. Although he continued to help his parents on the farm, he grew less obedient; except on holidays, he stopped going to church altogether. Nevertheless, he continued to think of himself as a good Christian, complete with all the Christian values he had been taught. And as he had done since childhood, he maintained friendships with people whose status, religion, and ethnicity differed from his.

As soon as he finished school, Josip found a job as a laborer in his home city of Vukovar, interrupting it to complete his military service and returning to it once he had been discharged. As he had been at school, he was popular at work, and was promoted to foreman. The work ethic he had learned on the farm served him well: He was a responsible, versatile worker, competent in building a house, tilling the soil, breeding cattle, building a boat, and catching fish. Moreover, he applied his values to his assessment of others. What was essential, he believed, was the quality of a person's work and the conscientiousness with which he did it. Political convictions, religion, or nationality did not change these verities.

Josip married in 1969, choosing on his own a woman of moderate means rather than having the traditional arranged marriage. His bride was Roman Catholic, like him, and, like him, a Croatian born in the Eastern province of Slavonia. He describes her as cheerful, light-hearted, and industrious, and their marriage as relatively harmonious. Their differences were minor and easily solved, they enjoyed economic stability, and they provided their daughters with a good education. Josip's adult relationships with his siblings were also amiable. His older sister graduated from college, married, and moved with her family to Zagreb; his younger brother completed an apprenticeship before moving overseas and establishing his own family, becoming financially successful enough to send money to their parents and also to Josip, to help him build his house. Josip's friendships included people of many nationalities, but his special friend and neighbor was Dusan, a Serb, whose two sons were also good friends of Josip's daughters.

Although Josip enthusiastically accepted the idea of an autonomous and independent democratic Croatia, he was not politically active. He had never been a member of the Communist Party in the former Yugoslavia, for example, nor, after the proclamation of the Croatian State, did he join a political party. Nevertheless, after one bloodstained conflict between Croatian police and some Serbs, in which several Croatian policemen were killed, Josip volunteered to join the Croatian forces, believing that danger now threatened his home, his people, and his country.

By the spring of 1991, Serbs had gradually separated themselves from Croats and begun cooperating with the former Yugoslav Army. An atmosphere of inter-ethnic strain and suspicion developed, and patrols were organized to protect the villages. During this time, Josip remained friendly with his Serbian neighbors, all known to him to be peaceful people. He was particularly close to his nextdoor neighbor, Dusan. They talked seriously and often, and Josip tried to persuade him to join the Croatian Army in the defense of their common homeland, Croatia. But Dusan was undecided. Dusan's wife appeared pro-Serbian and anti-Croatian, as did Dusan's elder son. Dusan and his younger son said that they accepted Croatia, but Josip noticed a hesitancy in their statements.

Then came an outbreak of violent attacks on Croatians by members of the former Yugoslav Army and rebellious Serbs. East Slavonian women and children were sent by their families to more peaceful locales, away from the immediacy of war. When a Croatian Army was formed, most Serbs joined the other side. By the summer of 1991, although some Croatian and Serbian civilians remained in their homes enduring worse and worse conditions, Josip's family had gone to Zagreb (in Croatia) while Dusan's had gone to Belgrade (in Serbia). Josip grew increasingly active in the Croatian forces fighting in Slavonia; Dusan hesitated, protecting his house but otherwise remaining passive. The two men saw each other less and less often, and finally stopped meeting altogether. At the same time, the war spread throughout the countryside. Former Yugoslavian soldiers and rebellious Serbs instigated violent attacks on Croats, setting houses on fire and leaving death and destruction in their wake. The suffering of civilians, especially children and women, was intense. Schools, hospitals, and churches were destroyed; innocent civilians were massacred. Josip lost many friends who had fought beside him, including his brother and his sister's husband. The full horror of war had descended on the country. Then, one dreadful day during the fighting in Vukovar, Josip, looking through the site of his rifle, was shocked to recognize Dusan among the enemy. Moments later, just as he caught Dusan's eye and the two men stood looking at each other face to face, Dusan was hit by a bullet and slumped to the ground, dead.

The town of Vukovar fell to the Serbs in that battle, and Josip, along with his fellow fighters, was captured. He stayed in the enemy prison camp for five and a half months, exposed to a horrific spectrum of mental and physical maltreatment and an atmosphere of fear, helplessness, and humiliation that every day grew more intense. Prisoners were locked in what had been stables. They slept on the floor in bitter cold, the air permeated by fecal odor. Meals were distributed to the prisoners accompanied by comments hardly fit for animals. Worst of all was the behavior of the guards who seemed to be specifically chosen to torture and systematically destroy the prisoners. Earlier in the war Josip had seen dead Serbians torn apart by dogs; now he was among the victims of the bestiality.

Josip described the methods of beating, explaining that he had witnessed the crippling of some men. Others were taken away from the camp, never to return. Afraid that he would be killed and afraid for his family, Josip tried not to be noticed. He listened to the guards' steps and observed them secretly. When sober, the guards were somewhat better to prisoners, but when they were drunk, they were savage. They yelled at, humiliated, and beat the men. The uncertainty of the prisoners' situation grew more and more unbearable.

Finally, international organizations intervened in an exchange of prisoners, and Josip was released along with a large group of other men. Although now a refugee he felt delighted to have been left alive and to be free. He visited his displaced friends, and they discussed plans to return home. During the first month of his stay in Zagreb, he did not feel disturbed by what he had experienced. He submitted to all medical tests and dealt with administrative matters routinely. He followed the news, celebrated the successes of the Croatian Army, and looked forward to the prosperity of Croatia. Meanwhile, the war continued.

Two months after he had left the prison camp that Josip's problems began to appear. He became more and more apathetic, had trouble falling asleep, and difficulty staying asleep. His nightmares recurred. At his family's suggestion, he was examined by a psychiatrist, who diagnosed him as suffering from depression and PTSD, and prescribed tranquilizers (diazepam). But Josip did not improve. During the day he became increasingly weary, especially when speaking about his return to and the possible liberation of his native Slavonia. He avoided people more and more and felt disheartened. He noticed that some other refugees were unhappy as well, but he felt tortured to see them try to drink away their troubles. Josip smoked heavily, but he tried to avoid alcohol because he noticed it made him even more irritable and often reduced him to tears. He began to worry about other refugees who were living in cramped quarters, with up to three generations in a small room. (Josip, his wife, and his father were living at his sister's in a comfortable house; his daughters were also safe, having gone to stay with his brother overseas in the summer of 1993.) He grieved because he had lost track of many people from his district, many of whom were considered by the administration to have disappeared. He observed sadly the many widows, dressed in black, who visited various offices asking about their dead and missing family members. He felt annoyed by the bureaucracy and insisted that the human tragedy of the refugee was not sufficiently respected. He felt like a stranger in Zagreb, believing that the contrasts between it and Vukovar, from which he had been exiled, were too great.

In short, he felt worse and worse. He returned to the psychiatrist and was given new drugs, antidepressants, but still made no progress. Dreams continued to torture him. During the night he would wake up and go to the kitchen so as not to disturb others. He felt listless, helpless, hopeless. Afraid of what was happening to him, he turned to a fellow refugee for advice, aware that his friend had been helped by a psychiatrist at the Centre for Psychosocial Help. Josip too visited the Centre and was accepted for evaluation by the same young therapist, under my supervision. During the screening interview, Josip was given the Hopkins Symptom Checklist and the Harvard Trauma Questionnaire (Mollica, 1992). His psychological testing showed above average intelligence but impairments in mental efficiency, concentration, memory, and capacity to organize work. Significant elevations in anxiety and depression were noted, and Josip was diagnosed as having PTSD.

More than six months after he had been traumatized, Josip reported the intrusion of recurrent painful memories of what he had undergone during the siege, in the prison camp, and at the sight of his ruined home. Strange feelings of sorrow overwhelmed him. He cried often, became anxious, irritable, emotionally unstable. His interest in everyday events deteriorated. He lost ambition and willpower, saw no sense in the future, and found it increasingly difficult to concentrate. At times he grew confused and forgetful. Although he tried to avoid thinking about those trau-matic events, he could never escape them. He suffered even when watch-ing TV, since the programs either reminded him of what he had experi-enced or symbolized those events in his mind. By day he talked about his ordeals; by night he dreamed about them. He had difficulty falling asleep and difficulty sleeping without nightmares, since in his dreams the dread-ful, frightening scenes forever replayed themselves.

Treatment Plan and Process of Psychotherapy

Josip was first examined by a professional team consisting of a psychia-trist, psychologist, sociologist, social worker, and neurologist. Individual psychotherapeutic treatment followed his initial examination. The psy-chotherapy was combined with pharmacotherapy and with an integra-tion of the traumatic events. Josip met with this therapist for twenty-eight weekly sessions of ninety minutes each. He was prescribed flurazepam as needed before sleep and amyzol only when his depressive condition was aggravated.

In the initial sessions Josip appeared deeply regressed. He felt inad-equate and had exceptionally low self-esteem. His speech was unfocused and, at times, incomprehensible. In later sessions he said he remembered the details from his past but found it very painful to recall those memo-ries. It was especially difficult for him to speak about his dreams, which often included sounds of the battlefield, fighting, and scenes of violence and death. In one particularly threatening dream, accompanied by the terrifying scenery of war, Dusan appeared in front of him and looked directly into his face before falling dead. Josip would awake from this dream in terror, a terror which fused anger, betrayal, and rage at his friend (for abandoning him and becoming the enemy); sorrow, grief, and mourn-ing (at the loss of his good friend and all their relationship had meant); and guilt (that he had failed to convince Dusan to remain loyal to that multiethnic home which they had shared).

At the beginning of each session, he tried to control his emotions, but they inevitably overwhelmed him. He reacted sometimes with anger, sometimes with aggression, often with tears. In his efforts to resolve his feelings of sorrow, guilt, and disappointment, he frequently spoke guiltily of his failure to live up to his religious principles. In referring to the con-flict in which Dusan died, he lamented that before the war they had been very good friends and neighbors. Josip counted on Dusan's taking his advice and joining Croatia's cause, but, to Josip's great disappointment, just the opposite transpired. "I am guilty of not persuading him well enough, so that his wife's anti-Croatian rhetoric convinced him."

As his psychotherapy progressed, Josip explained that he was no longer able to be like other people. He walked the empty streets, ate alone, avoided talking to others, and feared falling asleep. Every discussion, he said, was hard for him. His thoughts were chaotic and he was increasingly tortured by guilt, especially about Dusan; he had lost touch with Dusan's children and didn't even know their address. He felt sorry for them because he was certain they lived in bad conditions. Sometimes he felt a strange impulse to let them know how and where their father died. He was anxious about the fact that Dusan's children and his had been such close friends, had even loved each other in a way. Perhaps there was even more to his guilt over Dusan.

In later sessions, Josip talked about his dreams about the prison camp, but here too he had doubts: Although he clearly believed that the camp guards had behaved as beasts, in his dreams he tried to find in them some human traits. "In spite of the fact that they treated me awfully, sometimes there is some strange feeling in me that they should be forgiven. It is perhaps my deep Christian education that requires forgiving. But all that creates confusion, chaos in myself." After such words he would tremble, cry, and become angry with himself.

A clinical regression occurred between sessions 21 and 23 as his guilt about his own violent impulses, particularly around Dusan, became most important. There were images, for example, of a dead enemy being torn apart by dogs. This period was crucial as well for the therapist, who up to this point had empathized deeply with Josip's sorrow, but insufficiently with his rage. The shot which killed Dusan: could it not, in fantasy, have come from his own rage? By the end of this period an important shift occurred in Josip as he now felt he could acknowledge and accept the military impulse to shoot his own friend, a man whom he truly had loved. Here, his therapist's empathy helped him accept the paradox. He came closer to integrating good and evil in himself and therefore in others. In the 23rd session he said, "My dream started horribly. Dusan appeared again. This time, however, I saw him as a calm man looking into my eyes with a mild expression on his face. I was no longer afraid of him. After Dusan's face appeared, everything became more peaceful at the battlefield. I could see the blue sky of Vukovar again. Everything was full of green vegetation and I woke up with a pleasant feeling. In a way, I was sorry to wake up. It was a wonderful feeling, and it would be excellent to have it last. I have the feeling that this is a beautiful dream in which I am reconciled with myself, accepting life and wishing to live more every day."

Gradually Josip began to accept the reality of the past and of the present. Most important, he accepted himself. In objective terms, he could concentrate better, could recall the past events without fear, could feel the joy of living, and, more and more, could remember the beautiful moments from his past.

In his daily life Josip functioned more and more adequately, only occasionally falling into bad moods. He became increasingly aware of the people around him, enjoyed their company, and started arranging his sister's courtyard in Zagreb. He noted that he had begun to laugh again. By the time therapy was terminated, Josip was doing construction work for a private builder and making plans to build a small house with his wife.

The therapist was a young woman psychiatrist whom I supervised. She used a combination of psychotherapy and pharmacotherapy with Josip. Our procedure called for flexibility and an interdisciplinary approach, the aim being to relieve Josip's psychosocial difficulties and prevent an intensification of his symptomatology. We chose this approach because of the intensity of his experienced traumas, his situation before the exile, and the ongoing difficulties of life he experienced in the former Yugoslavia (the continuation of the war, the decline of social standards, the daily struggle with a host of administrative difficulties, and the ongoing uncertainty of the refugees about their return from exile, among many other expectations).

We determined that the level and condition of Josip's psychodynamic development at the start and duration of the traumatic events had an important role in the formation of his PTSD with a dominating depressive syndrome. That syndrome was probably also conditioned by Josip's separation fears. In his life before the war as well as during psychotherapy, he idealized places and people and found it difficult to separate from them. He idealized Vukovar, for example, the home he was forced to abandon; he nursed his very sick father until his father's death, never considering a hospital or nursing home in spite of all his own troubles. He idealized his relationship with Dusan and was blocked at mourning his loss. Even though Dusan, a Serb, ultimately allied himself with the enemy, Josip could not get past his great disappointment, guilt, and grief at the loss of his former neighbor and friend. During the initial phase of the therapy his therapist took a supportive empathic, almost nurturing, role. This position was natural for the doctor as she too had been exiled from her home during the war, so she comforted Josip much the way a dutiful daughter would support her anguished father. They spoke together of a longing for the peacefulness of the river of childhood.

Perhaps for those reasons, the therapist was reluctant to observe that Josip, often unconsciously, refused to accept his aggressive impulses and fantasies. Instead, he consciously wanted to attribute wishes to kill and destroy only to the enemy. His self-respect as a pious, decent man was dependent on external authority. He was submissive to his father, all of whose requests he wanted to satisfy. In the transference he accepted every kindness addressed to him by his doctor passively but with delight, as he had with his mother, who had complied with his wishes as a child. But he also wished to engage his therapist in the father transference: what did she think of his fear of being killed and his impulses to kill?

The war itself influenced Josip in many ways. It undermined his self-confidence, endangered his hope, shook his optimism, and transformed his purpose in life. It left him with doubt about himself and others as well as feelings of humiliation and inferiority. At the same time, his ethnic identification as a Croat from Vukovar grew progressively stronger as he identified the rebellious Serbs and former Yugoslavian Army forces as obvious aggressors. As his sense of belonging to his native region intensified, Josip longed for home, for Slavonia, and had difficulty orienting himself to the new environment. His dreams of Dusan, clearly defined as an aggressor at the manifest level, provoked ambivalence in Josip. He could not forget the pre-war situation when he had experienced Dusan as a good neighbor and friend, and his dreams of his former friend included feelings of guilt. He tried to resolve his conflict with Dusan and by the end of therapy, Josip had done much to integrate this ambivalence. He strengthened his identity and accepted the fact that, in certain circumstances, good people can change and do bad things. That understanding allowed him to accept reality and feel less disappointment in people like Dusan whom he once idealized. Finally, Josip settled down. His ability to adapt improved, he lost feelings of sorrow and guilt, he accepted reality and once more enjoyed life, and he became active in life and work.

The Therapist

A woman in her thirties and the mother of one child, the therapist was living through her first war. Like her patient, she had been driven from her home town by the Yugoslavian (Serbian) army. She had watched the town being shelled and could picture it being overrun. She too knew the pain and loneliness of the loss of friends, community and home, and the strangeness of life in Zagreb. In her early sessions with Josip, she responded warmly and openly to his longing for the sea and the river; his longing for home mirrored her own. She shared with him her own experiences of military siege, and of being a child in a patriarchal family. And, she extended the sessions beyond the usual time frame.

But she found this over-identification wearing and ultimately became distressed as Josip shared some of the hateful things he had participated in prior to his being captured. She found herself feeling resentful and even fearful of him in an understandable countertransference withdrawal. During the period of Josip's clinical regression, he felt disconnected from his therapist. Ultimately her withdrawal was changed by the work in the supervision (see below) and by her recognition that even in the midst of the worst horror Josip's compassion was never far away. For example, he quietly took the time to bury the enemy soldier whose dead body had been torn apart by dogs.

The Supervisor

Unlike the young therapist, I am a sixty-five-year-old man who has had several experiences with war. During my life, I have survived the birth and death of four political systems, each with opposing values. These experiences generated a series of crises in me concerning my origins, my identity, my values, and my recognition of the potential for brutality we all share. I adapted and survived in large part because I found a hard-won inner balance, a personal ethic existing in a world of violence and contradiction. My education—especially my study of psychoanalytic concepts such as our common drives and defenses and our individual search for personal meaning—certainly contributed to my understanding of myself. That education offered me a perspective on my past reality. I learned from it that I needed to adapt myself to precarious life conditions, and to confront and contain my emotions, especially during therapeutic work and especially in this brutal war, one which has led to hard inner conflicts and mental disorder in people who have been jeopardized, both directly and indirectly. As I listened to the therapist, I understood her over-identification with Josip and cautioned her to understand it, lest it wind up interfering with their work. Yet in this world of war I also understood that such strong ties between doctor and patient might evolve, and to some extent even have some beneficial properties. What became clear as the treatment proceeded, however, was that it was Josip's rage and his own violent impulses which he could not accept and which the therapist, in her over-identification with him, could not see.

As is sometimes the case, the supervision took on its own life. The therapist told me of her home town and of her losses. As I listened she became first more comfortable in sharing some of her grief and then more aware of her rage at what had occurred and her own violent impulses in response. More accepting of herself, the therapist was now able to be more understanding and less frightened of her patient's violent impulses and deeds, stories, and fantasies. Now she could hear him talk while retaining her own sense of value and identity. I believed the initial over-identification in this case was of less danger to the therapy than an opposite situation in which therapist and patient take an essentially different view of life and avoid therapeutically engaging the trauma and war. Helping the doctor to address her inner conflicts helped her patient to do the same. In this way, Josip's psychotherapy was carried out and, we believe, successfully concluded.

Reflections

In the more than sixty years in which my home has been in Zagreb, I have lived under four radically different regimes which have died: the monarchy of the Southern Slavs, the Nazi-dominated fascist dictatorship of the Ustashe and the concurrent civil war, Tito's Communist Yugoslavia, and the post-totalitarian Communist years; I now live under the current Croatian nationalistic government. These regimes and those of surrounding states held starkly contrasting visions of the present, the past, and the future. Each demanded harsh adherence to political doctrine in the present. Each called on its citizen alternately to remember or to repress cruelty or multiethnic civility, Serbs as enemy or as brother. Each utopian world-view when compared with the next regime was full of paradox and contradiction: chauvinism versus pluralism; ethnic revenge versus brotherhood of workers; investment in the State as an expression of group values versus fear and resentment of the State as the will of enemies. Maintaining continuity of an inner identity amidst political regimes which disrupt such continuity is a central task for many in my country, for the patients we see, and the doctors who treat them. And the recent bloody war which went on between Serbia and Croatia had terrors that are more horrible than those from World War II. New war for some patients revives old trauma. Yet in contrast to some in the West who view the "Balkans" as a vestige of ancient hatreds, I am more and more certain that atrocities between neighbors are the exception in our history and not the rule.

The span of my memory of events in Europe and in my country covers a longer period than my much younger colleagues from Eastern Europe who also take part in writing this book. I am closer to the age of their parents, a fact that is essential for an understanding of the thoughts and feelings I experience while seeing the people with mental disorders who are my patients.

In the end it is both the stability of my identity (professional and human) which has helped me to survive this series of political systems, and my ability to adapt which has enabled me to maintain that continuous sense of self.

Chapter Highlights

1. Among those at risk in the ethnic wars of the post-Soviet period are civilians armed and unarmed whose homes stand in the way of advancing military. They are exposed to trauma, loss associated with war, and the abusive violence associated with ethnic cleansing and deten-

tion camps. They then become refugees displaced by war. Soldiers of course may also experience trauma leading to PTSD. Dr. Muacevic describes strategies to offer services to both groups, the first in refugee camps and the second treating military casualties at the front and in civilian hospitals.

2. The collapse of the unifying superstructure of Communism has unleashed in the Balkans and elsewhere severe ethnic divisiveness. But rather than being a war of clans in mortal combat as one might deduce from afar, the actual surface of these wars (because of their complex histories) touch people whose closest friends are now enemies. Further, divisions in political loyalties in the twentieth century have been within the family as well as outside it. With such radical and sudden changes in the political/military climate, and the exacting tests of loyalty by new governments philosophically opposed to their predecessors, the problems of PTSD are overlaid with crises in personal and social identity.

3. For Josip and his therapist whom Dr. Muacevic was supervising, the critical moment in the treatment was when the patient was ready to reveal his exposure to abusive violence and his reactions to being treated like an animal. Countertransference revulsion on the one hand and over-identification with the abused victim on the other warded off and stirred ethnic passions in the therapist as well as the patient. Sensitive management in the supervision and in the treatments are essential to successful outcomes. While North American clinicians may prefer to see themselves as immune from the clinical problems presented in this chapter, we continue to see Vietnam veterans suffering the effects of abusive violence, we work with refugees from around the world subjected to the equivalent of ethnic cleansing, and we see victims and perpetrators of hate crimes in our own communities.

4. Like accounts of the nightmares of Viktor and of Josip, Dr. Muacevic's chapter is about old scars and new wounds, implying a complex history of injuries, attachments, and new injuries over the lifetime of his patients and over the centuries regarding his country. In the following sketch, Ivo Banac places these injuries and attachments in his historical context.

Historical Sketch: Croatia

Ivo Banac

Croatians in the Twentieth Century

The Croats, a branch of the South Slavic peoples, settled the western portions of the Balkan peninsula in the seventh century, and established their early medieval kingdom in the tenth century. The Croats entered into dynastic union with Hungary in the twelfth century. Although Roman Catholic by religion, they were unique in the Western patriarchate in having received the papal sanction for the use of Church Slavonic in liturgy. Their union with Hungary did not diminish their separate institutions (a parliament, separate mint, and armed forces) which provided the Croat nobility with extensive autonomy until the early modern period.

Late fifteenth and sixteenth centuries were the era of Croatia's rapid decline. Buffeted by Ottoman incursions, the Croats sought protection from the Austrian Habsburgs and other Christian rulers, thereby opening the gates to the partition of their lands among the Turks, Austrians, and Venetians. Their institutions were increasingly subjoined to Habsburg interests, their lands having become a war zone between Vienna and Istanbul. Moreover, the Habsburgs settled the frontier provinces next to Ottoman Bosnia with Orthodox Serbs, who, in turn, valued their independence as Habsburg frontiersmen over potential communal interest with Croatia. This grim situation continued until the early nineteenth century.

For Croatians, the idea of a common South Slavic state, or Yugoslavia, first took form in the nineteenth century, when the middle class began to assume leadership. A national revival brought about a high degree of cultural unity in all the Croatian lands, and promoted goals of greater autonomy and even independence from Austria-Hungary, the political entity of which they were a part. These goals were in part pursued together with the Serbs. In fact, by the beginning of the twentieth century the most influential Croat politicians favored a common Yugoslavia (together with Serbia and Montenegro).

The South Slavic or Yugoslav solution was tested after 1918, with the dissolution of Austria-Hungary in the First World War. Unfortunately, instead of national equality and a major role in the running of the new State, the Croats and the other non-Serbs discovered that the new state was effectively an expanded Serbia. The monarchy, the civil administration, and the army were all slightly adapted Serbian institutions. Although the Serbs represented only a third of the population of Yugoslavia, they effectively held the reins of power by patronage and a variety of electoral and economic manipulations.

The Croat opposition, however solid, was unable to provide a democratic cure. In 1928, a Serb deputy assassinated Stjepan Radic, the chief Croat leader, on the floor of the Belgrade parliament. The political disarray which followed provided King Alexander I with the opportunity to introduce his personal dictatorship in 1929. Political parties were banned and the king promoted his own version of Yugoslav unitarism, which was directed against Croat "separatism," but not against Serbian hegemony. This was the dark period of police terror and the rise of modern totalitarian movements. Both the Communists and the Ustasas (Croat fascists) sought to capitalize on national disaffection in Croatia. Behind them stood the Soviet Union and the fascist powers of Italy and Germany.

In 1934, King Alexander I was assassinated. Organized by the Ustasas and backed by Mussolini, this event provided an opportunity for a restructuring of Yugoslavia. Prince Paul, Alexander's cousin and regent of Yugoslavia, reached an agreement with the Croat leadership in 1939, establishing an autonomous Croatian banate or province. But this piecemeal solution was consistently undermined by all extremists who got their chance to change matters after the Axis attack on Yugoslavia in April 1941.

The occupying powers—Germany and Italy—dismembered Yugoslavia and created their nominally independent Croatian dependency out of rump Croatia (Italy having helped itself to sizable parts of the coastal province of Dalmatia) and Bosnia-Herzegovina. Ruled by the (fascist) Ustasas, this state terrorized Serbs, Jews, and Gypsies. It was a scene such as this, the men hanging from trees, which Dr. Muacevic recalls from his childhood. Massacres, concentration camps, and everyday forms of discrimination provoked partisan resistance, which was organized and led by the Communist Party. (It was in this context, fighting for the Communist partisans, that Dr. Muacevic's patient, Viktor, as a boy of seventeen, was captured, tortured, sentenced to death, and escaped.)

The Communists, in turn ruthless towards all those who stood in their way, used sometimes conflicting ideals to promote their own revolutionary goals: Croat and Serb patriotism, no less than the notions of Yugoslav and Slavic unity, the promise of a democratic future, and social equality. Communist forces could not be successfully countered by the collaborators who had compromised with the enemy, either Serb royalists (Chetniks) or Croat Ustasas, nor indeed by the weak democrats who had no armed forces in the field. After the Western Allies threw their support in 1943 behind the Communist leader Tito, himself a Croat by nationality, the Communists encountered less and less resistance in Croatia. By 1945 they commanded an army of over 150,000 Partisans.

The Communist victory brought Croatia the status of a federal republic within Yugoslavia, but on a fully centralized Soviet model that afforded little autonomy and less democracy. Moreover, the Communist victory was accompanied by widespread executions, massacres, and repression. The Yugoslav party's emulation of Moscow, sometimes even in excess of it, created strains in relations with Stalin, who provoked a conflict with Yugoslavia in 1948, hoping to purge Tito and make the Yugoslav Communists as obedient as the rest of the satellite leaders. Having survived this challenge, Yugoslavia, under Tito's leadership, changed course and increasingly drifted in the Western direction. (Dr. Muacevic, for example, unlike the other therapists in this book, identifies his psychiatric education as being Western.) By the mid-1960s, this led to more pluralism and greater self-rule by the federal units, including Croatia. This trend, however, had its limits. When the liberal Croatian Communist leadership opted for a political course that effectively promoted a confederation of Yugoslav republics, a market economy, and more openness in the media, it was quickly purged and replaced by "anti-nationalist" leaders, who kept the republic in deep freeze until the mid-1980s.

Tito's death in 1980 provided an opportunity for Serbian Communist leaders to begin revising the dead leader's federal system. They used the Albanian disturbances of 1981 to begin agitating for the change of the constitution. In time, after Slobodan Milosevic seized full reins of power in Serbia in 1987, Serbian pressures created enormous problems for the leaders of most other republics. Slovenian Communists were the first to respond, challenging Milosevic's hard-line and centralizing approach. By 1989, with the backdrop of Communism's collapse throughout Eastern Europe, the Slovenian lead was followed by the Croatian Communists. It seemed that the systemic endgame throughout the region provided the most logical exit from the Yugoslav State crisis. Slovenian and Croatian Communists, followed by their comrades in Macedonia and Bosnia-Herzegovina, opted for free elections in which they all lost power, mainly to nationalist leaders. Milosevic's response was to metamorphose into a nationalist himself. He then faced the new leaderships, especially in Croatia and Bosnia-Herzegovina, the republics with sizable Serb minorities, with the following dilemma: Either stay in Yugoslavia on my terms or leave after surrendering those of your territories that are by my yardstick properly Serb. The resulting warfare and "ethnic cleansing" are the historical backdrop for the cases presented in this chapter.

In June 1991, Croatia declared independence from Serbian-dominated Yugoslavia. A few months later Milosevic directed the Serbian-controlled Yugoslav People's Army to march on Croatia. It was this sight—troops wearing the uniform of his own former Yugoslav army invading his native Croatian town—which set off in Viktor, Dr. Muacevic's patient, the symptoms of delayed PTSD. As part of the same Yugoslav offensive in 1991, Serbian and Croatian elements in many towns, such as Vukovar, split into warring factions. It was in this context that Dr. Muacevic's second patient, Josip, fought against his Serbian neighbors, was captured and tortured, and later survived as a refugee. A similar process, in 1992, led to the Serbian attack on Bosnia-Herzegovina and, in 1999, an invasion of Kosovo. The results are well known and extreme in every fashion. This was a war, not just for territory, but for the reconfiguration of territory, "ethnic cleansing" being the handmaiden of new borders.

CHAPTER

Armenia

Editors' Note

Dr. Levon Jernazian grew up in Armenia and was a psychotherapist and school psychologist in a center of reform activity there in 1988. His grandparents escaped Armenia during the genocide of 1915, although his parents returned from the European Diaspora in 1952 in response to Stalin's propaganda about new opportunities in the new Soviet Armenian state. Well after Kruschev had cleared the path for critical thinking about Stalin's era, Dr. Jernazian conducted scholarly work in Armenia on the psychohistorical significance of the image of Joseph Stalin. Indeed the central point of that work was to critique Stalinist thought as a revived form of paganism.

During the epic events of 1988–89 Dr. Jernazian served both as psychological consultant to leaders in the reform movement and as a trauma therapist following Armenia's devastating earthquake.

In his first case, we observe a typically Armenian cultural attitude of "protecting" children by denying them access to the truths of disaster, trauma, and loss that are around them. We also see the earthquake and its aftershocks as symbol of devastation and rebirth. His second case highlights fundamental problems of split-off levels of awareness among officials in the Communist Party, of people who both perpetuate traumatic conditions and are mightily influenced by them. In this case, an outward effusiveness covers panic attacks, phobia, and self-depreciation.

Dr. Jernazian's colleague, Dr. Anie Kalayjian, also a grandchild of Armenian survivors of the genocide, is an Armenian American and a professor of education and psychiatric nursing at the College of Mount Saint Vincents in New York. She organized a mental health intervention in Armenia following the Armenian earthquake (Kalayjian, 1994, 1999). Her poignant clinical observations in this chapter focus on interventions with teachers and with her grieving KGB hosts.

We note here the symbolic role the 1988 earthquake in the trauma history of the Armenian people, and the perception of relief efforts at the time in shaping Armenia's current independent status from Russia (Goenjian, 1993).

Armenia: Aftershocks

Levon Jernazian
Anie Kalayjian

Introductory Reflections

Our story in this chapter is from two perspectives, that of Dr. Levon Jernazian, a native Soviet Armenian psychologist from Yerevan, and that of Dr. Anie Kalayjian, an American psychiatric nurse of Armenian background from New York City. We first met in Armenia several months after the massive Armenian earthquake of 1988. Like many other members of the international health community, we had been drawn to Spitak, the quake's epicenter, to try to be helpful especially to the children whose lives had been shattered by this disaster. It was at an elementary school near the site of the earthquake that we began working together.

For those of us who had grown up in Soviet Armenia, and were acutely aware of the rapid and enormous political events which preceded and would follow the earthquake, it went without saying that such a disaster would have major political overtones: that the survivors would experience the collapse of buildings, the massive human tragedy, and the delays in rescue operations in the context of a land run too long by a hostile Party apparatus.

For those of us with a Western perspective, it was difficult to integrate the harsh political dimensions of this natural disaster. Was this not the world of *perestroika*? Wouldn't relief assistance from the central government in Moscow be offered quickly and be gratefully received?

172

Dr. Jernazian's Story Begins

My part of the story begins the winter before the earthquake, when, on February 24, 1988, I was one of several demonstrators on the square in Yerevan, speaking out in favor of the Armenian democratic movement and the return of Nagorno-Kharabakh that was forcefully annexed to Azerbaijan by Stalin. Our families and friends warned us constantly of danger from the KGB, but each following day my friends and I returned, convinced that now was the time. And each day the crowd of demonstrators grew until, in just three days, it reached one million.

By February 27, 1988, after seventy long years of Soviet domination, I was one of the one million gathered in a spontaneous rally at that same square, now named Freedom Square, demanding the recognition of the Armenian people's cry for democracy and the recognition of our neighboring countrymen in mountainous Kharabakh as part of a legitimately restored Armenian people. Ours was a hope-filled show of solidarity before the Gorbachev government, an outpouring of long-repressed national and democratic strivings.

I felt swept up that winter day by powerful historical and moral forces, and by social psychological changes which, in fact, had been my academic interests for years. I wondered, for instance, about the enormous internal psychological changes the future would require of our people, as we were starting to throw off the "inner slave" in us all.

I felt especially close to those few with whom I had been in the square each day since February 24. In the days to come, many of my friends would be arrested. I would be lucky to be spared this fate but I would continue to feel deeply connected to those in prison, as I had gradually become the informal psychological consultant to those in leadership positions in the democratic reform movement.

Nine months later, on December 7, 1988, at 11:41 a.m., a catastrophic earthquake hit northwestern Armenia, leveling Spitak and Leninakan (presently Gumri) and badly damaging nearby cities. Surviving that earthquake, gradually becoming aware of its enormity, and choosing to participate in its aftermath as a trauma therapist placed me in yet another awesome context, one which included confronting unimaginable feelings of fear, rage, pain, and loss, all of which were aggravated by the State's failure to act responsibly, by bureaucrats who hid behind collective irresponsibility.

On December 10, behind the shield of Gorbachev's visit to the site of catastrophe, a new military commander was appointed back in Yerevan and the leading members of the Kharabakh committee (my friends) were arrested. They remained in prison for six months, until May 31. Their release signaled the beginning of a victory for Armenia, and national and world events moved quickly in the ensuing months. Their release was another momentous experience for me, encapsulating what seemed to me a dual renewal: Greeting my friends and understanding the implications of their return for the eventual independence of Armenia coincided with my experiencing the earthquake survivor's will to live beyond the initial trauma and loss. For me, these two events fused into one experience, transcending the usual psychological dimensions and bringing an existential, almost spiritual dimension to my work.

In September 1991, Armenia elected Ter Petrosian, former leader of the Kharabakh committee, president of an independent Armenian state, a political event nearly one thousand years in the making.

Dr. Kalayjian's Story Begins

My part of the story begins in the winter of 1989–90, as we received word in New York of the extent of the damage from the Spitak earthquake. Older members of my family recalled friends left behind in Armenia. We were concerned for their safety, stunned by the enormity of the devastation, and anxious to help in any way we could. My Armenian roots were never very far beneath the surface. I had been born in Aleppo, Syria, to an Armenian couple, one a survivor of the Ottoman Turkish Genocide of 1915–1923 and the other a child of a survivor. My father and his parents were forced to leave their ancestral home and lands, and to walk for several months through the desert to get to Syria. Although Syria was very hospitable at first, providing shelter and allowing Armenians to live there, later this understanding evaporated. In Armenian schools in Syria, I was not allowed to study Armenian history or religion. Arab inspectors, intermittently and without notice, popped into our classes to examine and inspect.

Also at this time (1967), the Syrian and Israeli conflict was ongoing. I have very vivid and traumatic memories of hearing Israeli planes flying so low and close to our house that they shattered our windows; they bombed civilian dwellings too. All too often we found ourselves with no school, no playing in the streets, no food, and no hope. Blackouts and running into dark and damp basements were an everyday experience. Oppression from within and threats of ultimate destruction from without were evident. Oppression was also experienced inside our homes, the Armenian homes, for women and girls. In a double standard my brother could go out to play when it was safe from the enemies, but I was forbidden to do the same because I was a girl. Most of my female classmates were forced to get married after completing the eighth grade. It was because I was fortunate to have an older brother, an Armenian Apostolic Priest, who was an American citizen and who sponsored our emigration from Syria, that I had more opportunities than my childhood classmates. I received my high school diploma in the United States, and masters and doctoral degrees from Columbia University in New York City. It was as a psychotherapist with a special interest in trauma and natural disasters that I developed a Mental Health Outreach Program post-quake for Armenia and sent over fifty mental health professionals to help the survivors. Despite a cold response from Armenian authorities, I pushed ahead and arrived in Armenia six weeks after the earthquake.

The Psychological Role of Armenian History

The Armenians are a people with origins in antiquity as were the Babylonians, the Syrians, and the Hebrews. Christianity was adopted as the State religion early in the fourth century A.D.; and since then the church has played a major role in sustaining our sense of national identity. In fact, it was our people's primary unifying factor in our many years without a national homeland. When Armenian communities would move to different locations around the world, the first thing that they would build was a church, a symbol of our viability.

Greater Armenia, located at the crossroads of Europe and Asia between the Mediterranean and the Black and Caspian Seas, spread out from the mountain of Ararat, the legendary landing place of Noah's ark. What remains of our homeland is now southeast of its original location, sitting below the Caucasus Mountains and the former Soviet Georgia at the eastern edge of what modern cartographers delineate as Europe. As one of the few Christian nations in that area, we have been for centuries in constant conflict with our neighbors. Our villages and towns were repeatedly destroyed. Time and again, the Armenian peasant had to pick up the pieces of his life and start over.

In this long history of strife and devastation, a crucial event is the genocide of 1915, when one million and perhaps as many as two and one-half million Armenians were exterminated as Western Armenia was absorbed into Turkey (Hovannisian, 1988; Kupelian, Kalayjian, & Kassabian, 1998).

Between 1908 and 1912, the "young Turks," originally a force for liberal change in Turkey, took a militant turn. In 1915 Turkey determined to solve the "Armenian question" by annexing Western Armenia, driving its people into the desert, and annihilating them. It seems impossible that this genocide could go unnoticed in world affairs, but that is precisely what transpired. Initial cries in the Western press were drowned out by the rapid developments of World War I nearer home. Even today, Turkey officially denies the genocide. The Russian stance, consistent with Soviet ideology, was that the genocide had been a kind of bourgeois revolution occurring within Turkey. No one in the world even seemed to know or care that a whole people was being slaughtered. Hitler's question illustrates how completely this event was eradicated from the world's memory: In answer to whether there would be independent protests against his "final solution to the Jewish question," he asked, "Who remembers the Armenian genocide now?"

Two years after the Armenian massacre, Russia erupted in revolution, and by 1921 that battle, too, was exported to Armenia. Through a minority party, the Bolsheviks used terror and the massacre of dissident Armenian party members to take control of the country. As it fell under the shadow of revolutionary Russia, Armenia could not have been at a lower point in its history. By 1923, Lenin had put Stalin in charge of the Trans-Caucasus provinces (Georgia, Armenia, and Azerbaijan). And Stalin, in one of his many moves to destroy the nationalism of these ethnic groups, redrew boundary lines, awarding Kharabakh, a mountainous region populated by Armenians, to Azerbaijan. Unable to grieve its massive losses, truncated in its geography, Armenia during the years between 1921 and 1939 plunged into the dizzying changes of forced collectivization and the purges of the bourgeoisie, intellectuals, and even its own old-guard Communists.

Despite the catastrophes in Armenia at the end of World War II, when Stalin called for the survivors of the genocide to return to the homeland as repatriates from Europe and elsewhere, his call was heeded. After all, Russia had long been Armenia's benefactor; "modernization" was evident; the Soviet Republic of Armenia had preserved the ancient language and proclaimed itself to be the carrier of its culture; and an ideal state was still in the making. Yet this rationale for return proved faulty, and those who returned were shortly to be bitterly disappointed—among them, my parents.

Dr. Jernazian's Story Continues

By the time I was born in Armenia in 1958, my parents had fallen from great hopefulness to great despair, for they, too, were among the Armenians of the Diaspora whom Stalin had seduced back to the homeland to build an idealistic socialist state. In Armenia, as everywhere in Stalin's empire, paranoid purges wiped out all potential enemies of the State. Free speech was abolished, and my parents quickly learned they must be silent if they were to survive: Many Armenian "repatriates" were being sent to the gulag in Siberia. Nevertheless, in our home my parents' European education and values were never far away.

Also of great influence upon me were my four grandparents, all survivors of the Armenian genocide by the Turks. They had survived genocidal marches into the deserts of northern Syria and had emigrated to Europe and the Middle East. They kept alive the hope that in better times our people would return to Armenia, but they could never forget the horror of the genocide.

Asking my grandparents directly about their experience of the 1915 massacre left me frightened and bewildered about events I could picture but not understand. In response to my questions, my normally stoic patriarchal grandfather wept uncontrollably, saying only "such horror." In my mind's eye I saw skeletons, especially skulls, littered over a desert; I saw brute sadistic faces butchering innocent, defenseless people, beating and raping them. I remember the story my grandmother told about a girl and her mother who were starving to death in the Der-Zoor desert and smelled meat cooking at the neighboring campfire. They were cooking human flesh. When the mother asked for some meat for her starving child and was refused, the little girl said: "Don't you worry mother, when I die you can eat my flesh but not give any to them." (Today, I use this story to illustrate psychological differences between human and animal instincts at my psychology classes.) And yet I also remember my grandparents explaining to me that it was Turks, friends and neighbors of my grandmother's family, who had saved them all. "Don't speak of all Turks as evil," they told me. "Some of them saved our lives."

While my parents had learned quickly that they must be publicly silent about their thoughts, they maintained our home as a sanctuary where they could express their true feelings. Thus, throughout my childhood, I recall in their daily homecoming the release of all the frustration and tension which they had kept pent up throughout the day. For me home became a place of truthful reflection, of open bitterness, sorrow, and anger.

It seems to me that as early as I can remember my education ran always along two tracks. One followed the official system, which demanded conformity to Marxist-Leninist doctrine (however it was currently interpreted); the other was driven by a ruthless search for truth, first because that was my parents' passion and ultimately because it became my own. Officially I was a bright student, although somewhat suspect as the son of "repatriate" Armenians. I mastered the official doctrine easily, learned to report what was expected—and disbelieved this level of discourse from the moment I was conscious of it. Yet I made no official or public errors, a record which aided me in standing for my dissertation at the age of twenty-four.

I developed a passionate hunger for knowledge of another kind. It was this side of my education which led to my lecturing in my 8th grade class about the Armenian genocide (an interpretation of events "disavowed" by the official Kremlin line); choosing the Western topic of empathy as the subject for my dissertation, informally and secretly examining the myth of Stalin from a psychological perspective, and studying psycho-analytic psychotherapy extensively, especially Jungian theory. It now seems to me that my choices were dictated by my conscious and unconscious defiance of the regime and its ideology.

The worst of Stalin's crimes were behind us but adherence to doctrine was stultifying. I was acutely aware of how the Soviet system, in fostering slavish dependency, continued to sap any potential for initiative and responsibility in people. My parents' silent critique of the Soviet system found in me a ready listener. By 1990, the USSR had taken an official anti-Stalin attitude, and that gave me the opening to pursue the publication of my research on Stalinism. How ironic that the opportunity to use my mind in the service of critique and responsibility was open amidst the general repression of our lives.

In the 1980s I had studied and semantically analyzed the excessive flattery of official writing and poetry in praise of Stalin. During the time that I was conducting my "top-secret" studies behind closed doors I did not even dare to imagine that some day I might think about their publication. But the compulsion of my unconscious anger and revenge for my parents and all those who were oppressed was imperative. Content-analyzing this source material, I proposed the view that, on the larger psychohistorical scale, Stalin's reign represented an arrest in spiritual development with a regression to the phase of religious idolatry or paganism. I argued that the God of Christianity, a God of love and forgiveness, had been overthrown, and an all-powerful, ruthless, archetypal god-hero, Stalin, had taken the pedestal. Marxist-Leninist theory stated that the great force of Communism was to be led by a dictatorship of the proletariat. Once Stalin personified the leader, however, that concept soon came to mean loss of responsibility for the individual, with total dependence on the god figure. Concepts of universal love and brotherhood of man were replaced with selective solidarity of proletariat against the "class enemy" of world bourgeoisie and imperialism. Stalin represented a personification of an archetypal god who is all-knowing, all-powerful, all-seeing, all, all, all—except one. He was not immortal. This is where the myth of Stalin-god betrayed millions of his worshippers. He betrayed by the mere fact of his death. Here, according to my interpretation of official poetry, is where mass anger led to a frantic search for substitute gods especially in those who followed him.

These broad brush strokes do injustice to my studies but at least offer a perspective on some of my work. Upon completion of my dissertation I began my clinical work as a psychologist in Armenia. At the same time I read extensively and gained training from a Jungian perspective, which greatly influenced my work. I was struck in these years by the terrible cost of having to say things one way in public, and being able to say things another way in private, to speak the truth only to one's closest friends and family.

By 1988 my life had led me to what was, given my education and my values, perhaps an inevitable political involvement. I had become deeply committed to the movement for an independent democratic Armenia, which was already well underway, and deeply involved with its leaders. The leaders of this movement were people I had known for many years. Our paths had crossed in the intellectual life of Yerevan, and some of our families had distant ties. We knew and respected each other, personally and politically. Gradually these leaders turned to me in my role as a psychologist: They wanted my help in assessing the psychological strengths and weaknesses of our opponents inside the power structure, in predicting the reliability of those who wished to help us, and in determining the veracity and management of information leaked from the government. They also turned to me in less overt ways as we all struggled with matters of courage, fear, and guilt. After all, at any time any of us could have been arrested, and the need to survive such an ordeal with integrity plagued us all. Each of us feared the specter of imprisonment and physical torture. Each of us privately wondered how we would withstand pressures to retreat. Each of us feared the blow to ourselves if we were to endanger others.

When the time for arrest came, I was spared the ordeal. Indeed, I thought this would be the case when the KGB did knock on my door and searched my office. But they could not find any incriminating papers, and abandoned their search.

In the end, I believe we all learned something of the power of our own private fears. As one of those imprisoned commented to me after release: "What is 'fear'? It is only my idea of it."

We shall present briefly four therapeutic encounters, two from my work and two from Dr. Kalayjian's work. The first gives a glimpse into what it was like conducting psychotherapy in the Brezhnev years, at the height of the "double speak" when our public words and private thoughts were so disparate. The second is a trauma therapy with a child survivor of the Armenian earthquake. The third is with a KGB host during outreach to earthquake survivors. The fourth is with teachers at a school affected by the earthquake. The first two are presented by an Armenian who has, from his earliest historical memory and at the deepest level, been opposed to the Soviet Communist regime and what it did to the initiative and responsibility of the Armenian people. The last two are presented by an Armenian American learning freshly the impact of the Soviet legacy.

Vahan

Hedrick Smith (1976) described individuals within the formal Soviet bureaucracy who illustrated George Orwell's concept of double-think most dramatically. I (Dr. Jernazian) find these people enforce sharp boundaries between themselves and others. These boundaries then detach their communication, that is their movements, behavior, and words (which must always be consistent with current Party dictates), from the much more complex world of awareness in which they consciously scan their environment, gather input, and process their ideas and perceptions. In this sharply bifurcated existence, people will often say one thing and be aware that quite the opposite is the case. An incongruity between action and belief almost goes without saying.

This kind of Soviet bureaucrat does not acknowledge feelings, which are seen as troublesome, brewing in an unconscious mind, which have no place in the "real-politik" of everyday life. Thus feelings are repressed and detached; awareness is screened and censored; and words and behavior are devoid of the richness usual in other societies. The result is a mask, friendly enough on the surface, but a mask nonetheless. My first case is my psychotherapy with such a man.

In the early 1980s, at the time of this psychotherapy, I formally held the position of head of the psychology and sociology department at the Scientific Method Center in Yerevan, a branch of the State's Ministry of Culture. The position was as high as I could go without compromising myself by joining the Communist Party. But even in this position, as head of psychology, I could not officially see patients at the Center on a confidential basis. When patients wished to see me for psychotherapy, therefore, we would meet in my home in order to preserve confidentiality.

It was in this way that I began to see Vahan G. in the early 1980s. This was the period when the government, in the form of totalitarian Communist ideologues, was violently repressing everything that was alien to the principle of Marxist-Leninist philosophy in an attempt to compensate for the apparent lack of its effectiveness. Behind the bright facade of official propaganda, a new class structure and class psychology were being developed with opposing sets of class interests. The social, political, and psychological gaps separating the workers from the intelligentsia, and the powerful elite of Party bureaucracy from either group, was growing. The result of this opposition was an increasing hostility.

It was in this atmosphere that Vahan, a forty-three-year-old Armenian man, came to my office—a self-referral, with multiple psychosomatic and phobic complaints. He had a history of duodenal ulcers and severe migraine headaches and was afraid of airplanes, elevators, dogs, the dark, and closed spaces. His symptoms (his phobias and psychosomatic illness) and his relationships with others were wrapped together in a vicious downwardly spiraling cycle. Efforts to extinguish the symptoms behaviorally and return him to his previous level of adaptive functioning not only did not help but further intensified his pain. Psychiatric medication had failed, and Vahan was desperate.

In our sessions, I learned that Vahan, a talented individual, was the oldest of four siblings raised in a traditionally patriarchal Armenian family. His father, an industrial worker, was strict and distant; his mother, was submissive and accepting of the father but withdrawn, depressed, and ungiving to her son. Vahan was now married with three children and had become a highly placed bureaucrat in the Armenian Soviet Republic. Nevertheless, he found himself unhappy in his work, especially around issues of authority, and dissatisfied with his wife, who turned away from him, and his children, who feared rather than loved him.

By the time he began therapy, Vahan's phobic symptoms and his duodenal ulcer were seriously impairing his capacity to work, yet air travel was necessary for his many trips to other republics to plan and arrange the flow of materials and goods to Armenia. It was especially important for him to fly to Moscow, where the crucial official decisions were made. Once he arrived in Moscow, he was faced with having to ride in elevators and to sit through long hours of meetings in windowless rooms.

Before Vahan's therapy began, we had agreed on a private fee, but curiously, he insisted on paying me "extra" for each session. Usually these "gifts" consisted of items such as Western cigarettes which were impossible for normal Armenians to buy but which were plentiful among Party officials. I would refuse the gifts; he would persist even more adamantly. Eventually I became aware of a vulgar, depreciating characteristic of this gift-giving: It struck me that it was a bribe.

My approach to Vahan in the treatment was quite straightforward. Using the positive paternal transference that was mobilized, I took direction of the steps he should take. I instructed him to carry out deep breathing and relaxation exercises in the office, and we imagined together the phobic tasks, using the new technique to gain control of his anxiety. Then I instructed him between sessions to practice certain behaviors, getting him closer and closer to carrying them out. Sometimes I would structure an assignment using paradoxical intentions. The results were good, and his phobic symptoms were alleviated.

In the more psychotherapeutic aspects of the case, Vahan gradually opened up regarding the unhappiness in his life, speaking about the coldness and lack of intimacy in his marriage and his problems in sustaining an erection during sex. While to the world outside the Party he appeared powerful, within the Party and in his own unconscious view of himself he felt closed in and helpless, depreciated and devalued. Now as he described the way he degraded himself by rushing to offer the biggest bribes to officials in Moscow in order to achieve something at home, he understood the terrible price he was paying. And I understood better why he didn't want to fly; why he didn't want to go in elevators or sit in closed-in rooms; and why he reversed this state by trying to bribe me with expensive gifts as well.

Countertransference: Dr. Jernazian's Story Continues

At this point I was also better able to articulate a countertransference reaction I had to Vahan from the very beginning, one based on our radically different political and world views. Vahan was by all external standards handsome, intelligent, verbal, and particularly successful in the Party. But he was a party-industrial bureaucrat, and I lived on the other end of the class structure with my family and my personal animosity about the system and its representatives.

My first reaction to this realization was to refer Vahan to someone else, and I had begun considering ways to make this transition easier for him. Before I could take any practical actions, however, we had already established an excellent rapport. Moreover, I found it interesting that none of my negative feelings surfaced during the sessions. Indeed, our sessions went very smoothly, with a lot of sharing and direct mutual communication, and it was clear that Vahan was already making some progress. After the sessions, however, I had a hard time. It seemed as if I was forcing myself not to like Vahan, to view him in terms of the value system imposed by my personal and family history.

My conscious attempts to resolve my dilemma only intensified the conflict. On one level I was enjoying working with this patient while on the other I was experiencing a sense of betrayal. It seemed as if I were betraying my friends and the friends of my family who had been repressed by Stalinist purges, betraying the sacred soul of hostility and nonacceptance of the system which bound me to my frustrated parents repatriated from the West.

Ultimately, my incongruent feelings started to show in my work. I became aware that I sometimes became overly directive, less responsive, and more and more forgetful—for example, about giving Vahan a new appointment at the end of each session. Finally, when I abandoned attempts to force a rational resolution to the problem, my resolution of the conflict came through, and I felt that I understood the nature of Vahan's conflict: he, like me, was just another victim of the faceless and repressive system, but on a different level. He was even more of a victim than I was because he did not have the privilege of maintaining a dignified silence or expressing his divergent views either privately among friends or in carefully circumscribed innuendo in public and professional appearances with peers. In both his outside and inside world he had to talk, and talk convincingly, about things and ideas in which he did not believe. Incongruity between his feelings, his awareness, and his efforts at communication generated the unconscious conflict that resulted in his symptoms, symptoms which inhibited his carrying out actions that went contrary to his true beliefs, symptoms which transferred inhibitions and suffering onto himself. In other words, the notorious resilience of Homo Sovieticus to feel, think, and act on three different levels gave way to the truth of the unconscious.

The effect of this realization on me and my relationship with Vahan was immediate. The channels of emotional closeness and empathy were finally open, and I started to perceive and interpret him in a completely different light—the light of the person-centered emotional understanding when "I" and "thou" are not separate entities but parts of an organic whole of the universal human cosmos.

Grigor

On December 7, 1988, I (Dr. Jernazian) was in the middle of a typically busy day in my job as head psychologist at School #183 on the outskirts of the city. My duties included testing teachers, counseling teachers and students, and conducting research in teaching methodology.

It was going to be a busy but routine day. I had appointments scheduled for the whole day and a meeting that evening. I do not remember my first thought when I felt the earth shake, but my first emotional reaction was one of uncertainty. I heard someone yelling that we should run out of the building, while someone else was telling us to stay where we were. Panic seized the school. By the time I realized I should leave my office, and the building, the strongest quake was over. Then I was consumed with worry about my family. Thank God, I thought, when I found that the telephone lines were not damaged. My family was fine.

Although aftershocks were felt for a couple of hours, I continued my work, dutifully according to my schedule, as if nothing had happened. Under a cloak of denial and repression, I covered up all thoughts and feelings about the earthquake for the sake of the tranquil predictability of my daily routine. I didn't even think (maybe I did not want to) about the possible destruction and victims. In fact, I didn't hear until my evening meeting any hint of the devastation, but that night the first reports about destruction and victims came in from Spitak and Leninakan. Even then the initial reaction of those of us at the meeting was denial. The air was so full of rumors that it was hard to trust anything you heard. The truth, however, emerged the next day with the first official communication. It was horrible.

My first direct experience with the tragic consequences of the earthquake was at Yerevan Hospital #8. There I found workers transporting the survivors, women, men, and children, from ambulances to hospital rooms. I had never seen so much bloody suffering in my life. At first I could not register individual faces or specific people; I was too stunned by the scene, the oppressive black cloud of bloody bandages, pain, suffering, and indescribable tragedy. It was already dark by the time I reached the hospital, and that made everything feel like surrealistic fantasy. The dark, faceless crowd, and the screams and suffering of the victims made me panicky. A feeling of impotence crawled all through me like a snake: the feeling that I knew I could and had to do something, but there was nothing I could do.

In the days that followed I saw patients at Yerevan Hospital #8, but I wanted to work closer to the major devastation, especially with children. In Spitak, an Italian agency had set up a temporary home for displaced children. It offered the opportunity to join a treatment group without being part of an official Party-organized relief effort. This suited me well since my rage at the government was continuing to mount now that I was witnessing first hand the incompetence of Soviet-based assistance.

At the home for displaced persons, I saw Grigor, an eleven-year-old boy who had lost his entire family. Although it was now a month after the earthquake, nobody had yet told him that his family was dead. He was living in a temporary relief village on the outskirts of Spitak with his distant relatives, and he had developed numerous phobias of strangers, robbers, darkness, earthquakes, etc. As a part of my getting to know him better, I offered him white paper and colored crayons and invited him to draw. Then, as he became more comfortable, I asked him to draw his fears. I felt tears swelling in my eyes as I watched what he drew. He seemed to be calm while he was obsessively going over the details of his picture with the black and red crayons he had chosen. It took him an hour and three continuous standard-size papers to complete his drawing. Using only the red and black colors, he drew overturned buses, destroyed houses, coffins, and crushed people. As he worked his way from left to right across the page with his ghastly images, I simply added the next page until he had finished his kaleidoscopic vision of disaster. At the same time I tried to track my own images as he worked. In my interior "drawing," I found myself as a boy confronting a monster and then a huge wall, tall and impenetrable; then my images took me inside the wall into a very dark tunnel which twisted and turned in frightening ways. This blackness was not only my reaction to Grigor's despair as he chronicled his images on the paper. It was also a countertransference confirmation that he knew his parents were dead. Then in my mind's eye I saw a small light; it signaled my resonating with a latent hope in Grigor that he would find his way through this terror. When he was finished drawing, I knew that he was aware that he would never see his family again. Spontaneously, I took his hand and held it tightly.

At that moment I did what I had never done before: I laid aside everything I learned in graduate school and instead I tried to face and overcome my own fears as they resonated with Grigor's to take him on the archetypal journey I had experienced while watching him draw. "Would you like to make a trip with me?" I asked him. He was apprehensive but agreed. I closed my eyes and asked him to do the same; together we went on a dream trip of light and darkness, of a boy's conquering the monsters and walls of his fears. And I took him to that image of light which I had seen. In the final stage of our image journey, Grigor stayed with me as we entered a purifying river, a symbol, I thought, of acceptance. When we had finished, Grigor went outside, joining his friends with a boyish energy where earlier there had been a total void.

For me, conducting psychotherapy would never be the same.

Dr. Kalayjian's Story Continues

My part of the story begins with the earthquake. Like Dr. Jernazian, once I had learned of the devastation it caused, I too felt compelled to try to use my professional training to address the emotional needs of its survivors. But because I was based in New York City at the time, doing so proved quite a challenge. As an American mental health professional asking to gain access to the Soviet Union in order to organize and deliver a mental health outreach program, I met with a cold response. The initial reaction of Soviet authorities was, "We don't need psychologists or psychiatrists; we need medication, surgical equipment, and disposable syringes." From their point of view, accepting mental health assistance was tantamount to admitting that they had lost their minds. Perhaps they suspected that Americans would come in and "read or control" their minds. After all, they had used psychiatry in this fashion when handling their own political prisoners. A Soviet official from Moscow stated explicitly, "We lost some lives, arms and legs, but we did not lose our heads." These responses can easily be identified as resistance, since the casualties of the earthquake, according to some reports, had climbed from 25,000 to 130,000. Such discrepant figures were in part due to poor systems of reporting under the former Soviet regime, but mostly due to the more than 300,000 Armenian refugees in Nagorno-Karabagh who had escaped Azeri oppression and pogroms and had fled to Armenia. In the end, some 25,000 Soviet Armenians had died, and another 500,000 were left homeless, handicapped, or otherwise affected: A calamity of this magnitude had to have an emotional impact.

Only after six weeks of ongoing communication, negotiation, and persistence, was I permitted to go to Soviet Armenia to conduct an on-site assessment and to develop and implement the Mental Health Outreach Program (MHOP).

On day one in Soviet Armenia, I was called to come down from my hotel room to meet members of the Ministries of Health and Education. As I was leaving the hotel, I saw a group of middle-aged men in dark suits and solemn faces waiting by a black, unmarked van. The sight of the black van startled me. At first I did not understand my reaction: chills running up and down my spine, my heart racing, my knees shaking. Then it dawned on me where these strong negative feelings had originated. I remembered visiting my uncles and cousins who had immigrated from Soviet Armenia and had settled in California in the early 1970s. I remember them as filled with so much pain, fear, and resentment, and I remember their stories of horror about the Communist regime, about oppression, deception, and fear. We had spoken, debated, and cried from dusk to dawn. A system nourished by oppression, deception, and fear had stripped them of their right to be responsible, to be human; and it had replaced those rights with terror, dependence, and an existential vacuum.

Their stories of horror always involved a van. I had learned all those years ago that a black, unmarked van approaching a house was the ultimate nightmare in Soviet Armenia. It marked you for a life without life. The van could take you away in the middle of the night; no one would know where you had gone or when you would return—if ever.

My trance was interrupted by a stern hand touching my shoulder. "The people in the van have been waiting for you." So, it was the KGB who were to escort me to schools in Yerevan, Leninakan, Kirvakan, and Spitak to conduct the first phase of the Mental Health Program needs assessment.

When we arrived at the first school, I found myself surrounded by tears and sorrow, and devastation of a magnitude I had never before witnessed. There were piles of steel, chunks of concrete, leveled buildings, and the stench of corpses. People wandered about wearing inadequate clothing, their eyes filled with tears and grief, shock and disbelief. They were terrified of impending aftershocks, and their hope of finding their loved ones was shrinking rapidly. Most of all, they asked "why?"

Mr. R.

For a few days we were escorted around by the solemn men, wearing dark suits and a flat affect with a depressed undertone, in the black, unmarked van. In time one of them, Mr. R. developed an attachment to me and began to open up about his own story.

On day five, we passed through fifty-six villages, all reduced to rubble and stripped of their humanness: Witnessing this we couldn't help but cry. It was then that Mr. R.—one of the men in black who had been assigned to escort us—also broke into tears. His crying soon turned into uncontrollable sobbing. He looked away from me and mumbled that he was sorry to have disappointed me by losing control and crying. I held his hand, gave him tissues, and told him that it was okay to cry. I was pleased that he had been finally able to express himself. Together we left the van and began walking the deserted streets, but even then he continued to look around suspiciously and asked me not to share this information with his superiors or colleagues.

What was amazing to me was that he claimed to be sobbing not because his daughter—twenty-four years old with two children—had died in the rubble in Leninakan, but because he was furious at the Soviet regime. "They" (the Soviet system) had made it impossible for his daughter to buy or rent a house in Yerevan, the capital, where the rest of his family lived. He said no one had a choice; the system made decisions as personal as choosing a dwelling; the system controlled their lives, their relationships, all communication; the system had looked the other way while the Azeris oppressed Armenians in Nagorno-Karabagh, a 4,000-square-kilometer enclave originally ruled by Armenians, mostly populated by Armenians, but governed by Azeris since 1923 when Stalin just gave the region to the Azeris. Mr. R. told me about the massacres and pogroms in Sumgait and Baku, where dozens of Armenians had been killed, houses burned, women raped, and set on fire.

He then went on to tell me how he had not been able to express his happiness when he had first heard about Stalin's death. Instead, when his son had come home crying that the teacher had said "Stalin Daddy" had died, he and his wife had shed false tears so that their child would not naively tell his teacher that his parents hadn't cried, much less that they had felt happy upon learning of Stalin's death. He then described the horror of Siberia, the perpetual terror it had instilled in them. He explained how, in the street where he grew up, their neighbors all kept their bundles (*dzerar*) ready by their doors; after all, no one knew who would be next to go to Siberia.

He also told me about his recurring nightmares in which he is forcefully being taken to Siberia to clean up the rubble. His personal guilt in not being able to save his only daughter was coupled with the guilt instilled in him by the system. He felt he was betraying the system by criticizing it, yet he was paranoid about all other Soviets. He said, "With you I feel safe; you'll be going back to America in two weeks. But I can't trust my own wife or child. They could be bribed or used as informants. Many people had been caught that way." Feelings of guilt and anger caused him many sleepless nights; working endlessly to cover up the painful feelings had been his only recourse.

I discovered that the earthquake survivors expressed their anger very frequently. This is contrary to previous research in this area, where natural disasters are referred to as "Acts of God," a label which automatically eliminates human involvement and leaves no target of resentment and anger. The targets of anger in Armenia included the Azeris, the Turks, and, most of all, the Soviet regime, the Soviet authorities, the Soviet caregivers, and the Soviet builders.

Ms. M.

Although there were a handful of trained and educated psychologists at the sites I (Dr. Kalayjian) visited, survivors expressed distrust and discomfort at reaching out to them and getting help from them. Survivors stated that the Soviet "doctors" didn't care, that they weren't trustworthy like the ones from America. As a result, dozens of people waited for hours in the hotel lobby from dusk to dawn just to talk with me. Most did not want to talk in the hotel since they believed the rooms were bugged. They said, in Armenian, "Sister, you don't know the Soviet system; I've lived here all my life. Here, the walls have ears."

The walls may have had ears, but the people did not. . . .

On day six, we went to Leninakan to continue the assessment phase. I found myself working with fourth graders under an army tent, in mid-January, in sub-zero weather. As a tool for diagnosis I asked them to do a structured drawing: to draw their homes after the quake. As I was going around giving paper, pencils, and pens to the students, I noticed that their teacher was walking up and down the aisle with a ruler in her hand, looking over the children's drawings critically and instructing them to draw "straight." Even the demolished houses the children were drawing were expected to be "straight." This outrageous instruction exposed the inflexible structure, the pressure to be in line with the system, and the control over free expression. I was furious when I heard her words. Indeed I was impressed by the intensity of the rage and anger I felt toward her. I knew it was taboo for a therapist to identify with her clients in this fashion, so I began talking to myself: "Anie, you are not angry at her;

you're angry at the system, the oppression, the distrust, the emotional imprisonment, which is similar to what you felt growing up in Syria." In the meantime, a few students had noticed my anger and were absorbed in wonderment and adoration.

By this time I was playing the role of "dedicated therapist," feeling an intense pressure to help everyone, and working at least eighteen to twenty hours a day. It seemed everyone, without exception, needed some form of psychiatric treatment, not just those surviving the earthquake. At first blush, one could loosely diagnose everyone as paranoid with a depressed undertone. But as one took the system into consideration—the Soviet environment and conditions in which they had lived—one realized that they had perhaps a healthy reaction to an unhealthy environment.

On the seventh day, I toured the schools in Yerevan, continuing my assessment. I had a group meeting, debriefing teachers, half of whom had been directly affected by the earthquake and had come from Leninakan to Yerevan for shelter. I began the session by giving didactic information about disasters and their impact. Then, I opened the group to the members, encouraging them to talk about their own experiences and feelings. There were four men in this group of twelve. As Ms. M., a teacher from Spitak, the quake's epicenter, described how she had witnessed the death of many of her students and how she had felt helpless and guilty, a large crystal-like teardrop rolled down her right cheek, so slowly that it seemed as if she was willing it to stop, but in vain. The moment defied description. As group members watched helplessly, she described the full horror of the earthquake and the ensuing devastation. Everyone was tightly clutching the seats of their chairs as though they would otherwise fall off. When they saw the teardrop, all eyes rolled toward me, seeking my reaction. I felt an initial identification with their feeling of helplessness but immediately pulled myself out of it. Before I could say or do anything, however, the teacher sitting next to Ms. M. pinched her and whispered in Armenian, "Girl, it's shameful {amot eh}." All eyes rolled back to Ms. M. to make certain that she stopped crying; then the eyes rolled back to gaze at me once again. But now tears spilled down my cheeks, and I said, "It's okay to cry. There is no shame, no 'amot' in expressing your feelings appropriately; it is healthy for all of us." As I relive that moment in writing, tears are again in my eyes; but these are tears of joy—joy at being a part of the transformation of the oppressed into the free, of *peristroika* and democracy.

I looked around the room, my eyes still wet, and was relieved to see more tears on more faces, perhaps for the first time. As handkerchiefs were passed around, so were feelings of connectedness, acceptance, and freedom. Initially there was some resistance by the men in the group, but then one of them asked bluntly, "Do you mean to say that it's healthy for men to cry too?" I was silent and looked around in elicitation of group input. After a long pause, Ms. M., who had become the initiator for the group, said humorously, "You always think you're special, different, don't you?" Everyone cried and laughed together.

Concluding Reflections

The sequence of events in 1988–89 taken together make a story which for us is greater than the sum of its parts. Despair at the arrests and the earthquake coupled with hope provided by the prisoners' releases and the survivors' will to live was so intense, so beyond our imagining, that living through them and to some extent transcending them has literally made us different persons. Our stunned grim despair at the scene of death in Spitak, our fury at the system which intensified that suffering, and our terror at the arrest of colleagues combined to reduce us to an emotional nadir in which we were overwhelmed by a sense of helplessness. Dr. Jernazian's quiet confidence that Grigor would see his way through his tunnel of despair, his certainty that change was possible for the Armenian people, and his joy and relief that his friends were free—these were the dawn of something new. Dr. Kalayjian's feeling the presence of tears and then seeing the earthquake survivors—including a KGB member—break through years of suppressed sorrow gave her access to the potential for transformation.

The earth's plates shifted at the eastern-most edge of the European continent causing the tragic quake in Soviet Armenia. Simultaneously, the Soviet Union attempted to shift from a vertical society, in which decisions are handed down from above, into a horizontal society in which decisions will be made increasingly by the people themselves.

Transcending the fear of the pagan-Communist god, transcending the grim death of the earthquake, transcending our people's subservience to masters throughout much of our history—these are powerful times and powerful ideas. For us they have existentially altered who we are.

Chapter Highlights

1. Survivors of the Armenian earthquake of 1988 experienced a horrific natural disaster. The psychological aftermath to this natural calamity, like the famine of 1937–38, became interwoven with a history of political repression thereby distinguishing it from most natural disasters in the West. One cannot view this trauma population without reference to the political backdrop. It occurred in a setting in which build-

ing structures were inadequate, relief efforts tardy and lacking in coordination. The aftermath reinforced a general conviction on the part of Armenians that the Soviet government would not and could not protect its citizens. On the other hand, there were important similarities to disasters in the West which provided opportunity to implement creative mental health care as described by Dr. Kalayjian. Significantly this was one of the first times many Western mental health trauma professionals worked side by side with their Eastern counterparts.

2. Dr. Jernazian presents the case of a bureaucrat, a party member within the Armenian Soviet Republic's hierarchy. Here we see the crushing psychological impact of a corrupt and eroding social/economic structure on an individual trying to balance obeisance and the wielding of power. His symptoms of impotence and phobia take on a wider psychosocial symbolism.

3. One critical moment in the psychotherapy of eleven-year-old Grigor is the timing of identifying hope poised next to despair. Dr. Jernazian underlines the critical role of authentic hopefulness and directness in the treatment of bereaved children who are survivors of disaster. North American clinicians are well aware of adults who wish to protect children by shielding them from tragic news. In Armenia such attitudes appear endemic, as does the attitude of public composure rather than expression of emotion. In her school consultations, Dr. Kalayjian helps to establish a climate in which responsible adults are permitted to feel and express emotions, even to model such feelings in the service of facilitating mourning in the larger community.

4. The chapter has an existential and holistic, almost religious, tone to it. The tone reflects Armenia's history, an ancient Church-oriented culture which has survived great hardships, being surrounded by enemies for centuries. In addition to the trauma of the Soviet era it has experienced a genocide, and a diaspora in the twentieth century. Arthur Martirosyan and Yitzhak M. Brudny explain this unique history in the following historical sketch.

Historical Sketch: Armenia

Arthur Martirosyan
Yitzhak M. Brudny

When Mikael Gorbachev turned the world stage of diplomacy to Armenia in the wake of the tragic earthquake of 1988 he faced there not only the devastation of natural disaster but a rapidly unraveling political situation set in motion in part by his own policies of glasnost. *Reform-minded Armenian intellectuals like Levon Jernazian and his friends were raising issues of ecological ruin, russification, and territorial injustices. Massive rallies in Yerevan, capital of Armenia, first directed themselves at the threat of nuclear and chemical ecological disaster—"the white genocide." Soon, however, demands for reunification of Armenia with Karabakh, the territory transferred to the Azerbaijani jurisdiction in 1923 and predominantly populated by ethnic Armenians, became the main political thrust of the movement. In an unexpected move, the Karabakh legislature, previously a rubber stamp for Party policy, voted 110 to 17 to intercede with the USSR Supreme Soviet for the transfer of Karabakh to Armenia. This legislative initiative triggered pogroms of Armenians in Sumgait, Kirovabad, Baku, and other Azerbaijani cities with significant Armenian population. By late 1988, tens of thousands of Armenian refugees began to leave Azerbaijan for Armenia in what turned out to be the beginning of the bloody war between the two republics. Ironically many of these refugees had settled in the Armenian cities of Leninakan and Kirovakan just a few days before the massive earthquake of December 7, 1988, devastated these places and left 20,000 dead and half a million homeless. This, then, was the immediate historical setting in which Dr. Jernazian, a member of the reform movement, and Dr. Kalayjian, a Western colleague, began their work with survivors of the earthquake.*

The events in the late 1980s were further steps in trends which had arisen earlier. As in other Soviet republics, the post-Stalin era witnessed the rise of a nationalist movement in Soviet Armenia. On April 24, 1965, an unsanctioned demonstration commemorating the fiftieth anniversary of the Armenian genocide took place in the capital city of Yerevan. In the 1970s, a variety of dissident Armenian groups advocated issues ranging from defense of human rights, preservation of the Armenian language as the official language of the republic, to independence.

Still, these events occur in a much larger context of Armenian history spanning three millennia. The Armenians are descendants of Proto-Indo-Europeans. There are about 6.9 million Armenians in the world with an estimated 3.3 million living in the Republic of Armenia, 1.4 million in the states of the former Soviet Union, 1 million in North and South America, 650,000 in the Middle East, and 500,000 in Europe. The nation itself emerged as a result of a fusion of Indo-European tribes which settled in Anatolia around 1,200 B.C. and merged with other tribes inhabiting the plains of Mount Ararat. The city Erebuni (the capital of Armenia, Yerevan) was founded in 785 B.C.

The Armenian state expanded under Tigran II and stretched from the Caspian Sea to Palestine, from the Black Sea to the Mediterranean. The empire of Tigran the Great was defeated by the Romans in 69 B.C. and the once-powerful kingdom, reduced to its original borders, became a subject ally to Rome serving as a buffer zone between Asia Minor and the Parthians.

Beginning with the second century A.D., Christianity became a significant religious force in Armenia. In 314 A.D., Armenia accepted Christianity as state religion. The new religion, fundamentally different from that practiced by Rome and Persia, had political implications throughout Armenian history.

The Golden Age in the Armenian history began with the development of the Armenian alphabet (36 characters, two more added in the twelfth century) by Mesrop Mashtots in 404 A.D. After translating the Old and the New Testament, a cultural movement promoted by a group of clergy known as the Translators produced a galaxy of able scholars and historians (Koriun, Pafstos, Yegishe, Parpetsi, and others). In that period the Armenian kingdom became a battleground between the Persian and Byzantine empires.

On May 26, 451 A.D., Armenians fought in the Avarair battle against the Persians who had long been trying to have Armenian nobility renounce Christianity. Outnumbered, Armenians lost the military battle but won a spiritual victory which for centuries to come would stand for all Armenians as a symbol of integrity and loyalty to the Christian faith, one of the strongest elements of Armenian identity.

The rise of Islam for Armenia marked the beginning of a new epoch of struggle for identity. With the exception of the ninth and tenth centuries, Armenia was beseiged by Arabs, Mongols, Seljuk Turks, and Ottoman Turks. Then, for five centuries, Armenia was divided between Safavid Persia and Ottoman Turkey.

The rise and expansion of the Russian empire in the end of the eighteenth century began a new chapter in the history of Armenia. As a result of a series of Russo-Turkish wars, Russia advanced in Transcaucasia and established control over Armenian lands (1828) which came to be known as Eastern Armenia. The Eastern Armenians fared well under the Russian czars who accepted Armenians as faithful subjects. The Armenians in their turn regarded the Russians as their liberators and ultimate protectors against Turkish oppression.

Tension began to develop both in the East and the West towards the end of the nineteenth century. The Russians sought to russify the territory of Eastern Armenia and to force the Armenian Church to accept the authority of the Russian Orthodox Church. With the rise of nationalism and the emergence of revolutionary parties, the situation became even worse in Western Armenia where the Armenians demanded self-determination and the Turks took punitive measures prompting several large scale massacres of the Armenians. Then, on April 24, 1915, the government of the Young Turks began to implement a systematic and well-organized genocide of Armenians. More than a million Armenians were exterminated in three years in the Ottoman Empire as Drs. Jernazian and Kalayjian attest. To this day, the tragedy of the genocide has strong implications for the political and psychological mentality of the Armenians.

In the summer of 1918, following the collapse of the Tsarist Empire, Armenia declared its independence. However, the independent Armenian Republic lasted only until December of 1920, then the Red Army occupied the state and made it a part of the emerging Soviet Union. The seventy years of Soviet rule brought modernization of the Armenian society. A predominantly agrarian society without significant industrial base in the early 1920s, Armenia became predominantly urban and industrial. The Soviet government used Armenian development as a propaganda tool inviting those of the Armenian diaspora in Europe and the Middle East to repatriate to Soviet Armenia. In the 1940s, this campaign was successful as tens of thousands of ethnic Armenians like Dr. Jernazian's parents resettled in the republic. However, the Soviet rule in Armenia was not without its dark sides: the collectivization of the Armenian agriculture in the late 1920s to early 1930s resulted in arrest and deportation of tens of thousands of Armenian peasants and intellectuals, including the writer Aksel Bakunts and the poet Eghishe Cherents. Moreover, many Armenian repatriates were arrested soon after their arrival on the suspicion of being Western spies and exiled to Siberia and Central Asia. And others, like Dr. Jernazian's parents, lived in fear of such treatment.

We have, earlier, discussed the impact of the post-Stalin era, the dissident movements, popular support for reunification with Karabahk, coinciding with the earthquake in Spitak.

Gorbachev's insensitive response to the earthquake and his inability to satisfy Armenian's demands in the Karabakh case provided a major catalyst in the growth of popularity of the independence-oriented Armenian National Movement which swept into power in the aftermath of the first free elections in the spring and summer of 1990.

The failed August 1991 coup in Moscow triggered the collapse of the Soviet Union and paved the way for Armenian independence. The independent Republic of Armenia was proclaimed in the fall of 1991, following a popular referendum on the issue, and was internationally recognized in 1992. In the years since independence, the Republic of Armenia has made some serious progress in introducing market reforms: Armenia was the first to privatize land in the former Soviet Union; its national currency has been stabilized; and after a severe economic crisis, caused by the economic blockade and shortages of power, the Armenian economy has begun to grow again. The transition to democracy in Armenia has been less spectacular mostly because of the ongoing conflict with Azerbaijan over Karabakh and other factors such as a lack of strong democratic institutions.

Invisible Walls

Jacob D. Lindy

Psychohistory Trauma and Countertransference

Erik Erikson, trained as a teacher and clicinian, applied a psychoanalytic lens to understand more clearly the individual dynamic tensions and unconscious motivating forces behind creative figures such as Martin Luther (Erikson, 1958) and Mahatma Ghandi (Erickson, 1969). He studied available primary and secondary sources regarding their lives, their times, and their backgrounds including early childhood. Applying his knowledge of psychodynamics, he discovered a fit between the individual great person in history and the emotional dynamics of his times. These men, in striving to resolve the tensions in their own inner lives, came to resolutions that changed history.

Robert Lifton, also originally a psychodynamically oriented clinician, examines ordinary people who have survived or become caught up aggressively in extraordinary events and often traumatic historical events, events that in turn have affected the lives of all of us, such as the nuclear blasts at Hiroshima and Nagasaki (Lifton, 1968, 1995) and the actions of Nazi doctors during the Holocaust (Lifton, 1986). In addition to available historical sources, he adds semi-structured in-depth interviews with ordinary people who are survivors and perpetrators. By analyzing the interviews, he studies and identifies psycho-social-historical themes which characterize their adaptations, giving all of us greater understanding of the extraordinary and traumatic times in which we live.

Both Erikson and Lifton apply their knowledge of the psychotherapeutic situation to the gathering of knowledge on a broader scale, namely psychohistory. But what of the psychotherapeutic situation itself as a source of knowledge about history and trauma? Is the two-person arrangement and interchange in psychotherapy not a microcosm of the world in which we live? The two individuals, in their attention to the arrangements of the treatment, must address matters of time, finances, confidentiality, and safety. In their attention to the value of each layer of thought and feelings between them, they will reproduce role expectations and unconscious contributions to them characteristic of their society: giving/receiving; interrogating/responding; setting expectations/meeting or resisting expectations. As each participant in the therapeutic encounter attends to his or her private thoughts, associations, and memories, the origins of the emotions they experience while in each other's presence become clear. Each becomes aware of struggles within, struggles involving opposing sides of themselves: standing up for oneself/giving in; blaming/being blamed; hurting/being hurt. Finally, it is in the nature of the psychodynamically oriented clinical interaction that parent–child and sibling roles from the past will become alive in the therapeutic setting as well: teaching/being taught, loving and hating/being loved and being hated. It stands to reason that in these three spheres—tensions in interactive roles, within the self, and across generations—therapist and patient will reflect others in their social and historical environments.

In the past twenty years a new diagnostic entity, Posttraumatic Stress Disorder (PTSD), has developed in the mental health field depicting the long-standing psychological symptom picture which attends certain traumatic events. In the study and treatment of survivors with this disorder, clinicians, too, hear and try to make sense of traumatic experiences with historical implications. Here clinicians, bound by confidentiality, find themselves in the role of psychohistorian, for the stories of trauma often contain information about our times that is not otherwise available, such as the extent of the tactical war of horror with which we were engaged in Vietnam (Haley, 1974). While the subject may be incest, rape trauma, war or political trauma, or natural disaster, it is rare that understanding does not require consideration of the larger historical perspective. In this role we trauma clinicians silently record the unseemly underbelly of the history of our times.

Occasionally it becomes possible to collect such cases, and bring them together so as to bear witness to larger historical events, as in the American experience in the Vietnam war (Lindy, MacLeod, Spitz, Green, & Grace, 1988). Here we are using the clinical situation, with its set arrangements and predictable replication of roles, including internal conflicts and conflict between generations as played out in transference and countertransference experiences, as a primary source of data, one that not only offers insight into a medical condition and its recovery but also into the psychohistorical forces which brought it about, and the likely consequences of these forces on many other similarly affected individuals. Of course adequate protection of confidentiality is crucial as well as the commitment of the persons in the patient role to the value of bearing witness to their experience in a publicly available forum.

At times, in work with PTSD, the therapist will have experienced traumas similar to those of the patient. Here, the vividness of transference and countertransferences increases, causing both greater risks for the neutrality of the treatment, but also the opportunity for greater poignance of understanding.

We have already learned in this book that in Russia and throughout Eastern Europe, the impact of political trauma has been so pervasive for three generations as to have affected nearly every family; that is, nearly every patient and nearly every therapist will have been affected. Turning the clinical setting inside-out as it were, what can these treatments then teach us of the forces which kept people in a captive state of mind (Milosz, 1990), and what is entailed in the exit from that captive mind?

Using Empathic Strain as a Method of Psychohistory

In this chapter we shall draw upon the case studies in this book to suggest psychohistorical principles pertaining to trauma and loss in the Soviet era. We shall review some of the most poignant moments presented in Chapters 3 through 8. We shall focus on the barrier which blocks communication between two East European people, one as a doctor and one a patient, people who are trying to understand the internal world of one of them, but who in the process cannot help but exacerbate pain in the other. The moments of special interest here are ones when understanding temporarily fails, moments when therapists temporarily cannot accept in themselves the same phenomenon which they are trying to understand in their patient. We call these moments of *empathic strain*. These awkward moments mark the point where trauma and loss of the patient unexpectedly cross paths with trauma and loss of the doctor. The therapist's discipline requires that she pursue the inner dynamics of this moment, that is that the clinician allow herself the freedom of association to identify that painful memory or affect/object configuration within which she will identify the troubled spot. It could be, for example, a moment of shame covered by a culturally common defense; a moment of helplessness covered by guilt; a moment of yearning covered by defensive rejection; a moment of fear covered by counterphobic action.

By glimpsing the source of comparable conflicts in the internal world of the therapist, the therapist is able to return to the blocked understanding of the patient. The insights gained from the reflective work on these moments open a unique window onto the workings of roles, conflicts, and intergenerational communication in the larger world of trauma and loss which they both share, elucidating the invisible walls which unconsciously perpetrate the mentality of adaptation to the Communist totalitarian world.

Two Types of Invisible Walls

We have identified in our East European colleagues and their patients persisting psychological walls from Soviet trauma in two locations: walls that unconsciously preserve outmoded ways of adaptation, and walls which maintain silence between generations. The first kind of wall represents the enduring personality traits and unconscious emotional defenses reinforced during the Communist era, which persist today as internal blocks to adaptation in a freer society. The second kind of wall divides an older generation who hid the identities of parents and grandparents from a younger generation who grew up angry that they did not know who they were.

Enduring Traits

The first type of invisible wall consists of a particular grouping of unconscious defenses. Most of them can be found in any population, but because these defenses have become selectively valued and rewarded in this particular culture over several generations, they have become indelible and endemic parts of the psychological landscape. We believe that these intrapsychic mechanisms originally gained ascendancy as a response to specific traumatic aspects of Communist political culture. Yielding traumatically to authority resulted in dissociating and dissembling, thereby sacrificing, one's authentic self. Accommodating to an all-pervasive yet irresponsible leadership that intruded traumatically into people's lives meant assuming a guilt that belonged elsewhere. Depending absolutely on the State for the distribution of basic needs meant regressing to a permanently dependent condition for sustenance. Surviving in an informer ecology raised universal suspicion; surviving in a culture of terror meant accepting the dual states of being cruel and enduring cruelty. Succumbing to absolute collective power meant despairing of individual hope and initiative. We see these traits enduring beyond their usefulness in the cases of Mihai (Dr. Cucliciu), Karl and Hans (Dr. Bernhardt), Vahan (Dr. Jernazian), and Josip (Dr. Muacevic). We see empathic therapists becoming aware of similar traits in themselves, and in the psychological work that follows this insight, moving beyond these old and now harmful adaptations. Their painful efforts help us to appreciate better the many who are not able to outgrow this impact on their minds.

Gaps Between the Generations

The second kind of invisible wall is a powerful block to communication between child and parent around the most central issues of identity. As a result, young people sense that their identities are incomplete and discover discontinuities within themselves and in their connection to their lineage. This kind of wall may first feel like a void or empty space close to the core of the personality or as anger at the silence and deception that produced it. Here we have young people discovering their own incongruent identities built on incomplete or inaccurate stories of their parents and grandparents, lies woven to protect the younger generation from the dangerous truths that the older generation has chosen to keep to itself.

Such lies hide the epidemic of traumatic loss of parents and grandparents in purges and in the Holocaust. Silent walls of intergenerational discontinuities are especially clear in the cases of Dima (Dr. Konkov) where the father–grandfather–son theme is discontinuous, and Mr. E. (Dr. Csiszer), where the father–daughter theme is disrupted. Finally, with Dr. Katona, the mother–daughter theme reaches center-stage as does the special issue of the denial of Eastern Europe's generation of hidden Jews.

We turn then to specific moments of empathic strain in the therapies, which offer insights into enduring traits, and to gaps between the generations. And as we do so, we also ask to what extent are these also reflections of the psychohistory of the larger world to which they belong.

Adaptation to Political Trauma

Yielding, Dissimulating, and the False Self

We turn first to Dr. Cucliciu's work with Mihai (Chapter 5, Romania). Dr. Cucliciu observes that his patient Mihai is consumed with an unbidden image from the past. Mihai gesticulates with his left hand in a forceful, repetitive manner, raising a separate finger for each of the assaults by his torturers: forcing him to eat from a trough, commanding him to eliminate waste on command, confining his body in a fixed posture for hours, beating him almost to the point of death, and torturing him for failing to reveal what the torturer wished. Yet above all this, Mihai explains, in a separate category, which he emphasizes by using the index finger of his right hand, is the matter of yielding to the appeal of the chief torturer and the new way. Being forced to behave in a bestial manner is one thing; yielding to his view of the world and becoming someone other than oneself is something else. Mihai's face revealed his agony as he repeated this shameful narrative.

Dr. Cucliciu felt blocked trying unsuccessfully to listen to this powerful material. He could not recall the details, as though wishing not to hear. He taped the interview to be sure he could listen thoroughly. At first he wondered if his discomfort came from guilt, that his prodding elicited such deep pain in himself. Perhaps this was causing his inability to listen. But, despite this awareness, Dr. Cucliciu's distress at listening continued (we shall return to this theme below). With further self-awareness, he realized that in addition to guilt, he was more importantly angry with Mihai, as the man he had been listening to, a man whom he admired, had yielded to the new way. Thus, this period of empathic strain was characterized at first by avoidance on the therapist's part, then guilt, but most importantly blame and anger. A wall had come between patient and doctor, because the doctor could not tolerate in himself the idea of yielding to the torturer.

The moment of empathic strain produced the therapist's own associations to a moment in his own life when he was being interrogated by the secret police; he was at first reassured that in his memory he held his own against the interrogators and that his goal of unalloyed resistance was intact. Indeed, he had not yielded. But then a troubling detail returned. As Dr. Cucliciu was about to be dismissed, his interrogator casually inquired, "By the way, would you join us in the Communist Party if we asked you to?" Quite automatically he answered in the affirmative, sliding into the dissimulated state that on the one hand denied authenticity (it is a lie that he would join the Communist Party) and on the other hand betrayed his own self-preservative instinct. (Intuitively he understood that if he could not lie according to the rules of real politik he would be dangerous to the regime and in real danger.)

Recognizing his all-too-human slide into dissimulation himself, his "yielding" even in this conditional sense, allowed Dr. Cucliciu to resume an empathic listening posture with Mihai.

Dr. Cucliciu argues that his own slide into dissimulation, like most others in Romania, is an adaptive ego mechanism brought into play whenever the circumstances call for it. Similarly, the interrogator, using an Orwellian logic, intuitively knows that the citizen who holds dissenting views is not the problem; it is the citizen who has lost the capacity to dissimulate who has become dangerous to the State.

Mihai is lamenting the period in his life when he gave way to a false self based on yielding to the chief torturer and his own false memory. His capitulation was paradigmatic of a generation of Romanian students and intellectuals who were forced to discard their Western tradition and to some extent accepted a false self and a false world-view in order to survive. Nearly two generations later Dr. Cucliciu unconsciously complies with the regime's prerequisite that he be capable of slipping into a false self even if only temporarily so that he can demonstrate to the secret police that he can still dissimulate by offering seemingly spontaneous loyalty if the situation requires it.

This capacity for dissimulation, this presence of false-self fragments has gained cross-generational endurance. What for Mihai became a momentous although brief yielding to the new order became for Dr. Cucliciu in the next generation an ingrained habit of personality: when endangered, dissimulate.

The capacity for dissimulation is fundamental to the totalitarian and to the post-totalitarian state. Milosz (1990) describes the phenomenon by analogy to medieval Muslims who had to hide their religious philosophical views in alien mind-sets. They became experts at pretending, a circumstance that they labeled *ketman*. Once the new way lost its own ideological moorings and even the leaders no longer believed, a new culture had grown which valued this capacity to pretend, this *ketman*, this dissimulation.

Against the backdrop of Western life, such phenomena appeared sociopathic. But in the East, *ketman* insured survival; it was understood and rewarded for what it was; it enabled vast spy/informer networks to exist; it was fundamental to the concept of real existing socialism, namely, the living with the contradictions of ends and means that characterized loyalty to Communism. This explains the indifference with which many informers greeted the news of the discovery of their deeds during the regime of the German Democratic Republic (GDR). What happens to this mechanism when there is a change in society that permits more open discourse and authentic interaction between people? Where, within the newly emerging structure of Eastern European societies, will these adaptive capacities find a new home?

Enduring Cruelty and Being Cruel

Earlier we noted that Dr. Cucliciu, working with a survivor of intimate cruelty, found that in his search to reach the depths of his patient's experience, he sometimes felt like a prodding torturer. In the transference/countertransference configuration we have a repetition where the patient, again, endures cruelty as victim and the therapist, because he is prodding with painful questions, feels like the one being cruel. This, we noted, was one of the elements in the first moment of empathic strain which interfered temporarily in the work with Mihai.

A second period of strain with Mihai occurred earlier as he had begun to trust his doctor and he was telling his story. Dr. Cucliciu noted that he felt tense and uncomfortable sitting with Mihai. He noted that the pain of Mihai's story was so riveting it diverted him from other duties in his life; that Mihai's penetrating questions forced him to doubt his own motives, that he even felt obliged to bare his soul in order to face the depths of Mihai's suffering; in short, he felt as though his patient were keeping him hostage and tormenting him.

What is crucial here is a transference/countertransference configuration in the same case which finds the patient and the therapist switching roles: each feeling alternately cruel and being treated cruelly in response to the other. We may understand this as the traumatized person forming a split in the ego making it possible for both these capacities, being victim and being perpetrator of cruelty, to exist side by side. In Mihai's case, as in many others in the Soviet era, we note also that the torturer insisted Mihai be both victim and torturer. The contradiction can be paralyzing. When we as therapists are able to recognize both tendencies in ourselves, we are better able to accept that enduring cruelty and being cruel can and do coexist in the same person. Being able to empathize with this split rather than being repelled by it catalyzes the healing process.

The moment of empathic strain that gives way to understanding the reciprocity between perpetrator and victim is particularly useful as a window for understanding the larger psychological consequences of Soviet trauma. A wall develops in the self between the capacity to be the torturer and the tortured, between the capacity to endure cruelty and the capacity to be cruel. The creation of this characteristic constitutes a second enduring psychological element of the Communist State. Indeed, creating and preserving the presence of a persecutor/victim split within the self was essential for the maintenance of the entire paranoid system. Each person, fearing cruelty, is afraid of being turned in and so, cruelly, turns in others to protect himself. This phenomenon was true of Stalin, of the Communist states in their most brutal form, as in beating one's fellow students close to death in Piteshti, or in a less brutal but still oppressive form, as in the vast informer system of the post-Stalin years. It becomes an adaptive although unstable situation in which the State profits from the inherent instability. The Communist State supports guilt and fear, which in turn play important intermediary roles in maintaining the persecutor/victim split. As Mihai explains, the chief torturer filled the minds of the tortured with self-loathing. They were victims because they were guilty of opposing the direction of history and of the new man. Yet the torturer, too, must fear the day when he becomes expendable. As the political picture shifts, the torturer would later stand trial for his crimes; he becomes the victim, just as he forced the victim, through yielding, to become a torturer.

Refusing to Be Free

Dr. Bernhardt's patient, Karl (Chapter 4, German Democratic Republic), refused to accept his work assignment in the hospital. Instead, he regressed to his intrapsychic dungeon. Like others of Karl's symptoms (e.g., theft, addiction), this symptom took a behavioral form. Karl preferred the regressive dependency of having others care for his basic needs even if they did so cruelly, rather than to step into the unknown external world and meet demands being placed on him. Dr. Bernhardt anticipated the moment when she must confront him about his refusal to work, and felt dread. Not only did she feel badly that Karl was reacting to her instruction to work with withdrawal, recalcitrance, and regression but also she objected to being in the role of insisting that Karl work because it made her feel like the harsh, humiliating teacher from her own childhood. Dr. Bernhardt, in this moment of empathic strain, found herself angry, wanting to punish Karl for placing her in such an unempathic and authoritarian role. She felt strongly that youth should wish to establish autonomy, not fear it. She wondered aloud, was this not the problem of many youth from East Germany as they dreaded the future?

Karl, like others in his generation, wished to remain in the protective prison-like atmosphere of the East. Here one will always find meals and shelter. Here one does not need to address problems that require personal autonomy, decisions, and consequences. Here, an all-powerful and sadistic authority punishes autonomy by imprisonment. Here passivity and dependency are valued. For many in his generation, responding to State control of basic necessities without humiliation, indignation, and rage was an adaptive habit. It began in the State-run nurseries and continued through school and military service. And now many of these young people are not yet able and prepared to be free. Dr. Bernhardt leaves us in the air about the outcome of Karl's unwillingness to be free. Indeed, the years since the fall of the wall have continued to be difficult for the youth of the former GDR.

Absorbing Undeserved Guilt

Hans was once again compulsively washing his hands in the psychiatric hospital as Dr. Bernhardt watched and felt uneasy then deeply moved. She knew that his symptom expressed an irrational, intense, and persistent sense of guilt, a sense of being contaminated, of being unworthy and inadequate, particularly in his mother's eyes. At first Dr. Bernhardt too, in her own countertransference reaction, felt helpless incompetent and irrationally guilty as she watched the hand-washing. She remembered feeling the wrath of Hans' mother who chastised her for not getting her son better more quickly and thought this is what Hans must feel. She also felt angry. She knew from the outset that both of Hans' parents had been active functionaries in the old regime, and had been complicit in spying on colleagues for the secret police. She knew that they hid their shameful past from their son. Indeed, Dr. Bernhardt became aware of the wish to punish the parents for projecting guilt on to Hans, and she was angry at them for informing on people like herself. Her feelings towards her patient's parents were those of citizen/reformer against those who corrupted her State.

As Dr. Bernhardt continued to reflect in response to this moment of empathic strain, she was struck by two overlapping images: in one, Hans' mother says of her political behavior during the Communist regime, "my hands are clean"; in the second image, her son absorbing the guilt his parent denies, cannot do enough to scrub his hands clean of all the filth and contamination he imagines to be on them. Dr. Bernhardt now recognized the psychological mechanism of projective identification (Kernberg, 1980), for she too had experienced this projected guilt directly when Hans' mother who denied her own role in her son's illness blamed the therapist for failing to cure him. "The mother must be right," she had reasoned. " I must not have been doing things in the right way." Dr. Bernhardt stepped back from the projection, and saw that the guilt rightly belonged to the mother who had disavowed it. Then she was able to feel her own pent up rage. Dr. Bernhardt thought that understanding how mother's ability to split off her guilt, to unconsciously place it into others, and then to be indifferent or angry towards those others is an important mechanism for the GDR. Accepting projected guilt had become an element in adaptive survival in the Communist era. (see also Csiszer and Katona chapter on institutionalized sacrifice).

On a larger scale throughout the GDR leaders denied their guilt over failures in the economy and civic progress and projected the responsibility on to others. They used a guilt-prone philosophy and world-view which chastises the citizen for falling short of the ideal of Communist Man to their own advantage. The citizen, especially if trained to believe so in childhood, is likely to absorb this projected guilt as his own, accepting such responsibility with self-recrimination. And indeed the ability to do so was amply rewarded by the State. Thus, actively projecting guilt on to those who are not responsible but who nonetheless accept the responsibility is a fundamental mechanism in perpetuating the collective irresponsibility of the Eastern European authoritarian regime.

Dr. Bernhardt's guilt, then anger at Hans' parents, was a product of the anger Hans could not afford to feel plus anger at her own informers. Upon reflection, she could return to the riveting image of Hans washing his hands to remove guilt and could more neutrally focus on establishing realistic goals as his doctor rather than feeling inhibited by guilt. She encouraged Hans to proceed in an autonomous direction consistent with his developmental needs and not tied pathologically to his parents' conflicts. But for her country, the problem of guilt and anger remain.

Corruption and Despair versus Initiative and Hope

In Chapter 8 (Armenia) Vahan brought to his therapy certain character traits and habits which, partly because they were endemic in the powerful class of Communist functionaries, his therapist found offensive. These included an overbearing jocularity and loquacious, a hail-fellow-well-met attitude, accompanied by an outpouring of superficial interest and concern. Consistent with these character traits, Vahan would produce "gifts" for the therapist at the end of his session, such as cigarettes, which the therapist could not afford and very much wished to have. These behaviors created awkward moments which were offensive reminders to Dr. Jernazian of the reality of a corrupt economic system, one which, in contrast to its ideology, depended heavily on barter and bribery. It was this character picture and the uncomfortable dilemma around refusing gifts that one very much wished to have, rather than the specific symptoms which set off an empathic strain.

In response, Dr. Jernazian found himself irritable and rejecting. He wondered, why was he treating someone who represented everything he despised? Yet, as he reflected, Dr. Jernazian became aware of opposite feelings as well. In fact the sessions themselves went quite smoothly; they were even enjoyable. How could Dr. Jernazian account for the paradox?

Acknowledging that he liked Vahan despite feeling defiled by him enabled Dr. Jernazian to arrive at an empathic insight: Vahan, too, might have felt humiliated within the Party structure where he was feeling defiled. His therapist could see that Vahan was being humiliated every day as he accepted and gave bribes, only to be toyed with by those with greater power. The insight opens onto a wider view of the decay implicit in a bribery/corruption-ridden, social-economic fabric. People do not feel good about themselves nor about others.

In this light, Vahan's symptoms become analogies for a culture: impotence, lack of intimacy, and fear.

Grigor, a child orphaned by the Armenian earthquake, but not yet informed that his parents were dead, sat with Dr. Jernazian in dark despair. As he struggled, Grigor found himself in a dark tunnel of overwhelming hopelessness. As Dr. Jernazian confronted the full blackness of Grigor's despair, it was as if both patient and therapist faced an immense and immovable wall of death and loss, of collapse and feared annihilation. As Dr. Jernazian followed his associations in a Gestalt manner, he became aware as well of a light that would lead Grigor and himself out of this darkness. As a result, he and Grigor were able to move beyond their impasse—they could speak of Grigor's parents' deaths and to go on. As he later reflected on this, he felt that the darkness also represented the plight of Armenian people within the Soviet system. In the treatment as in the political turmoil outside it, Dr. Jernazian found hope, hope for Grigor, for his country and for himself.

Perhaps despair, as an adaptation, is the other side of the coin of participating in corruption. One can adapt to a corrupt system by becoming embroiled in its machinations (as did Vahan) or become withdrawn into an isolated, helpless, and despairing state. Both adaptations will interfere with societal advancement in a post-Communist world.

Discontinuity

The State's use of sudden arrests, political detention, labor camps, involuntary psychiatric hospitalization, torture, and murder on a vast scale— all these constitute a powerful discontinuity of individual lives and of family ties. The impact of building the Soviet machine by destroying so many of its citizens has affected nearly everyone who survived. Not only were individual people lost to their families during the height of their adulthood but the memory of their lives was often lost as well. During their absence, the stories of the lives they had been living and the causes to which they were committed were wiped clean. They became shadow figures to children who would grow up never truly knowing their parents, with the central features of their lives altered so that the next generation might have a chance for success in the new State. Discovering who these lost relatives were is one of the great reconstructive tasks of the post-Soviet world. Integrating their memory into future generations is a difficult yet necessary task for the present and the future. The tasks facing our East European colleagues and their patients in this regard was a consistent theme throughout our work.

Intergenerational Deception and Void

We have noted a second type of invisible barrier in these treatments, the wall of silence between generations; the barrier of missing or deceptive information passed on to children about their parents and grandparents who suffered under Communism. Here the empathic strain in the doctor–

patient relationship is of a different type. In the first instance powerful traumatic events revived in the treatment evoke powerful memories in the therapist who finds himself or herself an unwilling player in another's internal world. In the second category there are only indirect inferences that something is wrong or missing in the life narrative of the patient and the family. Sometimes the treatment evokes a troubling void in the therapist's personal narrative as well. The therapist, having inferred a missing piece, a gap, in the patient's life story is momentarily adrift because this has stirred an analogous gap in his or her own life narrative. The disconnections felt in the therapeutic situation then become windows into the discontinuities in a society. They separate generations; they disconnect personal authenticity on a vast scale. They describe in a psychohistorical sense the ways in which Communism intended to cut itself off from the pre-revolutionary past and from the continuity of cultures which made up that past. Such disconnections have lasting impact on the identity of the survivor and the family, and the country.

The first group to experience traumatic disconnection are those who personally survived the *gulag* and its Eastern European equivalents. Today, such emotions as numbing, loss, betrayal, and alienation, along with the effects of PTSD, are not uncommon in former political prisoners.

Arrested Grief

For children and grandchildren growing up in such truncated families, there may be lasting effects as well. We know a great deal about the impact of parental loss on children (Fleming & Altschul, 1963). Here we have an epidemic of parental loss with fabricated stories regarding those lost parents and grandparents being passed on to the subsequent generations. The result is an arrested grief. Its impact affects both psychological development and fundamental questions of identity.

During *perestroika*, the younger generation began to ask questions about missing parents. Often they met silence. More often a series of clues began to take form. As the surviving children and grandchildren came to understand something of the real parent who was lost, awesome personal tasks remained: (a) recognizing anger at the deception, (b) absorbing previously missing information, (c) coming to know the real parent who disappeared and accepting the loss of that real parent, (d) grieving the loss of the fantasied parent, (e) returning to points of developmental arrest for further psychological work, (f) integrating the real parent in the further development of a more complete identity, and (g) finally developing empathy for their parents and grandparents who saw no alternative but to hide the truth.

In their work with their patients, all the therapists in this project discovered some aspect of their own personal discontinuity. This form of empathic strain sends the therapist on a personal journey in search of continuity of self, and continuity of internal dialogue with the intrapsychic representation of the lost family member. Therapists, too, learn the details of the lives of missing people and discover that the values of these real people persist in their own lives. They also struggle angrily with the impact of parental deception, the coloring or omission of the past in order to adapt to the present. In the end, the search for connections which occurs in these therapies, and in the therapists themselves, provides a model for communication within families and for the process of healing in the aftermath of the trauma of the Soviet era.

Gaps Between Father and Son

In Dr. Konkov's treatment of Dima (Chapter 6, Russia), discontinuity between fathers and sons spans three generations. It was not a dramatic event in the treatment but rather the tremulous quality of Galena's voice, as she told Dima to stay safe, that led Dr. Konkov to intuit a gap in the historical narrative of his young patient. The tone of voice stirred memories of his own mother and of a history with some parallels to his patient. He saw that the brash youngster, by threatening suicide, was also desperately trying to claim a personal space, one that would be free from grandmother and mother. Somewhere in the thin story of Dima's grandfather, a cardboard hero of the revolution who supposedly died for the great cause, and father who disappeared without a story, is a core of missing relationships and missing masculine role models for identification.

While empathic with Dima's search to find the missing pieces to make sense of his own history, Dr. Konkov is not particularly empathic with Dima's mother for the lies she and the grandmother have told Dima about his grandfather. Like Dima, Dr. Konkov has spent much energy trying to understand and to integrate the voids in his own past. Dima did not know his "hero" grandfather. Dima wanted to admire this hero and in his latency dreams imagined himself reaching such heights of glory. But how could this hero have had such a fuss-budget for a wife, always snooping into his affairs, never respecting his privacy, always dictating what everyone will do? On the sands of misinformation, Dima tried to build an internal construct, a powerful man who would have known how to navigate the difficult waters of human affairs and his troublesome family; instead he was relying on a defensive fantasy structure whose fragility would surely not suffice as an internalized imago to help him navigate life. Galena's tone of voice when she warned Dima to stay safe tapped into Dr. Konkov's experience with his own mother, and this brought back all he didn't know about the men in his own family. For Dr. Konkov, there were the hidden emotions of father, and the silence that guarded father's views on life and inner feelings during much of the time he lived at home. Father had been a military man, belonging to the military establishment, not to his son. Also he and mother had hidden the identity of Dr. Konkov's paternal grandfather who, in truth, had been a murdered priest. Dr. Konkov, bolstered by the relative freedom of *perestroika*, tried to provide the safe place where gaps in family information could be filled and new identity forged.

For Dima, parental lies had arrested grief and mourning. In this situation the lie interferes with the integrity of the introject. The view of father as hero was inconsistent with the many other clues about who the missing parent was. What was Dima to make of the discrepant parts of himself which were genuine unconscious and genetic identifications with the lost figure? The task in working through the arrested grief of a lost parent with a false history, for the child, concern current issues of self-image and self-continuity. We suspect that Dima's and Dr. Konkov's experiences have been repeated in hundreds of thousands if not millions of homes in Russia and Eastern Europe.

Gaps Between Parent and Daughter

Dr. Csiszer's patient, Mr. E. (Chapter 3, Hungary), wished to clear his name of an earlier politically motivated psychiatric diagnosis. He had endured physical disability, imprisonment, harassment, marginalization, and loss of his daughter as a result of standing up against two totalitarian regimes. Yet the central core of his moral fabric remained in tact. While a little distant, he was hardly the kind of individual one would expect to elicit anger from his skilled and sensitive therapist. Yet this is precisely what happened to Dr. Csiszer as she listened to his story. Through peer supervision Dr. Csiszer confirmed what she suspected: that she was unconsciously identifying with Mr. E.'s daughter and her rage at having been abandoned by her own father. The story within the story gradually becomes clear when we see in Mr. E.'s extraordinary efforts to clear his name, a specific wish that he be rehabilitated before *this* doctor, a woman the same age as his daughter. For a time, Dr. Csiszer became the unconscious substitute for Mr. E.'s daughter, while Mr. E. became the unconscious substitute for Dr. Csiszer's missing father.

At this point we are addressing two previously unacknowledged traumatic losses: one belonging to the patient, the second belonging to the therapist. What was in Mr. E.'s daughter's mind at the time of his disappearance? What has she thought subsequently about all those important times in her life when he was not there? What was in the father's mind at the time of the trauma? Did he ever miss his daughter or imagine her and her life without him? How did he feel about the way in which fate seemed to cut her off from him? Did he ever imagine a time when they might be reunited? Here a discontinuity in the epigenetic development of the father–daughter relationship is being confronted. The psychological implications are far more than an absent father, or a stigmatized father, or an ostracized father, or an admired father who chose honor over continuity of relationship with his daughter—although these are all part of the picture.

The central question is one of revivifying the missed relationship in the present and in this present tense manner confronting the past, and trying to integrate a life-span interaction, father with daughter, daughter with father, so that both can go on with their remaining years. Each person in the father–daughter pair has built a defensive structure around the disappointment of this truncated path in the life cycle. Each has a frozen emotional state attached to that defensive structure. For example, the daughter may have come to a defensive posture in which she understands father as an impulsive, naive zealot, who would have caused trouble even if he had been around; it is a relief to feel him absent. Anger at him for these presumed characteristics protects against the hurt of his absence. Confronting the traumatic loss involves loosening these defensive structures, and experiencing the affects, both defensive and primary which accompany them, and entertaining new fantasies as well as learning new facts about who he is or was. These have as their purpose a more constant, more reliable, more accurate, and more useful internal image which will then be of help later in the life cycle.

With Dr. Katona we come in contact with the silent or missing generation, children of the post-war era whose Jewish parent or parents had survived the Holocaust by taking on another identity, denying their Jewishness. Here the barrier of silence between the generations had been complete. Parents refused to speak of the war years, or religion, or any other facet in mother's background. No surviving relatives could fill in details.

Dr. Katona, in her research, found herself more and more drawn to studying and talking with Jewish survivors of the Holocaust. Their steadfastness in their identity as Jews without resorting to suicide fascinated Dr. Katona as she pursued her research interests in the traditionally high rate of suicide among Hungarians. Clues to her own false identity had been available to her for years including the repetitive childhood dream of hiding in a concentration camp. Nevertheless, coming upon incontrovertible evidence that her own mother was hiding her Jewishness was a shock. It confronted her directly with the task of re-working her own identity and that of her children, a task that led her to reclaim her Jewish identity and even for a time live in Israel. We do not know the actual number of such families.

Discontinuities Within the Self

It is not primarily parental loss or deception which is at the heart of Dr. Muacevic's work with his patient, Viktor (Chapter 7, Croatia), but rather the sudden radical shifts in identity that successive authoritarian regimes thrust on him. For Viktor the trauma of Communism, and of post-Communism as the trauma of Nazi occupation, was one of civil war. As a partisan, Viktor broke from his father during the occupation; as a Croat he broke during the recent war from the Yugoslav Army which had been his home. Each break was occasioned by the threat of real physical violence or the threat of death. Each was accompanied by symptoms of posttraumatic stress disorder. He sought in his therapy with Dr. Muacevic a way to reintegrate himself and his values within a radically changed political climate. His struggle to maintain a steady bearing amidst radical change is reflected in the therapist's struggles to keep a steady course during these shifts as well. For Dr. Muacevic also lived as a child during Nazi atrocities, as a young adult during the disillusionment with Tito's Communist State, and as an academic elder during the shift to radical nationalism. For him, maintaining a humanistic core has been a central task.

Another form of discontinuity within the self occurs during wars in which abusive violence becomes temporarily legitimized. This is the discontinuity of humanistic values. And here countertransference reactions are an expectable accompaniment of accessing the central traumas (Haley, 1974). The psychotherapy literature includes many variants on these countertransference reactions (Wilson & Lindy, 1994). The case of Josip is illustrative. As Dr. Muacevic was supervising his younger colleague in the case of Josip, he suspected that the patient was ready to talk about abusive violence but his therapist was still uncomfortable listening. It was necessary to allow his supervisee to express her own feelings about her village when it was overrun by the Serbs, before she could address the feelings of her patient. It was only then, after she was in touch with her own revenge fantasies, that Josip could safely open his shame at acknowledging his own bestial impulses which had surfaced after he had treated like an animal in the detention camp.

To some extent the trauma of radical discontinuity to Croatians, Bosnians, ethnic Albanians, and Serbs in the area of the former Yugoslavia has been another feature of the post-Communist era. Building continuity amidst the events of radical discontinuity is a theme which we continue to address in the next chapter as we widen our lens from an applied psychoanalytic view to a psycho-social-historical one.

CHAPTER

History as Trauma

Robert Jay Lifton

Those of us who seek to comprehend the psychological impact of the Communist era—that combination of forces involving history, trauma, and person—are presented with a daunting task. Commentators like myself need to maintain an emphasis not only on what we think has been taking place but, equally, on what we learn from experiences we ourselves have not had. The trauma operates on many levels and its complexities defy our ordinary categories. It lacks the structure and limits of a discrete disaster, such as an earthquake. Natural disasters have something approaching an end point: The effects reverberate over years or even decades, but the catastrophe itself is over. What we are discussing here is on the order of a sustained catastrophe that never goes away, of threats, dangers, and pressures towards betrayal that become perpetual. The pressures are both acute and chronic, both individual and societal. For the individual person caught up in these traumatic historical forces, fear and pained ambivalence to the regime are transmitted from the moment of birth and before and extend throughout the life cycle.

It may be that we do not quite know how to evaluate that kind of trauma, to conceptualize it or even how to talk about it. Yet we must try. In doing so here, I shall focus on that elusive realm of interaction between the individual person and intrusive historical forces. Indeed we might think of the whole process in terms of *history as trauma*.

Generational Transmission of Trauma

The family, which we usually think of as one's main source of protection, can become, instead, a transmitter and even a locus of trauma itself. However protective the intent, what was transmitted in the families described in this book, and over their generations, was the threat of death, literal or psychological, together with the costs of survival.

Dr. Fyodor Konkov refers to early childhood memories of "feeling my mother's anxious tone of voice in the years of greatest danger," when the anxiety conveyed could have to do with anything from a nagging concern about the family's status with the regime to an ominous late-night KGB visit. In either case it is important to understand that behind that "anxious tone" was a message about the immediate danger to and overall precariousness of life.

At the least extreme end of the spectrum, and contributing more indirectly to the psychological equivalents of death, are what Dr. Heike Bernhardt terms the "traumatizations of everyday life"; at its most extreme end is the message of brutal threat to the physical and psychological self, which Dr. Ion Cucliciu describes in the Piteshti prison.

What was done in the Piteshti prison was a systematic undermining of identity and belief, the elaborate manipulation of guilt and shame, all in the service of reconstituting the self according to existing Communist requirements. The regime's ultimate impact had to do with its complete control over the individual and its manipulation of death or its equivalents, including extreme separation and loss, psychic numbing with general stasis, and anticipation or experience of personal disintegration. That led in turn to control over the prisoner's continuing life inside or outside the prison. In such cases, the individual person becomes inwardly motivated to embrace the regime and plunge into its enterprises. The process resembled the Chinese Communist thought reform programs I had studied in the 1950s and 1960s (Lifton, 1961). The Piteshti experiment differed from Chinese thought reform in its insistence on extreme forms of physical abuse rather than seeking to achieve the same results primarily through psychological means.

While the extremity of Piteshti had to do with the special cruelty of the Romanian Communist dictatorship, some such set of death-haunted images, however amorphous, became a worst-case scenario transmitted over generations to large numbers of families in Eastern Europe.

In the end, parents and children can become dangerous to each other. Parents feared having or attaching themselves to children who might then become used as threats to make the parents conform to the regime. Children could also be dangerous to parents by speaking or acting in such a way as to bring shame, danger, and punishment to the family. Similarly, the parent disappearing in the night who is then vilified by the State brings shame and outcast status to the family. Because the ecology of informing intruded into the family structure, full authentic expression of emotions about current experiences and past family memory was sacrificed. In this atmosphere falsehoods replace the ordinary stories of familial continuity told over generations. Adolescents come to be disillusioned and angry at having been denied knowledge of their parents and grandparents, and therefore of who they themselves really are.

Dr. Bernhardt speaks of the "subtle daily traumatization of the German Communist system" (Chapter 4) beginning in nurseries before age two and continuing in pre-schools, and in elementary and secondary education. In these compulsory state institutions, conformity and dependency replaced authenticity and autonomy. Daily wariness towards a massive informer network eroded trust. All of these factors had profound impact on family efforts to transmit adaptive psychological traits.

We are speaking, then, of multiple levels of trauma involving the immediate and extended family, as well as virtually all social institutions, as transmitted. And what happens over generations can have the most extreme psychological reverberations. Where children strongly sympathize with their parents, the family can become an oasis of relative security. But where deep distrust intrudes into the home itself, children are more likely to be confused and angered, with a resulting family dynamic of ever-increasing tension and anxiety. Feelings between the generations are then poisoned at the root by the transmission of death anxiety.

Facing the Past

Facing one's past includes drawing upon, letting in, the actuality of one's personal family and social history in a way that can provide at least a modicum of a sense of continuity. And everyone requires some connection with a personal and social past as a source of self and of personal agency. But actually facing an extraordinarily traumatic past can only be done in fits and starts, with elements of denial and avoidance, and with every variety of subtle psychological maneuvers. Indeed, no person, and no group, fully faces the past. For a nation or society to face its past is even more haphazard and often begins as an expression of a determined, articulate minority. Yet the whole experience of post-Communist Europe and of the writers of this book has made clear the psychological and moral imperative of such an effort, however limited and imperfect it may be.

Facing the past has to do with bearing witness, with opening the self to much of the pain in order to tell the tale. In this sense, therapists are always in a position of bearing witness, both in enabling their patients to tell their stories and in taking in, and themselves retelling, those stories. Under repressive Communist regimes they have a special vantage point for witnessing what these regimes have done to the inner life of human beings. In that way the therapist is what I call a witnessing professional. His or her stance ordinarily requires a measure of detachment towards the narrative encountered, but here she, too, is a survivor, likely to have experienced no less trauma from the regime than her patient. The therapists in these chapters had to combine roles of survivor, witness, and witnessing professional, and drew special insights precisely from this excruciating amalgamation of roles.

When in the past I worked with American veterans of the Vietnam war (Lifton, 1973), or with survivors of Nazi genocide (Lifton, 1986), each of our statuses was clear. They were survivor-witnesses and I was a witnessing professional. While I was by no means immune from their pain, nor should I have been, I had the good fortune and security of having lived essentially outside of their experiences of trauma. The therapists in these chapters had no such security. They lived out the pressures of the regimes even in their roles as psychiatrists and psychologists and they told us about it just a few years later. As they did so, everything they had gone through still reverberated actively within them. How could it be otherwise?

Yet the writers of this book at times performed a task similar to that which I carried out with Nazi doctors. Dr. Cucliciu bore witness to the Piteshti project, struggling to uncover the full narrative of evil and to probe the psychological and historical conditions conducive to evil. In the process he had to maintain the emotional and intellectual distance necessary to the witnessing professional, even as he tried to cope with his own painful experiences as survivor-witness. Under Communism, the witness of all these therapists had to do with both the nature of evil, and with the troubling extent to which ordinary people can be socialized to evil, again close to my own task in studying Nazi doctors. In the work reported here (in, for instance, Dr. Levon Jernazian's patient, Vahan, and the parents of Dr. Bernhardt's patient, Karl) we have strong indications that talented people under special circumstances can all too readily undergo that socialization to evil. I thought of the Nazi physician/biologist I interviewed who spoke of his early ideological fascination with the Nazis as "youthful folly" but in that youthful folly managed to provide a "scientific" rationale for the Nazi racial vision.

Breaks Without Transitions

The traumas with which we are dealing here occurred in great sudden breaks with the past (as in the radically different vision of the Communist world-view supplanting that of Nazism); and in continuous yet unpredictable individual traumatic happenings (such as the serial traumas Dr. Nora Csiszer describes in her patient, Mr. E.), causing radical breaks in personal experience and identity. These breaks did not permit the kind of healing so crucial to any significant transition: clarifying and working through disillusionment, grief, and mourning, and absorbing elements of sudden change into a new, protean whole. Rather than give rise to a more inclusive and mature self, the breaks led to troubled, improvised, and a more dissociated self.

There can have been very few historical sequences comparable to that from Nazi occupation to Communist control in much of Central and Eastern Europe following World War II. On the one hand, there was in that sequence an odd psychological continuity of totalism and vicious suppression; on the other, there was a radical undermining of the idealistic visions that motivated much of the struggle against the Nazis at the time of World War II. Miloscz, in his *Collected Poems* (1988), tells of the horror of returning to Warsaw, "a horse-flesh city in ruins," and to Kracow where he saw "scores of young men behind barred windows on the ground floor" who were only yesterday courageous young soldiers of the Polish Underground fighting against the fascists, and today imprisoned by the Communist regime as "agents of the class enemy." Bearing witness to this radical change, and anticipating its long-term results, he wrote, "Let the dead explain to the dead what happened. We are fated to beget a new and violent tribe." To be sure, large numbers of people originally embraced the new Communist regimes. But looking back at the subsequent combination of repression and disillusionment, we can see that many were overwhelmed by precipitous shifts in their landscape that they could neither comprehend nor psychologically absorb. The same was true in connection with sudden policy changes on the part of the established regime—changes that greatly affected therapists and patients by legislating what was either no longer or once more permissible.

Dr. Bernhardt used the phrase "break without transition" in describing how her parents, faced with such an abrupt subversion of ideals, simply traded their brown Nazi Youth shirts for the blue kerchiefs of the Communist Pioneers. Dr. Bernhardt also tells of her patient, Karl, whose mother was a Stasi informer. With the downfall of the Communist regime, Karl's mother never looked back as she and her husband plunged immediately into successful entrepreneurial activities; and that mother's mother had earlier experienced a different kind of break upon returning from Nazi occupied Poland as an outcast refugee, forced to restart her life as though no trauma had intervened. In all of these cases, there was a partial illusion of seamless transition, of simply taking the next necessary step. But what was underneath the outward adaptation were combinations of severe psychic numbing and seething but unacknowledged psychological and ethical conflicts.

Illusory adjustment in the presence of abrupt change is not, of course, limited to the Eastern European experience. In America and other non-Communist societies, we, too, deceive ourselves with seemingly successful adaptations which, at a cost, leave out the psychological dimension. For example, in my recent work with Aum Shinrikyo, the extremist cult which released lethal gas in Tokyo subways in 1995, I have been concerned with those consequences in Japanese society. While the lust for Armegeddon is by no means unique to this group, one gains the strong impression that its emergence had much to do with the extraordinary upheavals in Japanese society; notably its sudden emergence from feudalism in the late nineteenth century, its abject and humiliating defeat in World War II, and its inability to confront its own wartime atrocities which were of a scale rivaling those of the Nazis. Here, too, there were breaks without transition, and here, too, the consequences have reverberated profoundly as an agitated underbelly of a seemingly stable society (Lifton, 1999).

We experience breaks without transitions in our own work as therapists, researchers, and university teachers. But we do not feel ourselves subject to the kind of reality shift that instantly reverses assumptions and policies lived out over years, decades, or generations. At issue here is the degree of absence of an adequate psychological process, individual or collective, for absorbing these changes. Again we lack precise knowledge of the consequences of such dislocations, but we can be sure that they are considerable.

The cost is always there, though it may not show itself (as in Japan) until many decades later. The therapists in this volume tell us that the costs in their patients are both immediate and sustained. (Dr. Vasco Muacevic, who has experienced at least five radical shifts in government in Zagreb during his memory, found that his patient, Viktor, experienced nightmares and psychic numbing accompanying these shifts in Yugoslavia during World War II; Viktor experienced a recurrence of those symptoms when his former Army invaded his home, now as the enemy, four decades later.) The therapists make clear that they themselves are hardly free of those consequences, but that their work made some contribution towards providing at least temporary psychological transitions, for their patients as well as themselves.

Dissembling and Dissociation

Adapting to multiple sudden breaks without transition, along with the continuous fear instilled by Communist regimes, led to walling off certain

features of behavior from an authentic self. Role and self became en-
tangled in a double life.

Even when one sees oneself as playing a role necessary for survival,
there is a sense in which one becomes that role. Or to put the matter
another way, there is no such thing as a mere role since the self is in some
measure present in what one is actually saying or doing. Here we enter
the realm of dissociation which, simply put, describes one part of the self
divided off from another part of the self. Dissembling is close to pretending, a relatively conscious activity; dissociation is unconscious and more
profound; much of the time it is difficult to distinguish between the two.
The Communist State always requires both, given its combination of radical
shifts and continuous claim to absolute truth. Dr. Cucliciu's patient, Mihai,
dissembled and dissociated during his thought reform experience, while
Dr. Cucliciu himself dissembled to pass the police interrogator's final test.
For Dr. Berhhardt's patient, Karl, his parents dissociated in splitting off
their guilt as informers, while Karl struggled with those dissociated aspects of their guilt which he himself carried within him.

The social and historical pressures which bear on these therapies ren-
der them a laboratory for examining the ingredients of dissociation and
dissembling in patient and therapist alike. While psychotherapy as we
know it in the West was anathema to the Communist State (because
therapy values self-reflection and strives for self-fulfillment rather than
for subsuming the self to the larger entity defined by the Communist
State), some physicians, nonetheless, did work hard (especially in the era
of *perestroika*) to create a space where they could assist individuals in seeking to recover the truths of their personal experience. But all therapists in
the Soviet era were citizens and employees of the State, rendering their
therapy highly vulnerable to many threats and demands of that State. We
recall the pressures brought on Dr. Konkov both to join the KGB and to
subvert the purpose of the suicide hot line by revealing the contents of
his therapeutic work. Dr. Bernhardt learned later from her Stasi files that
she had been spied upon and manipulated by Communist authorities
throughout her therapeutic activities with patients. And beyond such glar-
ing examples, there were more subtle ways in which therapists and their
patients alike sensed the danger of full exploration of any personal experience, lest it contradict the perceived truths of the regime, and endanger
either party or both. Can we conceive of what we call the therapeutic
alliance, with its special requirement of trust, ever being realized under
such duress?

Therapists faced the constant danger, or temptation, of having their
work distorted to serve the regime. The specific Soviet-style abuse of psychiatry—labeling dissidents as mentally ill—was likely to find some expression in all Communist countries, whether emanating from design or

slightly more indirect expressions of the totalistic claims of the State. Hence, there were specific professional pressures towards dissembling and dissociation experienced by all who did psychological work.

Our therapists' efforts to explore these issues with us was an important step in the direction of authenticity. But in both Communist and post-Communist countries, this is by no means a mere psychological problem. Overcoming dissembling and dissociation as lasting personal defenses requires a social environment that encourages trust in one's individual experience and safety in revealing it. As always, the political process becomes inseparable from psychological struggles. While post-Communist countries vary greatly in their political climates, none is without formidable confusions and contradictions which discourage one from surrendering by-now-established patterns of dissembling and dissociation. Having said that, we can trace overall tendencies, however imperfect, towards overcoming the specific forms of dissembling and dissociation so characteristically produced under Communism.

Betrayal and Self-Betrayal

Under Communist regimes, virtually everyone was constantly on the verge of betraying someone or something. That betrayal could of course take the most egregious form of one's secret denunciation to the regime of a friend or family member. But the process could be much more subtle. If people were less than enthusiastic about official policies, they could be accused of betraying their nation or something called "the future." That lack of enthusiasm could in turn adversely affect their family, whom they could then be accused of betraying. Or perhaps most typically, people in the professions could accede to Party policies here, hold back on them there, and then tread a fine line of compliance and a stance closer to reluctance than resistance. What is bound to result from all this is a heightened susceptibility to guilt and shame.

One then experiences a sense of badness and humiliation because one falls short of what one perceives to be required of one, either by the large impersonal forces of the State or by those to whom one is most intimately connected. In one way or another the accusations of betrayal can be internalized; the feeling then becomes one of self-betrayal.

We recall that Dr. Cucliciu focused strongly on what his research subject called the "moment of yielding"—of giving in completely to the chief torturer and thereby to the new regime. Dr. Cucliciu had difficulty grasping this moment until remembering a lesser personal incident in which, when interrogated by the secret police himself, he answered affirmatively to the question of whether he would join the Party if asked. His subsequent feeling involved a combination of self-betrayal for what he viewed as a false expression of compliance, and of empathy for those who had "yielded" because he himself, albeit slightly and almost automatically, had done the same.

Psychotherapist and patient would inevitably struggle with these emotions in themselves. Therapists, in addition, could be placed under pressure to betray their patients by reporting on them to the regime or undermining, on behalf of the regime, their struggles for authenticity and independence. It was also true that patients could in turn betray therapists by reporting on them or in some way spreading deleterious rumors about them. At the very least, both had to be on their guard concerning danger from the other.

The case of Mr. E., as presented by Dr. Nora Csiszer and Dr. Eva Katona, illustrates many of these levels of betrayal. Mr. E., whose archeological ambitions led to his being falsely accused as a heretic, was betrayed not only by the regime but by the psychiatric profession which established his label. In the case report in this volume, his new psychiatrist not only helps him to reverse that decision but chooses to bear witness to his story.

In doing so, Drs. Csiszer and Katona seek some moral rectification of both Mr. E. and their own profession. It is a story of a father seeking acceptance from his alienated daughter; of a dissident seeking rehabilitation from a reform government; and of a profession seeking to face its past and to set aright wrongs committed and professional compromises made.

Who is it that compromised with the Communist regime? Elsewhere in their story, Drs. Csiszer and Katona say, "We continued to adapt best by compromising outwardly and inwardly" (Chapter 3, p. 38). Later they comment "We were all part of the old regime and we have to face that truth and go on from there" (Chapter 3, p. 40).

I have a personal inkling of what a therapist's sense of self-betrayal is like. Some years ago, when serving a required tour of military duty as a psychiatrist, I was asked (ordered) by the head of our psychiatric unit to treat his wife. I did so, somewhat flattered that he had chosen me over other, more experienced psychiatrists, but began to have difficulty when he made regular inquiries about her progress. I knew that he had considerable control over my military status and could, for instance, have me transferred to an undesirable or dangerous place. While I had her permission to talk to him and did not disclose any confidential details, I found myself telling him a little more about the therapy than I would ordinarily have done with a spouse. I recall having an uncomfortable feeling that in some small way I might be betraying my patient and my professional responsibility. The matter was further complicated, as I soon discovered, by the fact that a major circumstance in his wife's seeking the therapy had been her husband's extended sexual betrayal of her. While the episode seems trivial in comparison to the content of this book, it does suggest a vicious circle of betrayal and self-betrayal that certain kinds of environments can engender.

Hannah Arendt, in her controversial study, *Eichman in Jerusalem*, wrote critically of Jewish leaders in ghettos because of their collaboration with Nazi officials in turning over Jews who would be sent to their deaths. But in later correspondence with her, Gershom Sholom, the great authority on Jewish mysticism and a longstanding friend of hers, pointed out that she had failed to grasp the terrible pressures these leaders had been under, and faulted her for the Jewish shortcoming of "lack of love for your people." What the story suggests is the sometimes indeterminable line between betrayal and something closer to coercive compromise or even protection. Guilt and shame follow wherever the line is blurred. Under such extreme conditions, one must recognize as the ultimate betrayer the group or regime that creates these structures of betrayal.

Case History and History

This work is a direct extension of an axis of inquiry begun by Erik Erikson in his explorations of great figures in history who could, in their personal breakthrough, reveal much about their era. But in my work, as in our approach to this volume, the focus is on the experiences of ordinary people from which we can draw inferences about the psychological meaning of extraordinary events. Erik Erikson taught us that we cannot take the case history out of history, and also that we cannot take history out of the individual case. From the anguished group of case histories presented in this book we learn much about Communist history that could not be learned in any other way. But we also find that we cannot comprehend any individual story without some grasp of the specific Communist history within which it takes shape. My own way of continuing the spirit of Erikson's work has been to carry out studies of people who have in various ways been acted upon by, or have themselves acted on, a particular historical event or sequence. They have included people subjected to Chinese Communist thought reform, survivors of Hiroshima, Vietnam veterans, and Nazi doctors. In each of these very different groups I found what I called "shared themes," which said something about them, their societies, and their times. Thus, by studying specific groups of people caught up in powerful historical events we can begin to record and better understand some of the mysteries of what we call the historical process, or, at the very least, learn something about the inner struggles of ordinary men and women in the wake of that process.

The reports in this volume suggest the profound revelations about a society that may be drawn from the psychotherapeutic process, and from ways in which that society permits, encourages, or undermines such a process.

The piece of history we look at in this volume is not a pleasant one. It, in fact, takes us to experiences of extreme cruelty and degradation. But we see much gained by confronting what we can of this history and take that confrontation to be an act of hope. The hope lies in our belief that our joint effort can contribute, however modestly, to the continuous struggle required against systems that institutionalize trauma, betrayal, and self-betrayal. The struggle reflects our commitment to alternatives based on decency, trust, and genuine healing.

AFTERWORD

Today's Headlines

Ten years after the fall of the Soviet empire, headlines from the former East Germany, from Poland, and from Russia seem troubling and puzzling. Teenage skin heads in the former GDR brutally murder a black man; Poles attack each other over what secret police files may show; Russia endangers trapped sailors out of fear of foreign rescue operations. For those who anticipated that Eastern Europe should have accommodated to the end of the Cold War with the same integrating energy as Western Europe after the end of World War II, these are troubling signs. Instead, we believe, these headlines reflect the continuing presence of personality traits that are remnants of trauma of the Soviet era, traits that because they have been so adaptive for so long, will be with us for some time to come: traits that engender suspicion, distrust, and projection.

In this book we have looked carefully at the origins of such behavioral attitudes and have traced them to the legacy of Soviet terror, trauma, and loss. East German schooling reinforced the projection of evil onto the outsider, the one who was different. Xenophobia was another form of intolerance of the way of the other. Today the foreigner is no longer the capitalist from the West, he is an African living and working on German soil. If youth, like the patient Karl, continue to have psychological difficulties especially with autonomy, work, and identity, the risk that they discharge these rageful feelings on foreigners is real.

We know that suspicion, fear, and rage among East Europeans over informers remains high. Many feel that the injustices of the past have not been fully addressed. Others, like Hans' parents, deny and suppress the moral impact of their informing. Tensions between informers and the people who were their targets have not disappeared, nor between the generation that endorsed such behaviors and the generation that protested against them.

For many in Russia, distrust, especially of the West, along with patriotic self-sacrifice and stoicism continue to be highly valued. In some ways, the mentality of the post-Stalinist state continues. The need to hide shame and to deny danger, even impending death, is real. As in the times of Dima's grandmother, the story of stoic Russian seamen seems preferable to a story of human defect and the need for help.

Enduring Traits

In these incidents we see the continuing workings of the multigenerational consequences and symptomatic behaviors of Soviet trauma and loss. For those who might have wished otherwise, it may be sobering to realize that these psychological walls have not disappeared in a decade. Tension remains between the generations, within individuals, and within the culture. As we have seen in this book, these and other phenomena were born out of the reign of Soviet trauma and loss and are part of its legacy.

Definition of Trauma Revisited

We began this project without limiting ourselves to a rigid definition of political trauma, hoping to learn from our colleagues who have endured so much of it, what their experience would add to our concept. Dr. Muacevic largely limits himself to those clearly defined massively traumatic events which are beyond expectable life experiences, as in the trauma of war and refugee experiences: experiences already defined as traumatic by the field of PTSD. He implies, of course, that these events are not so rare, and indeed they are characteristic of the life experience of many if not most in Eastern Europe today. But the younger authors tended to use the concept broadly, harkening back to Freud's idea that trauma influences character development. In their definitions of traumatizing events, Drs. Csiszer and Katona include the very climate and institutions that produced complicity. Dr. Bernhardt includes a pedagogy which praises conformity while shaming individuality and creativity as traumatically deforming character. She argues that a society which insists on the premature separation of children from mothers also produces insecurity when a later developmental phase calls for autonomy. Dr. Jernazian spans the bridge between political trauma and natural disaster, pointing out how an imposed totalitarian and pagan State that fails to protect or offer effective relief, and which blames the victim, is experienced as an agent in natural calamity. Dr. Konkov underlines that trauma as a psychological event does not end with one generation: on the contrary, traumas especially of historical dimensions, are multigenerational phenomena calling for psychological adaptations in each generation if they are to be processed.

Multigenerational Challenge

Drs. Cucliciu, Konkov, Csiszer, and Bernhardt point out that Soviet-era trauma affected the generations differently. Original victims of Soviet-era trauma hid their suffering, alienation, depression, paranoia, and PTSD. Their children, under continuing exposure to the same institutions of political trauma, adapted self-protective character traits. But arrested grief, in children and grandchildren, underscored fault lines in their own development and identity. After the fall of the Berlin Wall, when the institutions of trauma (such as secret police) lost much of their power, and a safer and more open environment began to form, pressures emerged to end the hidden suffering, to break barriers of silence, to give expression to repressed trauma memory, and to reengage the task of mourning. Equally, counter-pressures formed to keep the barriers of silence in place. In this new setting, each generation has its own challenge. The first (like Mihai) tries give voice to its legacy without sacrificing structures of the mind that have helped them endure, insulate, and protect. For them the challenge is both integrity and survival. The second, like Dr. Cucliciu, experiences the trauma of their parents' generation vicariously. In Dr. Katona's case, what she has not been told haunts her dreams, and as with Dr. Konkov, it unconsciously organizes patterns of interpersonal relationships. It is this latter generation's role to learn about the suffering which they have already experienced unconsciously so they may organize an understanding consciously, and in so doing, free themselves for a separate life. The third generation wants to know "the truth," feeling cut off and empty because what little they know has been doctored. But the task before them is complex. Having deconstructed the reality they were told as children, their challenge is to discover a new multigenerational history. Yet in the end this, too, they will acknowledge is incomplete.

Populations of Survivors

Throughout this book we have looked at specific populations of trauma survivors, former political prisoners and their families, survivors of politically charged traumas of war, genocide, and disaster, both victims and perpetrators and their families. Further, we have narrated how sensitive mental health professionals have responded to the needs of individual survivors and their families in individual psychotherapies. They did this while operating within a field that had lost much of its credibility because of its connection with the secret police in controlling and managing political dissent. As we conclude, we must look at how the mental health institutions are faring since the fall of Communism. Are the mental health systems in these countries independent of police ties? Are they better prepared to take on such public health tasks as programs for trauma survivors and their families? Have they addressed the abuses of the past? What is the health of spontaneous, supportive survivor-based networks? Are today's professionals prepared to network with such indigenous support groups to offer creative ways of healing the past?

Changes in Mental Health in Eastern Europe and Russia

Changes in mental health institutions in Eastern Europe have generally been positive, but have a long way to go. The Geneva Initiative on mental health reform, which was supportive of this project, has fostered an international support group for those inside the former Eastern bloc countries and former Soviet republics to establish rights for the "user" of psychiatric facilities, particularly inpatient facilities. It also assists professional groups in establishing ethical grounds to protect mental health from abuse by government.

Romania has taken steps to restructure psychiatry with a set of ethics that separate it from government control. But a ten-year retrospective study of families of psychiatric patients in Bucharest, Romania, shows that much remains to be done. Ordinary citizens feel powerless in the face of authoritarian psychiatry. "The results outline a relationship indicative of totalitarian scars . . . relatives take refuge in a passive and uncritical role . . . (there is an) abnormal tolerance of . . . double standards (which) . . . shows the impact of the totalitarian experience"(Andreescu, Grigorescu, & Teodorescu, 1999)

In Hungary, a self-help group for former users of psychiatric facilities, called Voice of Soul, has developed to offer opportunities for reform and empowerment. It joins a coalition of ex-users/survivors, family organizations, and reform-minded professionals in the Hungarian Mental Health Interest Forum (Gombos, 2000).

An Armenian Mental Health Foundation is lobbying the legislature to protect the rights of the mentally ill. Supporters are optimistic that soon Armenia will follow Estonia, Latvia, Poland, and Russia with laws that guarantee human rights for psychiatric patients. But "proper legislation is only the beginning . . . it would be naive to think that legislation alone will solve the problems of the field" (Vardanyan, 2000).

In the former East Germany, folding its mental health institutions into the organization and laws of the Federal Republic of Germany has led to the most complete change of the former Eastern bloc countries. Also, under the auspices of the Gauck Commission, careful study of Stasi (secret police) files has been under way. One objective has been to ascertain the degree to which Soviet Russia's use of psychiatry in its anti-dissident policy was replicated in the GDR. A report by the former East German psychiatrist Sonya Suess, who assisted us in this project, has appeared under the title *Politically Abused? Psychiatry and State Security in East Germany* (personal communication). She finds that there were individual East German doctors whose attitudes and behaviors were consistent with Russian doctors who hospitalized people because of dissident views. However, she finds no definitive evidence of systematic policy-level measures to hospitalize dissidents in East Germany through psychiatric diagnosis.

Croatian psychiatry has directed itself with energy in the study of those traumatized by war, and in the introduction of up-to-date treatment protocols (Klain, 1992). Psychiatrists have addressed the special problems of the deportation camps (Jukic, Dodig, Kenfelj, & DeZan, 1997) and refugees (Mandic & Bosnic, 1992), but are relatively silent on the influence of totalitarian trauma.

Memorial: A Non-Professional Support Network

Of all the spontaneous support groups in Russia and Eastern Europe, perhaps the most successful is Memorial. In Russia, a group of descendants of those killed by Stalin's purges has formed under the name Memorial. The group provides support for relatives of those persecuted by the Communist State, seeks proper burial of remains, and appropriate statements from the government. It also assists relatives in learning of the fate of their kin through KGB files. The group has sponsored church-sanctioned burial rituals for those interred in mass graves. Memorial sponsors publication of literature about its activities and functions as a support group outside the government.

Trauma's Legacy: Illness of the Soul or of the Mind

In the West, the notion of PTSD has gained significant currency. A sociocultural mind-set has grown that empathizes with the suffering of survivors of trauma. An increased awareness of the traumatic experiences of American soldiers in the Vietnam war and survivors of the Holocaust has led to the building of the Vietnam Memorial Wall and the American Holocaust Museum. These are sanctioned places for education and multi-generational healing. The success of self-help groups such as Vet Centers, survivor groups for incest and rape victims, and the collateral support of professional groups such as the International Society for Traumatic Stress Studies (ISTSS) speaks to this confluence of supportive forces. Here the concept of the multigenerational legacy of trauma finds legitimacy and hope.

In the East, such a consensus does not yet exist (Merridale, 2000). The concept of PTSD as a legitimate medical condition does not match easily with the stoic, suppressive, minimizing adaptations to trauma and loss. Trauma reactions in the West stand out precisely because they appear in sharp contrast from expectations of the population as a whole. But in the East, trauma and its reactions do not stand out. Rather, they are typical of the sufferings of most if not all. Trauma seems to have been too frequent, too severe, too long-standing, and too institutionalized to allow the emergence of a concept of how it is processed. A truly supportive recovery environment, one with socially sanctioned ritual to help this working through, has been too recent to allow alternative organizing concepts to emerge. Also, some argue that the official stigma associated with the purges has been too internalized and is too well integrated with denial, even the cult of forgetting, for the general public to embrace Western notions such as PTSD. And so, change is slow.

Still, as in Memorial above, progress towards healing is being made. Hopefully we move gradually towards an environment in which survivors and their families have access to: a political climate open enough and stable enough to tolerate the telling of the stories of the past; art, film, literature—arenas for ritualized memory which convey to the broader public the impact of Soviet-era trauma over the generations; mental health professionals who are self-aware enough to listen effectively to those who must tell their stories; and open communication between the generations. In the minds of survivors and clinicians, trauma and its consequences must be given a place where it does not stigmatize or penalize those who experience continued suffering

Parallels in North American Society

Recently, a growing exposure of Eastern European art, film, and literature is expanding the West's base of knowledge regarding those who lived through these years in Russia and Eastern Europe. However, the enormous waves of violence and death that have covered Russia and Eastern Europe in the twentieth century, and the specifics of Communist political repression, remain difficult for the North American reader, who has not experienced total war on his or her own soil, to comprehend. Political trauma arising out of ethnic hatred and genocide, an ecology of informing, persecution of "enemy elements" under cover of war—all seem at first blush foreign to the American experience. But psychological analogies in our own history and personal experiences are not really so far away.

A broad historical perspective makes parallels with our own history more possible. The legacy of the trauma of slavery and genocide, indeed, may be so longstanding and so deep that it is difficult to limit in definition—but it would be hard to dismiss as unrelated to slavery and genocide the widespread poverty, fractured families, and endemic drug and alcohol addiction traumatizing a large proportion of African Americans (Cross, 1998) and Native Americans today (Duran, Duran, Brave Heart, & Davis, 1998). While this is beyond the scope of this book, it is important to acknowledge the magnitude and span of this trauma. For therapists, it would be helpful to view this trauma as we have characterized trauma in Eastern Europe—as a phenomenon whose effects can be passed on through many generations.

We in the West have experienced to a lesser extent some of the trauma of the ecology of informing. During the McCarthy era, in selected subcultures of our country (e.g., entertainment and media, universities) widespread informing occurred along with the expectation that all good citizens were on the look-out for "pink Commie sympathizers." We turned, venomously, on those accused, and we watched on TV as previously admired figures squirmed under public scrutiny. We ostracized people on the basis of half-truths, and were complicitly silent as their lives were ruined. Those who experienced this shunning were tainted and their children spent at least another generation trying to rehabilitate the names of those accused. Some bystanders took risks and stood up to the pressures, but most did not.

During war, we also have blurred the line between legitimate internal security and political repression. American concentration camps for Japanese families during World War II created hardships publicly denied by the United States government for two generations.

And what of the Eastern European epidemic of disruption in multigenerational continuity? How might that resonate with the American experience? Many immigrants arriving in the United States during the past fifty years carry with them similar gaps in multigenerational identity which we have described among East Europeans, especially those fleeing extreme poverty, ethnic/racial/religious persecution, civil war, and dictatorship. North American mental health professionals who work with survivors of any of these conditions will find applications to their work and to understanding their clients' experience. Indeed the size of this population is considerable. The United States Committee for Refugees reports that 1.3 million refugees were admitted to the United States between 1986 and 1999 alone, including 600,000 from the USSR and Eastern Europe. Of these 100,000 arrived in 1998 and 1999 from the former Soviet countries and Bosnia, and 500,000 from East Asia.

Another population of Americans, unrelated to political repression, also deals with this multigenerational gap, namely, adopted children, cut off from their biologic parents. Some want to learn who these parents were in an effort to define more clearly their own identity. And they hope that filling in this gap in their self-knowledge will fill in a gap in themselves as adults.

Lessons for the North American Clinician

So, what have we learned that is of practical use for the North American clinician? Certainly we have an increased sensitivity to patients whose backgrounds reflect the historical trauma of the twentieth century, especially Eastern European immigrants and refugees, as well as refugees and immigrants from other war-torn areas of the world.

But there is much more. The treatments of our Russian and East European colleagues teach us much about the basic framework of the therapeutic encounter. It is possible to create atmospheres of trust even in the most distrustful of circumstances. The working alliance is a sturdy structure so long as the therapist reacts with integrity. Therapists who have been wounded by the same or similar forces as their patients are capable of helping their patients if they remain aware of the critical roles of transference and countertransference. Therapists, by virtue of their commitment to human growth, can be active elements in communities whose repressive measures, whether in the name of the collective or in the name of wealth and power, call for change and reform. Character traits and symptoms may reflect political trauma as well as psychosexual or developmental trauma. And the overcoming of such experiences is a multigenerational challenge.

The Therapists Today

Five years have elapsed since the therapists met together in Berlin. The therapists have accomplished much in that time, some of which has grown directly from interests they expressed in this book. Dr. Heike Bernhardt, now in the private practice of psychiatry and psychotherapy in Berlin, has published on euthenasia during the Third Reich (1994), and she has co-authored a book on psychoanalysis in the German Democratic Republic (Bernhardt & Lockot, 2000). Dr. Vasko Muacevic has translated a psychiatric text from English into Croatian and published several papers on PTSD (Muacevic, Simunovic, & Bamburac, 1995). Dr. Anie Kalayjian has published on delivery of mental health services in disasters (1994, 1999).

Drs. Levon Jernazian and Fyodor Konkov have settled in California where they have worked with Armenian and Russian immigrants. Dr. Eva Katona has remarried and settled in England where she treats drug-addicted patients. Dr. Ion Cucliciu has completed a fellowship in psychiatry in Paris, France. The intervening years have not been easy ones for these East European therapists. Changes in geographic locations brought with them the need to master new languages, differing criteria for practice, and a new culture. They have had to cope with distance from their families. Each spoke of the confusion created by open options in life. They struggled with unpredictable and unfair decisions from authorities and were confused by the seeming cacophony of motives which produced them. They found that prior templates from the world of Communist Eastern Europe for dealing with those who presented irrational obstructions to them were not helpful. In a way they lamented disappearance of the orderly and predictable. Their enthusiasm for change a decade ago is tempered by a more persistent distrust than they expected, by skepticism of causes, and by a reluctance to join the group. Some find themselves critical of the West which they idealized only a few years ago, now seeing its own social inequalities, disavowed trauma, and dishonest corporate rhetoric. Life and hope centers in their private lives and families.

Those clinician-reformers who have remained at home have also been quiet, as though to say that the burst of enthusiasm surrounding the revolutions themselves has been tempered by economic crisis at home, and painful awareness that proceeding on to a free-market, democratic world will not be a route with a straight line.

What Has Become of the Patients

These same forces, geographical mobility, career shifts, and economic crisis, have made it difficult for the therapists to follow-up with their patients. The best data are available for Josip, who remains in contact with his therapist. He has had several set-backs requiring medication and supportive psychotherapy, but he uses the resource of his therapist effectively to combat periodic symptomatic states and to adapt to his current world.

The Editors Today

Like the therapists, the editors have been busy. Dr. Lifton completed books on the Japanese cult that planned to save the world by destroying it (1999), and on the American use of nuclear weapons at Hiroshima and Nagasaki (1995). Dr. Lindy completed five years as director of the Cincinnati Psychoanalytic Institute and co-edited a book on the psychotherapy of trauma (Wilson, Friedman, & Lindy, 2001).

Like the therapists, we have continued to struggle with the personal meaning of the traumas of the Soviet era.

Use of this Casebook as Text for Russian Therapists

One of Dr. Lindy's activities in the past few years has been as psychoanalytic teacher to students of psychoanalysis in Moscow and St. Petersburg. In the course of this work, he has used texts from earlier drafts of this book as case material for study and discussion of psychotherapeutic work which addresses trauma and loss, transference, and countertransference, from within a current Russian and Eastern European perspective. Students reading the case material have reacted with evasion, denial, and protest. They have also reacted with great openness, warmth, pain, and understanding. Often in the small discussion groups afterwards there are memories of trauma to parents and grandparents and wounds still in the midst of healing.

Dr. Lindy also learned, in 2001, that his grandfather had left behind in Russia three cousins: the oldest, Max, was killed in the failed 1905 revolution against the Czar; the second, Aaron, was repressed in the early years of the Communist revolution, and spent many years in a prison camp before being released; the third, Moise, was repressed in the Stalin era, sent to a labor camp, and died there. Aaron's descendants are survivors of many of the displacements and traumas recounted in this book. I (Dr. Lindy) met in February 2001 (through the efforts of my cousin Elsa Kisber), a young woman pianist from Lithuania and Moscow, the age of my daughter. Olga is a descendant from that part of my family which had stayed in Eastern Europe. There, in my daughter's home in London, in the company of Dr. Eva Katona, we began to reconnect a familial link between us, one that had been broken for one hundred years.

We began this journey responding to the plea of our East European colleagues to help them tell their story to the West. We complete the journey knowing in fact now what we knew then only distantly—that their story is also ours.

Glossary
of Eastern European Terms

Antifaschistischer Schutzwall: Antifascist Protecting Rampart, East German
 term for the Berlin wall. The name implies the function of protecting
 the East from the evils of capitalism and the West.

Arrow Cross: Fascist ultranationalist Hungarians.

Chetniks: Serb royalists; in collaboration with the Nazi occupiers.

dacha: A Russian country house.

dzerar: An Armenian term for small bundle of belongings which one is
 ready to take at a moment's notice in case one is arrested by the
 secret police.

Domobran: A member of the Croatian home guard during World War II,
 allied with the Nazi occupiers.

FDJ: An abbreviation for the Freie Deutsche Jugend, or "Free German
 Youth," the youth organization of East Germany (GDR).

gegauckt: German word coinage derived from the Gauck Commission which
 has control over Stasi files. East German informers, discovered from
 the Commission's studies of the files, were denied access to government positions in the new united German government. This loss of
 employment was termed *gegauckt*.

gulag: Russian term for political prison or workcamp.

gulag archepelago: The network of prison camps for political prisoners mostly
 in remote areas of the Soviet Union.

HJ: An abbreviation for Hitlerjugend ("Hitler Youth"), the youth organization of Nazi Germany.

ketman: A term originally used to describe Muslims who preserved their
 heritage, while being prohibited from their religion by the Persians.
 They disguised themselves as wise Persian priests. This task of successfully hiding one's true self while seeming to excel in a role admired by the contrary world-view of the conqueror is a concept which
 Cseslaw Milosz used to describe the world of survival within a captive mind in the Eastern European countries under Soviet control.

Krippen: State nurseries for children one to three years of age in East Germany. Eighty percent of children attended.

kulak: Soviet term for prosperous or middle-class farmer. This designation would often mean forceful and shameful displacement to another region of the USSR.

moskal: Ukrainian term for Russian invader.

partisans: Term used throughout Western and Central Europe designating resistance fighters to the Nazi occupation. While this was usually a loose alliance of political groups, in the former Yugoslavia, the most powerful partisans were under Tito's Communist leadership.

Ustasas: Croat fascists collaborating with the Nazi occupiers.

Vergangenheitsbewaltigung: Confronting, or doing business with and getting on with the past, referring not only to Nazi Germany but also the years of East Germany.

weltanschauung: Worldview or overall philosophy/belief system.

Wermacht: German army in World War II.

Wiedervereinigung: German for wide sweeping changes, referring to the experience of the reunification of Germany, particularly from the Eastern side.

zagradotriad: A Soviet military unit instructed to kill "friendly" troops at the front, if, in the presence of advancing enemy, they try to retreat. This was done at Stalingrad with political prisoners released from camps to earn their freedom by fighting under intolerable circumstances for the homeland.

zek: Political prisoner of the USSR.

REFERENCES

Chapter 1 Introduction

Chukovskaya, L. (1988). *Sofia Petrovna*. Chicago: Northwestern University Press. (Original work published 1967)

Havel, V. (1993). *The garden party* (pp. 49–50). New York: Grove Press. (Original work published 1963 in Czech)

Havel, V. (1986). *Living in truth* (pp. 50–122). London & New York: Faber & Faber. (Original work published 1979 in Czech)

Havel, V. (1993). *The memorandum* (p. 128). New York: Grove Press. (Original work published 1966 in Czech)

Kundera, M. (1992). *The joke* (pp. 89–121). New York: HarperCollins. (Original work published 1967)

Lindy, J. D., MacLeod, J., Spitz, L., Green, B., & Grace, M. (1988). *Vietnam: A casebook* (pp. 244–259). New York: Brunner Mazel.

Manea, M. (1990). Three lines with commentary. In W. Brinton & A. Rinzler (Eds.), *Without force or lies: Voices from the revolution of central Europe in 1989–90* (pp. 305–332). San Francisco: Mercury House.

Miller, M. (1998) *Freud and the Bolsheviks* (pp. 131–146). New Haven, CT: Yale University Press

Milosz, C. (1990). *The captive mind* (pp. 54–81). New York: Random House. (Original work published 1953)

Solzhenitsyn, A. (1962/1991). *One day in the life of Ivan Denisovich* (pp. 9–10). New York: Noonday. (Original work published 1962)

Wilson, J. P., & Lindy, J. D. (1994). *Countertransference and the treatment of PTSD* (pp. 5–29). New York: Guilford.

Wolf, C. (1970). *The quest for Christa T.* (pp. 40–56). New York: Noonday.

Wolf, C. (1980). *Patterns of childhood* (p. 1), New York: Noonday. (Original work published 1976 in German as *A model childhood*)

Chapter 2 The Legacy of Trauma

Adler, N., & Glutsman, S. (1993). Soviet "special psychiatric hospitals" where the system was criminal and the inmates were sane. *British Journal of Psychiatry, 163*, 713–720.

Beevor, A. (1998). *Stalingrad: The fateful siege: 1942–1943* (pp. 406–417). New York: Penguin Books.

Croan, M. (1992). Germany and Eastern Europe. In J. Held (Ed.), *Columbia history of eastern Europe in the twentieth century* (pp. 345–393). New York: Columbia University Press.

Davies, R., Harrison, M., & Wheatcroft, S. (1994). *The economic transformation of the Soviet Union 1913–1945* (pp. 62–64). Cambridge, UK: Cambridge University Press.

deJonge, A., & Morrow, W. (1986). *Stalin, and the shaping of the Soviet Union* (pp. 329–354). New York: William Morrow.

Djordjevic, D. (1992). The Yugoslav phenomenon. In J. Held (Ed.), *Columbia history of eastern Europe in the twentieth century* (pp. 306–344). New York: Columbia University Press.

Ehlers, A., Maercker, A., & Boos, A. (2000, February). Posttraumatic stress disorder following political imprisonment: The role of mental defeat, alienation and perceived permanent change. *Journal of Abnormal Psychology*, 45–55.

Eros, F., Vajda, J., & Kovacs, E. (1998). Intergenerational responses to social and political changes: Transformation of Jewish identity in Hungary. In Y. Danieli (Ed.), *International handbook of multigenerational legacies of trauma* (pp. 315–324). New York: Plenum Press.

Green, B., Wilson, J. P., & Lindy, J. D. (1985). Conceptualizing post-traumatic stress disorder: A psychosocial framework. In C. R. Figley (Ed.), *Trauma and its wake: The study and treatment of post-traumatic stress dissorder* (pp. 53–69). New York: Brunner/Mazel.

Goenjian, A., Pynoos, R., Steinberg, A., Najarian, L., Asamov, J., Karayan, I., Ghurabi, M., & Fairbanks, L. (1995). Psychiatric co-morbidity in children after the 1988 earthquake in Armenia. *Journal of Child and Adolescent Psychiatry, 34*(9), 1174–1184.

Hanak, P., & Held, J. (1992). Hungary on a fixed course: An outline of Hungarian history. In J. Held (Ed.), *Columbia history of eastern Europe in the twentieth century* (pp. 164–228). New York: Columbia University Press.

Havel, V. (1986). *Living in truth* (pp. 50–122). London & New York: Faber & Faber. (Original work published 1979 in Czech)

Havenaar, J. M., Rumyantzeva, G. M, Van den Brink, W., Poelijoe, N. W., van den Bout, J., van Engeland, M., & Koeter, M. W. (1997). Long-term mental health effects of the Chernobyl disaster: An epidemiologic survey in two former Soviet regions. *American Journal of Psychiatry, 11*, 1605–1607.

Kozaric-Kovacic, D., Marusic, A., & Ljubin, T. (1999). Combat experienced soldiers and tortured prisoners of war differ in the clinical presentation of post traumatic stress disorder. *Nordic Journal of Psychiatry, 1*, 11–15.

Kuper, L. (1988). The Turkish genocide of Armenians, 1915–1917. In R. Hovannisian (Ed.), *The Armenian genocide in perspective* (pp. 43–59). New Brunswick, NJ & Oxford, UK: Transaction.

Loewen, J. (1995). *Lies my teacher told me* (pp. 139–170). New York: Simon & Schuster.

Martic-Biocina, S., Spoljar-Vrzina, S., & Rudan, V. (1998). Acute post-traumatic stress disorder in prisoners of war released from detention camps. *Drustven Istrazivanja* [*Social Research*], 7(3), 485–497.

Merridale, C. (1996). Death and memory in modern Russia. *History Workshop Journal, 42*, 3–4.

Merridale, C. (2000a). *Night of stone: Death and memory in Russia* (pp. 128–158). London: Granta Books.

Merridale, C. (2000b). The collective mind: Trauma and shell-shock in twentieth-century Russia. *Journal of Contemporary History, 35*(1), 39–55.

Miller, M. (1998). *Freud and the Bolsheviks*. New Haven, CT: Yale University Press.

Milosz, C. (1990). *The captive mind* (pp. 54–81). New York: Random House. (Original work published 1953)

Priebe, S., & Denis, D. (1998). Leiden bus heute: Uber die psychischen Folgen politischer Verfolgung in der DDR [Suffering until today: On the psychological sequelae of political persecution in the German Democratic Republic]. *Nerenheilkunde* [*Nervous Disorders of Medical Science*], *17*(2), 84–90.

Solzhenitsyn, A. (1991). *One day in the life of Ivan Denisovich* (pp. 9–10). New York: Noonday. (Original work published 1962)

Chapter 3 Hungary

Adler, N., & Glutsman, S. (1993). Soviet "special psychiatric hospitals" where the system was criminal and the inmates were sane. *British Journal of Psychiatry, 163*, 713–720.

Eros, F., Vajda, J., & Kovacs, E. (1989). Intergenerational responses to social and political changes: Transformation of Jewish identity in Hungary. In Y. Danieli (Ed.), *International handbook of multigenerational legacies of trauma* (pp. 315–324). New York: Plenum Press.

Havel, V. (1986). *Living in truth* (pp. 57–72). London & New York: Faber and Faber. (Original work published 1979 in Czech)

Laufer, R. S. (1988). The serial self: War trauma, identity and adult development. In J. P. Wilson, Z. Harel, & B. Kahana (Eds.), *Human adaptation to extreme stress: From the holocaust to Vietnam* (pp. 33–54). New York: Plenum Press.

Lifton, R. J. (1993). *The protean self: Human resilience in an age of fragmentation* (pp. 213–233). New York: Basic Books.

Manea, M. (1990). Three lines with commentary. In W. Brinton & A. Rinzler (Eds.), *Without force or lies: Voices from the revolution of central Europe in 1989–90* (p. 308). San Francisco: Mercury House.

McFarlane, A., & Yehuda R. (1996). Resilience, vulnerability, and the course of posttraumatic reactions. In B. van der Kolk, A. McFarlane, & L. Weisaeth (Eds.), *Traumatic stress: The effects of overwhelming experience on mind, body, and society*. New York: Guilford.

Miller, M. (1985) The theory and practice of psychiatry in the Soviet Union. *Psychiatry, 48*(1), 13–24.

Racker, H. (1968) *Transference and countertransference* (pp. 133–137). New York: International Universities Press.

Schwarzer, R., & Jerusalem, M. (1995). Optimistic self-beliefs as a resource factor in coping with stress. In S. Hobfoll & M. De Vries (Eds.), *Extreme stress and communities* (pp. 159–177). Dordect, the Netherlands: Kluwer Academic Publishers.

Wilson, J. P., & Lindy, J. D. (1994). *Countertransference and PTSD* (pp. 30–61). New York: Guilford.

Chapter 4 German Democratic Republic

Geulen, E. (1995, Fall), Nationalism: Old, new and German. *TELOS, 105*, 18.

Huyssen A., (1995). Marking time in a culture of amnesia. *Twilight memories* (p. 81, pp. 73–74). New York & London: Routledge.

Huyssen, A. (1991, Winter). After the wall: The failure of German intellectuals. *New German Critique, 52* (Special Issue on German Unification).

Israel, A. (1992). *"Spezifische Konflikthaftigkeit sozialer Bedrfrfnisse in der Kindesentwicklung im Kontext der Sozialisationsbedingungen in der DDR."* Zeitschrift ffr Gruppentherapie und Gruppendynamik. [Conflicts over aggressive needs in the socialization and early childhood development in the German Democratic Repbulic.]

Plog U. (1993). Vertrauen ist gut: åber den Mi°brauch der Psychiatrie durch den Staatssicherheitsdienst der DDR [Confiding is good; but was there abuse of psychiatry through the state security police (Stasi) during the DDR]. *Mabuse, 85,* 30–34.

SchrÜter, S. (1994). Schweigepflicht gebrochen: Psychiater im Dienste der Stasi [Broken confidentiality: Psychiatry in the service of the Stasi]. *Mabuse, 89,* 48–49.

Simon, A., (1994). Seelenblindheit: Åber die Folgen der verdrèngten Angst [Torn from blindness: The state which supplants fear]. *Mabuse, 88,* 38–42.

Statistisches Amt der DDR. (1990). *Statistisches Jahrbuch der DDR, Berlin.* [Bureau of Statistics for the GDR. (1990). *Statistical yearbook for East Germany, Berlin.*]

Statistisches Bundesamt. (1991). *Statistisches Jahrbuch fur das vereinte Deutschland, Weisbaden.* [Bureau of Federal Statistics. (1991). *Statistical yearbook for the united Germany, Weisbaden.*]

Wierling, D. (1993a). Von der HJ zur FDJ?" *BIOS, 6,* 103–118.

Wolf, C. (1970). *The quest for Christa T.* New York: Noonday.

Chapter 5 Romania

Adler, N., Mueller G., & Mohammed, A. (1993). Psychiatry under tyranny: A report on the political abuse of Romanian psychiatry during the Ceausescu years. *Current Psychology: Research and Reviews, 12*(1), 3–17.

Gilberg T. (1990). *Nationalism and Communism in Romania: The rise and fall of the Ceausescu cult* (pp. 11–137). Boulder, CO: Westview Press.

Lifton, R. J. (1961). *Thought reform and the psychology of totalism: A study of "brainwashing" in China.* New York: Norton.

Walker, L. E. (1985). The battered woman syndrome study. In D. Finkelhor, R. J. Gelles, G. T. Hotaling, & M. A. Strauss (Eds.), *The dark side of families* (pp. 31–48). Beverly Hills CA: Sage.

Chapter 6 Russia

Baker, K. G., & Gippenreiter, J. B. (1998). Stalin's purge and its impact on Russian families: A pilot study. In Y. Danieli (Ed.). *International handbook of multigenerational legacies of trauma* (pp. 403–434). New York: Plenum Press.

Havenaar, J. M., Rumyantzeva, G. M., Van den Brink, W., Poelijoe, N. W., van den Bout, J., van Engeland, M., & Koeter, M. W. (1997). Long-term mental health effects of the Chernobyl disaster: An epidemiologic survey in two former Soviet regions. *American Journal of Psychiatry, 11,* 1605–1607.

Kalayjian, A. S. (1999) Coping through meaning: The community response to the earthquake in Armenia. In E. Zinner & M. B. Williams (Eds.), *When a community weeps: Case studies in group survivorship* (pp. 86–101). Philadelphia: Brunner/Mazel.

Kindra, G. P., & Turakhodzhaev, A. M. (1994). The influence of post-traumatic stress disorders on adjustment of Afghanistan war veterans. *Journal of Russian and East European Psychiatry, 27*(2), 76–82.

Lifton, B. J. (1994). *Journey of the adopted self* (pp. 38–45). New York: Basic Books.

Miller, M. (1985). The theory and practice of psychiatry in the Soviet Union. *Psychiatry, 48*(1), 13–24.

Miller, M. (1998). *Freud and the Bolsheviks* (p. 128). New Haven, CT: Yale University Press.

Chapter 7 Croatia

Aarts, P., & Op den Velde, W. (1996). Prior traumatization and the process of aging: Theory and clincical implications. In B. van der Kolk, A. McFarlane, & L. Weisaeth (Eds.), *Traumatic stress: The effects of overwhelming experience on mind, body, and society* (pp. 359–377). New York: Guilford.

Freud, A., & Burlingham, D. (1943). *War and children* (pp. 175–185). Westport, CT: Greenwood Press.

Hartman, H. (1958). *Ego psychology and the problem of adaptation* (pp. 100–109). New York: International Universities Press.

Jukic, V., Dodig, G., Kenfelj, H., & De Zan, D. (1997). Psychic difficulties in former prisoners of detention camps. *Collegium Antropologicum, 21*(1), 235–242.

Kaplan, R. (1993). *Balkan ghosts: A journey through history.* New York: St. Martin's.

Klain, E., & Pavic, L. (1999). Countertransference in therapists/helpers working with psychotraumatized persons. *Croatian Medical Journal, 4*(4), 466–472.

Kozaric-Kovacic, D., Marusic, A., & Ljubin, T. (1999). Combat experienced soldiers and tortured prisoners of war differ in the clinical presentation of post traumatic stress disorder. *Nordic Journal of Psychiatry, 1,* 11–15.

Martic-Biocina, S., Spoljar-Vrzina, S. M., & Rudan, V. (1996). Anthropological and psychodynamic characteristics of family life of displaced persons and refugees: An example from the island of Hvar. *Collegium Antropologicum, 20*(2), 301–308.

Martic-Biocina, S., Spoljar-Vrzina, S., & Rudan, V. (1998). Acute post-traumatic stress disorder in prisoners of war released from detention camps. *Drustven Istrazivanja* [Social Research], *7*(3), 485–497.

McFarlane, A., & Yehuda, R. (1996). Resilience, vulnerability, and the course of posttraumatic reactions. In B. van der Kolk, A. McFarlane, & L.Weisaeth (Eds), *Traumatic stress: The effects of overwhelming experience on mind, body, and society* (pp. 155–181). New York: Guilford.

Milivojevic, L. (1999). Complexity of therapists feelings in the work with war-traumatized patients, *Croatian Medical Journal, 40*(4), 503–507.

Mollica, R., Casp-Yavin, V., Bollini, P., Tuong, T., Tor, S., & Lavelle, J. (1992). The Harvard Trauma Questionnaire: Validating a cross-cultural instrument. *Journal of Nervous and Mental Diseases, 180*(2), 111–116.

Op den Velde, W., Hovens, J. E., Falger, P. R. J., De Groen, J. H. M., Van Duijn, H., Lasschuit, L. J., & Schouten, E. G. W. (1993). PTSD in Dutch resistance veterans from World War II. In J. P. Wilson & B. Raphael (Eds.), *International handbook of traumatic stress syndromes* (pp. 219–230). New York: Plenum Press.

Vanista-Kosuta, A., & Kosuta, M. (1998). Trauma and meaning. *Croatian Medical Journal, 39*(1), 54–61.

Chapter 8 Armenia

Goenjian, A. K. (1993). A mental health relief programme in Armenia after the 1988 earthquake: Implementation and clinical observation. *British Journal of Psychiatry, 163,* 230–239.

Hovannisian, R. (1988). *The Armenian genocide in perspective.* New Brunswick, NJ: Transaction Publishers.

Kalayjian, A. S. (1994). Emotional and environmental connections: Impact of the Armenian earthquake. In E. Schuster & C. Brown (Eds.), *Exploring our environmental connection* (pp. 155–174). New York: National League for Nursing.

Kalayjian, A. S. (1999). Coping through meaning: the community response to the earthquake in Armenia. In E. Zinner & M. B. Williams (Eds.), *When a community weeps: Case studies in group survivorship* (pp. 86–101). Philadelphia: Brunner/Mazel.

Kupelian, D., Kalayjian, A. S., & Kassabian, A. (1998). The Turkish genocide of the Armenians: Continuing effects on survivors and their families eight decades after massive trauma. In Y. Danieli (Ed.), *International handbook of multigenerational legacies of trauma* (pp. 191–210). New York Plenum Press.

Smith, H. (1976). *The Russians* (pp. 273–301). New York: Quadrangle/New York Times.

Chapter 9 Invisible Walls

Erikson, E. (1958). *Young man Luther*. New York: Norton.

Erikson, E. (1969). *Ghandi's truth*. New York: Norton.

Fleming, J. & Altschul, S. (1963). Activation of mourning and growth by psychoanalysis. In S. Altschul (Ed.), *International Journal of Psychoanalysis, 44*, 419–431.

Haley, S. A. (1974). When the patient reports atrocities: Specific treatment considerations of the Vietnam veteran. *Archives of General Psychiatry, 30*, 191–196.

Kernberg, O. (1980). *Internal world and external reality* (pp. 111–112). New York & London: Aronson.

Lifton, R. J. (1968). *Death in life: Survivors of Hiroshima*. New York: Random House.

Lifton, R. J. (1986). *Nazi doctors: Medical killing and the psychology of genocide*. New York: Basic Books.

Lifton, R. J. (1995). *Hiroshima in America: Fifty years of denial*. New York: Putnam.

Lindy, J. D., MacLeod, J., Spitz, L., Green, B., & Grace, M. (1988). *Vietnam: A casebook* (pp. 244–259). New York: Brunner/Mazel.

Milosz, C. (1990). *The captive mind* (pp. 54–81). New York: Random House. (Original work published 1953)

Wilson, J. P, & Lindy, J. D. (1994). *Countertransference in the treatment of PTSD*. New York: Guilford.

Chapter 10 History as Trauma

Lifton, R. J. (1961). *Thought reform and the psychology of totalism: A study of "brainwashing" in China*. New York: Norton.

Lifton, R. J. (1973). *Home from the war*. New York: Simon & Schuster

Lifton, R. J. (1986). *Nazi doctors: Medical killing and the psychology of genocide*. New York: Basic Books.

Lifton, R. J. (1999). *Destroying the world to save it. Aum Shinrikyo: Apocalyptic violence and the new global terrorism*. New York: Henry Holt.

Milosz, C. (1988). *Collected poems*: (1944, p. 75) Flight, (1946, p. 85) Child of Europe, (1945, p. 90), Mid Twentieth Century Portrait. Hopewell, NJ: Ecco Press.

Afterword

Andreescu, C., Grigorescu, G., & Teodorescu, R. (1999). Families and mental health workers in a post-totalitarian society. *Mental Health Reforms, 2,* 2–5.

Bernhardt, H. (1994). *Anstltpsychiatrie und "euthenasie" in Pommern 1933–1945.* Frankfurt am Main: Mabuse-Verlag.

Berhardt, H., & Lockot, R. (2000). *Mit ohne Freud, zur geschichte der psychoanalyse in Ostdeutschland* [Without Freud: The history of psychoanalysis in East Germany]. Giessen: Psychosozial-Verlag.

Cross, W. (1998). Black psychological functioning and the legacy of slavery: Myths and reality. In Y. Danieli (Ed.), *International handbook of multigenerational legacies of trauma* (pp. 387–401). New York: Plenum Press.

Duran, E., Duran, B., Y. H. Brave Heart, M., & YH Davis, S. (1998). Healing the American Indian soul wound. In Y. Danieli (Ed.), *International handbook of multigenerational legacies of trauma* (pp. 341–354). New York: Plenum Press.

Gombos, G. (2000). Voice of soul: Run by users and survivors of psychiatry. *Mental Health Reforms, 1,* 2–4.

Jukic, V., Dodig, G., Kenfelj, H., & De Zan, D. (1997). Psychic difficulties in former prisoners of detention camps. *Collegium Antropologicum, 21*(1), 235–242.

Kalayjian, A. S. (1994). Emotional and environmental connections: Impact of the Armenian earthquake. In E. Schuster & C. Brown (Eds.), *Exploring our environmental connection* (pp. 155–174). New York: National League for Nursing.

Kalayjian, A. S. (1999). Coping through meaning: The community response to the earthquake in Armenia. In E. Zinner & M. B. Williams (Eds.), *When a community weeps: Case studies in group survivorship* (pp. 86–101). Philadelphia: Brunner/Mazel.

Klain, E. (1992). *Psychology and psychiatry of war.* Zagreb: Faculty of Medicine, University of Zagreb.

Lifton, R. J. (1999). *Destroying the world to save it. Aum Shinrikyo: Apocalyptic violence and the new global terrorism.* New York: Henry Holt.

Lifton, R. J. (1995). *Hiroshima in America: Fifty years of denial.* New York: Putnam.

Mandic, N., & Bosnic, D. (1992). Psychological state of the Croatian refugees in the Republic of Hungary. *Croatian Medical Journal (War supplement), 2*(33), 106–109.

Merridale, C. (2000). *Night of stone, death and memory in Russia* (pp. 412–441). London: Granta Books.

Muacevic, V., Simunovic, V., & Bamburac, J. (1995). Stress and depression. *Social Psychiatry, 23,* 164–179

Suess, S. (1988). *Politsch missbraucht? Psychiatrie und staatscherheit in der DDR* [*Politically abused? Psychiatry and state security in East Germany.*]. Berlin: Ch. Links, Verlag.

Vardanyan, A. (2000). Reforming mental health law in Armenia. *Mental Health Reforms, 1,* 8–9.

Wilson, J. P., Friedman, M., & Lindy, J. D. (2001). *Treating trauma and PTSD: A psychobiologic framework.* New York: Guilford.

INDEX